Holt School Mathematics

HOLT, RINEHART AND WINSTON, PUBLISHERS
NEW YORK • TORONTO • LONDON • SYDNEY

ABOUT THE AUTHORS

EUGENE D. NICHOLS is Professor of Mathematics Education and Lecturer in the Mathematics Department at Florida State University, Tallahassee, Florida.

PAUL A. ANDERSON is an elementary school teacher in the Clark County School District, Las Vegas, Nevada.

LESLIE A. DWIGHT is the former Head of the Department of Mathematics and Professor of Mathematics at Southeastern Oklahoma State University, Durant, Oklahoma.

FRANCES FLOURNOY is Professor of Elementary Education at the University of Texas, Austin, Texas.

ROBERT KALIN is Professor, Mathematics Education Program, at Florida State University, Tallahassee, Florida.

JOHN SCHLUEP is Professor of Mathematics at State University College, Oswego, New York.

LEONARD SIMON is Assistant Director, Planning and Curriculum, for the New York City Board of Education.

Photo Credits
Pages 21, 75, 113, 133, 187, 243, 271, 311 HRW Photo by Russell Dian
Pages 45, 90, 217 HRW Photo by John Running
Page 281 Courtesy New York State College of Ceramics at Alfred University, Alfred, New York
Page 351 HRW Photo by Paul Gignac

ISBN 0-03-018566-1

890123456   032   9876543

CONTENTS

v

1 NUMERATION

NUMBERS

The
counting numbers
1, 2, 3, 4, 5, 6, . . .

1. Look at the counting numbers. The three dots tell us the numbers continue without end.

   a. What is the first counting number?

   b. What is the next counting number after 1? after 6? after 9? after 99?

2. Count the pupils in your class.

   a. How many pupils are there?

   b. What number did you use first when counting?

3. Look at the whole numbers.

   0, 1, 2, 3, 4, 5, . . .

   a. What is the first whole number?

   b. What whole number comes just before 5? 6? 1? 100?

   c. What do the three dots tell us?

1. What are the first three counting numbers?

2. What are the first three whole numbers?

3. What is the next counting number after 8? 24? 100?

4. What whole number comes just before 10? 26? 102?

5. Is there a last counting number?

6. Is there a last whole number?

Add.

1. 7 +4	**2.** 9 +2	**3.** 2 +7	

Keeping Fit

4. 6 +4	**5.** 5 +5	**6.** 6 +8

7. 4 +4	**8.** 7 +2	**9.** 3 +3	**10.** 7 +3	**11.** 9 +5

12. 2 +8	**13.** 3 +4	**14.** 8 +8	**15.** 7 +7	**16.** 5 +7

17. 8 +3	**18.** 4 +9	**19.** 7 +8	**20.** 6 +6	**21.** 8 +9

22. 9 +3	**23.** 3 +5	**24.** 9 +9	**25.** 5 +8	**26.** 6 +9

1

Numbers can tell "how many."
There are **five** children in all.

Numbers can tell "which one."
The child with the bat is **second** in line.

1. Look at the picture above.

    a. How many children are wearing hats?

    b. How many children are not wearing hats?

    c. How many children are wearing jackets?

2. Numbers can tell "which one." This tells **order** or **position** of a member in a set.

    a. Which child has the ball?

    b. Which child has the tennis racket?

    c. Which child is wearing a sweater?

    d. Which child is wearing a red hat?

3. List the numbers that tell "which one."

    a. From first to fifteenth

    b. From thirtieth to forty-first

Here is a list of the first 10 presidents of a club.

1. Which president was Marie Battista?

2. Which president was Thomas Black Hawk?

Louis Bing
Christina Sanchez
Gill Diaz
Shirley Robinson
Fran Cohen
Thomas Black Hawk
Marie Battista
Stanley Craig
Marita Gomez
Joan Royce

3. How many presidents had a last name that began with the letter B?

4. How many presidents had a last name that began with the letter C?

5. Which president was Joan Royce?

Is the number used to tell "how many" or "which one"?

6. Susan lives in the tenth house on Stanley Street.

7. Susan has two dogs.

8. Susan is reading the third chapter.

9. There are twelve chapters in the book.

Here are some numerals the Romans used.

Roman Numerals	I	V	X	L	C
Our Numerals	1	5	10	50	100

X I I I	C L X V I
10 + 1 + 1 + 1	100 + 50 + 10 + 5 + 1
13	166

1. Write our numerals.

    a. VII   **b.** XXVIII   **c.** XVI

2. The Romans used subtraction in special cases.

    $IV = 5 - 1$, or 4 $XL = 50 - 10$, or 40

    Write our numerals for these special cases.

    a. IX   **b.** XC

3. We use the special cases this way.

    Example
        CCXLIX   *Steps*

    C   C   (XL) (IX)   Circle special cases.

    100 + 100 + 40 + 9   Show our numerals.

                249   Add.

    Write our numerals.

    a. XXXIX   **b.** XLIII   **c.** XLIX   **d.** CCXXXIV

4. We can write Roman numerals for larger numbers.

Example $234 = 200 + 30 + 4$
                 CC + XXX + IV
                 CCXXXIV

Write Roman numerals.

a. 65   **b.** 49   **c.** 236   **d.** 244

EXERCISES

Write our numerals.

1. LXV   **2.** LIX   **3.** LIV   **4.** CXIX

5. XVII   **6.** CCLIV   **7.** XLI   **8.** XCV

Write Roman numerals.

9. 24   **10.** 36   **11.** 145   **12.** 304

Brainteaser

Some ancient people used letters as the names for numbers. Let's use our letters to name some numbers. The chart shows the code.

1 A	10 J	100 S
2 B	20 K	200 T
3 C	30 L	300 U
4 D	40 M	400 V
5 E	50 N	500 W
6 F	60 O	600 X
7 G	70 P	700 Y
8 H	80 Q	800 Z
9 I	90 R	900 *

Examples $ME = 40 + 5$ or 45
              $36 = 30 + 6$ or LF

What numbers are named?

1. PA   **2.** ZF   **3.** YOG   **4.** SRH

Use the code to name these.

5. 49   **6.** 63   **7.** 732   **8.** 456

5

Subtract.

1. 17
− 8

2. 4
−2

3. 18
− 9

4. 3
−2

5. 16
− 7

6. 4
−3

7. 15
− 9

8. 5
−4

9. 14
− 7

10. 6
−2

11. 15
− 8

12. 5
−3

13. 13
− 7

14. 7
−2

15. 14
− 9

16. 7
−4

17. 10
− 8

18. 12
− 5

19. 8
−2

20. 9
−7

21. 10
− 5

22. 13
− 5

23. 8
−6

24. 10
− 3

25. 6
−3

26. 8
−4

27. 13
− 6

28. 9
−4

29. 7
−5

30. 11
− 4

31. 12
− 7

32. 8
−3

33. 15
− 6

34. 11
− 5

35. 13
− 8

36. 14
− 6

37. 14
− 5

38. 12
− 4

39. 10
− 7

40. 12
− 3

41. 13
− 9

42. 11
− 8

43. 17
− 9

44. 9
−3

45. 16
− 9

46. 10
− 6

OUR NUMERALS

In our system we use these symbols, called **digits:**

0, 1, 2, 3, 4, 5, 6, 7, 8, 9.

We group by tens.

2 groups of ten and 4 ones
or 2 tens + 4 ones
or 24

1. Look at the picture with 42 stars.

   a. What does the digit 4 mean in 42?

   b. What does the digit 2 mean in 42?

2. Write our numerals.

   a. 3 tens + 2 ones   **b.** 7 tens + 9 ones

Write our numerals.

   1. 4 tens + 5 ones   **2.** 7 tens + 6 ones

   3. 5 tens + 0 ones   **4.** 8 tens + 4 ones

   5. 9 tens + 1 one   **6.** 6 tens + 6 ones

Complete.

   7. 35 means ___ tens + ___ ones

   8. 46 means ___ tens + ___ ones

7

UNDERSTANDING PLACE VALUE

Numbers can be named in different ways.

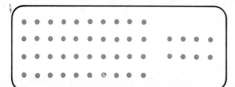

Standard Numeral
48

Expanded Numerals
4 tens + 8   40 + 8

1. **a.** Which numeral above shows the usual way we write forty-eight?

   b. Which numerals show the meaning of 48?

2. Complete to show expanded numerals.

   a. 51 = ___ tens + 1   **b.** 51 = 50 + ___

   c. 34 = ___ tens + 4   **d.** 34 = ___ + 4

3. Write standard numerals.

   a. 6 tens + 7   **b.** 4 tens + 1

   c. 80 + 3   **d.** 10 + 7

4. This place-value chart shows the meaning of 48.

   Place-Value Chart

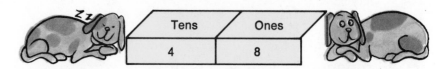

Tens	Ones
4	8

   What digit is in these places?

   a. The ones place   **b.** The tens place

Complete.

1. 63 = ___ tens + 3

2. 37 = ___ tens + 7

3. 34 = 3 tens + ___

4. 95 = 9 tens + ___

5. 86 = 80 + ___

6. 91 = ___ + 1

7. 38 = ___ + 8

8. 76 = ___ + 6

Write two expanded numerals for each.

Example　　73 = 7 tens + 3　　　　73 = 70 + 3

9. 34　　**10.** 93　　**11.** 87　　**12.** 85　　**13.** 56

In which place is each underlined digit?

14. 7̲1　　**15.** 9̲3　　**16.** 8̲5̲　　**17.** 2̲9̲　　**18.** 62̲

19. 3̲7　　**20.** 99̲　　**21.** 2̲3　　**22.** 30̲　　**23.** 1̲8

Write standard numerals.

24. 4 tens + 8

25. 7 tens + 5

26. 50 + 7

27. 70 + 1

28. Forty-six

29. Sixty-four

30. Ninety-seven

31. Seventy-nine

32. Fifty-five

33. Seventeen

34. Eighty-one

35. Thirty-six

HUNDREDS

When we have 10 groups of 10, we group again.

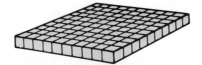

10 tens = 1 hundred
We write 100.

1. Look at these bags of marbles.

a. Tell the number of sets of 100; of 10; of 1.

b. How does 234 tell how the marbles are grouped?

2. We can write expanded numerals for 234.

Standard Numeral	Expanded Numerals
234	2 hundreds + 3 tens + 4
	200 + 30 + 4

Write two expanded numerals for each.

a. 458   **b.** 693   **c.** 701

3. We can show 234 on a place-value chart.

Hundreds	Tens	Ones
2	3	4

a. What digit is in the tens place? the hundreds place? the ones place?

b. The value of the digit 2 is 200. What is the value of the digit 3?

Write standard numerals.

1. 3 hundreds + 5 tens + 6   **2.** 400 + 70 + 3

3. 6 hundreds + 0 tens + 7   **4.** 300 + 80 + 7

5. 7 hundreds + 4 tens + 9   **6.** 900 + 0 + 5

7. 2 hundreds + 8 tens + 0   **8.** 700 + 30 + 8

9. Seven hundred   **10.** Three hundred eight

11. Nine hundred four   **12.** Two hundred ninety

13. One hundred fifty   **14.** Six hundred two

15. Four hundred forty-six

16. Eight hundred twenty-three

17. Five hundred thirty-seven

Write two expanded numerals for each.

18. 487   **19.** 598   **20.** 370   **21.** 249

22. 108   **23.** 948   **24.** 853   **25.** 789

What is the value of each underlined digit?

26. 4<u>0</u>7   **27.** 96<u>5</u>   **28.** 3<u>9</u>6   **29.** <u>6</u>90

30. 25<u>4</u>   **31.** 8<u>4</u>3   **32.** 76<u>2</u>   **33.** <u>5</u>04

★ **34.** What is the largest 3-digit number?

When we have 10 groups of 100, we group again.

10 HUNDREDS = 1 THOUSAND

WE WRITE 1,000.

1. We can show thousands on a place-value chart.

Thousands	Hundreds	Tens	Ones
2	4	5	3

What digit is in the tens place? the hundreds place? the ones place? the thousands place?

2. Complete to show the expanded forms for 2,453.

   a. 2,453 = 2 thousands + 4 hundreds
         + ___ tens + ___

   b. 2,453 = 2,000 + ___ + ___ + 3

3. The value of the 2 in 2,453 is 2,000.
   What is the value of the 4? the 5?

4. Write 2 expanded numerals for each.

   a. 3,496   **b.** 2,438   **c.** 5,370

5. What is the value of the 3 in each part of Item 4?

Write standard numerals.

1. 6 thousands + 9 hundreds + 8 tens + 5

2. 7 thousands + 0 hundreds + 9 tens + 7

3. 8 thousands + 8 hundreds + 0 tens + 8

4. 8,000 + 700 + 60 + 8

5. 4,000 + 70 + 6

6. 9,000 + 800 + 7

7. 8,000 + 7

8. Three thousand, four hundred sixty-three

9. Nine thousand, seven hundred eleven

10. Four thousand, nine

11. Four thousand, ninety

Write two expanded numerals for each.

12. 9,382   **13.** 7,654   **14.** 8,012   **15.** 3,641

What is the value of each underlined digit?

16. 9,876   **17.** 5,342   **18.** 9,604   **19.** 4,944

20. 2,063   **21.** 1,738   **22.** 8,543   **23.** 7,903

★ **24.** What is the largest 4-digit number?

EXTENDING PLACE VALUE

This place-value chart shows the first 6 places.

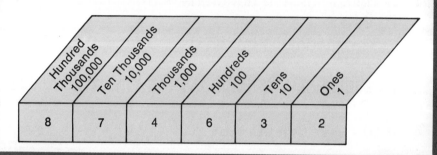

1. What place is just to the left of the thousands? the ten thousands?

2. In the numeral 874,632, the value of the digit 7 is 70,000. What are the values of these digits?

   a. 4   **b.** 8   **c.** 6   **d.** 3   **e.** 2

3. An expanded numeral for 874,632 is
   800,000 + 70,000 + 4,000 + 600 + 30 + 2.

   Write expanded numerals.

   a. 738,261   **b.** 496,285

4. In this chart the places are grouped into periods.

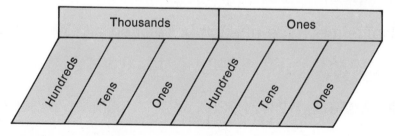

How many places are in each period? Name them.

5. Look at 738,261. What separates the periods?

6. We read 738,261 as seven hundred thirty-eight thousand, two hundred sixty-one.

   Read these.

   a. 34,894   **b.** 40,765   **c.** 56,139

   d. 263,147   **e.** 508,604   **f.** 840,003

What is the value of each underlined digit?

1. 38,271   2. 90,486   3. 76,392

4. 794,286   5. 297,484   6. 394,287

7. 380,076   8. 405,290   9. 863,081

10. 482,672   11. 136,048   12. 953,876

Write expanded numerals.

13. 39,286   14. 52,904   15. 84,736

16. 474,287   17. 963,470   18. 352,114

For 298,206 tell what digits are in these periods.

19. The ones period   20. The thousands period

Complete.

21. $9 + 1 =$ ___   ★22. $9,999 + 1 =$ ___
     $99 + 1 =$ ___ $99,999 + 1 =$ ___
     $999 + 1 =$ ___ $999,999 + 1 =$ ___

15

MILLIONS

Pretend you have a million dollars now. You spend $1,000 each month for 80 years. You would still have some money left over!

Your heart beats about a million times a week. It beats 100,000,000 times in about 2 years.

1. Here is a place-value chart for millions.

a. What place is just to the left of the hundred thousands place? What digit is in that place?

b. What digit is in the ten millions place? the hundred millions place?

c. What digits are in the ones period? the thousands period? the millions period?

2. We read 704,853,291 as seven hundred four million, eight hundred fifty-three thousand, two hundred ninety-one.
Read these.

a. 2,389,286 **b.** 4,200,391 **c.** 13,486,291

d. 68,297,401 **e.** 300,300,300 **f.** 714,000,603

3. Consider 368,402,195. The value of the 8 is 8,000,000. What is the value of the 3? the 6? the 2?

Write standard numerals.

1. Twenty-one million, six hundred twenty-eight thousand, four hundred eighteen

2. Eight hundred ninety-four million, seven hundred sixty-seven thousand, five hundred four.

3. Eight million, sixty-four thousand, twenty-nine

4. Four hundred million, nine hundred thousand

5. Nine million, nine

6. Seventy million, fifty thousand, thirty

7. Eight hundred million

8. Forty-five million, fifteen thousand, eighty

What is the value of each underlined digit?

9. 8,286,491

10. 7,271,106

11. 39,849,286

12. 55,798,287

13. 604,298,947

14. 306,276,100

15. 583,470,291

16. 849,614,153

17. 486,503,212

18. 256,349,007

★19. What is the largest 7-digit number? 8-digit number? 9-digit number?

COMPARING NUMBERS

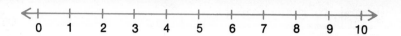

| 0 | 1 | 2 | 3 | 4 | 5 | 6 | 7 | 8 | 9 | 10 |

4 is to the left of 5
4 < 5
4 is less than 5

6 is to the right of 3
6 > 3
6 is greater than 3

1. Compare. Use =, >, or <.

   a. 3 ⬚ 9   b. 4 ⬚ 0   c. 7 ⬚ 7

   d. 32 ⬚ 35   e. 35 ⬚ 32   f. 28 ⬚ 78

2. Let's compare 7,632 and 7,629.

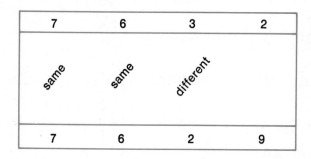

7	6	3	2
same	same	different	
7	6	2	9

   3 tens > 2 tens, so 7,632 > 7,629

   a. Tell why 4,746 > 4,499.

   b. Tell why 6,543 < 7,539.

3. Compare. Use =, >, or <.

   a.   473 ⬚ 474   b.   369 ⬚ 379

   c.   782 ⬚ 682   d. 4,286 ⬚ 4,386

   e. 5,739 ⬚ 5,739   f. 9,854 ⬚ 8,999

Compare. Use =, >, or <.

1. 8 ≡ 9

2. 76 ≡ 75

3. 98 ≡ 99

4. 52 ≡ 47

5. 346 ≡ 357

6. 298 ≡ 295

7. 601 ≡ 599

8. 847 ≡ 847

9. 701 ≡ 700

10. 485 ≡ 911

11. 4,782 ≡ 4,791

12. 1,349 ≡ 1,349

13. 7,806 ≡ 7,960

14. 4,287 ≡ 2,289

15. 4,076 ≡ 4,070

16. 9,782 ≡ 8,982

17. 6,004 ≡ 6,003

18. 8,944 ≡ 8,934

19. 7,099 ≡ 7,100

20. 6,123 ≡ 4,123

Solve these problems.

21.

Who weighs more?

22.

Which snake is longer?

23.

Which jar has more?

24.

Which town is further?

19

WHAT'S THE RULE?

Someone Says	Kathy Answers
5	8
7	10
0	3
11	14

My rule is add 3.

1. Find Deleon's rule and complete the chart.

Someone says	7	9	4	10	3	6	4	1
Deleon answers	6	8	3					

2. Find the rule and complete this sequence.

1, 4, 7, 10, ____, ____, ____, ____

1. Find George's rule and complete the chart.

Someone says	6	1	4	7	9	0	8
George answers	11	6	9				

Complete each sequence.

2. 2, 4, 6, 8, ____, ____, ____, ____

3. 0, 1, 3, 6, ____, ____, ____, ____

4. 36, 31, 26, 21, ____, ____, ____, ____

★ **5.** 1, 1, 2, 3, 5, 8, 13, ____, ____, ____, ____

20

SCHOOL LUNCHROOM MANAGERS

Mrs. Arnold is the lunchroom manager at Griffith School. Each year she makes a report about the lunch program.

1. During the school year thirty-six thousand lunches were served. Write a standard numeral for this number.

2. Forty-three thousand, two hundred four cartons of milk were served. Write a standard numeral for this number.

3. **a.** Find the number of school lunches that are served today. Ask the lunchroom manager for this information.

   b. Find the number of students in school today. Go to the school's office for this information.

   c. Do this each day for a week. Make a chart of the results.

   d. Compare the numbers in your chart. Use >, <, or =.

Date	Lunches	Attendance

CHAPTER REVIEW

1. Write the first three whole numbers. [vi]

Look at these 5 letters: A, B, C, D, E. [2]

2. How many letter A's are there?

3. Which one is the letter D?

Write standard numerals for each. [4]

4. XXVI   **5.** XXIV   **6.** CCLXIX   **7.** XL

Write two expanded numerals for each.

    Example   97 = 9 tens + 7   97 = 90 + 7

8. 58   **9.** 279   **10.** 8,504
[8]   [10]   [12]

Write standard numerals.

11. 8,000 + 700 + 70 + 5
[12]

12. 300,000 + 20,000 + 1,000 + 800 + 70 + 6
[14]

13. Four million, four thousand, four
[16]

For 3,287,145 give the value of these digits. [16]

14. 3   **15.** 2   **16.** 4   **17.** 8

Compare. Use =, <, or >. [18]

18. 476 ≡ 486   **19.** 7,248 ≡ 7,248   **20.** 985 ≡ 899

Complete this sequence. [20]

21. 0, 3, 6, 9, 12, ____, ____, ____

22

CHAPTER TEST

1. Write the first 3 counting numbers.

Look at these 5 letters: X, Y, Z, Y, X.

2. How many X's are there?

3. Which one is the letter Z?

Write standard numerals for each.

4. VII   **5.** CCXLI

Write two expanded numerals for each.

    Example   62 = 6 tens + 2   62 = 60 + 2

6. 38   **7.** 487   **8.** 2,786

Write standard numerals.

9. 4,000 + 90 + 8

10. 800,000 + 8,000 + 80

11. Ninety-three million

For 6,284,301 give the value of these digits.

12. 3   **13.** 6   **14.** 2   **15.** 8

Compare. Use =, <, or >.

16. 397 $\equiv$ 387   **17.** 3,498 $\equiv$ 3,599

Complete this sequence.

18. 1, 3, 5, 7, _____ , _____ , _____

2 NUMBER SENTENCES

A FUNCTION MACHINE

A function machine follows a rule. The rule for this machine is **add 2.**

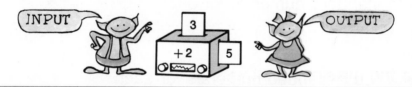

1. Look at these machines.

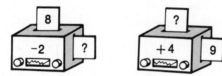

   a. What are the rules?

   b. Find the missing inputs or outputs.

2. The table shows some pairs of inputs and outputs. Copy and complete it. Use the rule on the machine.

Input	Output
8	12
5	
10	
1	
	4
	7

3. Copy and complete the table by finding the rule.

Input	Output
7	3
4	0
9	
	1
11	

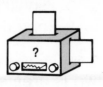

Find the missing inputs or outputs.

1.

2.

3.

4.

5.

6.

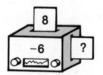

7.

8.

9.

Copy and complete the tables by finding the rules.

10.

Input	Output
9	15
1	7
8	
	13

11.

Input	Output
8	4
4	0
6	
	3

English Sentence	Number Sentence
Eight is equal to five plus three.	$8 = 5 + 3$
Forty-two is greater than forty.	$42 > 40$
Thirty-three is less than forty.	$33 < 40$

1. Read these number sentences.

    a. $3 + 6 = 9$ **b.** $9 > 7$ **c.** $7 < 8$

A number sentence with an equals sign, $=$, is an **equation.** Examples $9 = 7 + 2$ $4 + 8 = 12$

A number sentence with $<$ or $>$ is an **inequality.** Examples $9 > 4$ $7 < 4 + 9$

2. Which are equations? Which are inequalities?

    a. $9 > 5 + 3$ **b.** $8 = 4 + 4$ **c.** $7 + 3 < 7 + 4$

EXERCISES

Which are equations? Which are inequalities?

  1. $3 + 7 = 10$ **2.** $4 + 6 = 8 + 2$ **3.** $10 - 3 = 7$

  4. $8 > 7$ **5.** $12 - 5 = 7 + 0$ **6.** $9 > 8$

  7. $7 > 2 + 2$ **8.** $3 + 6 > 3 + 5$ **9.** $8 - 1 < 8$

10. $8 - 5 = 3$ **11.** $5 + 6 = 6 + 5$ **12.** $3 + 7 > 8$

13. $6 = 2 + 4$ **14.** $5 - 3 < 8 - 5$ **15.** $4 + 3 = 7$

English sentences can be true or false.

TRUE   The American flag is red, white, and blue.
FALSE   Babe Ruth discovered electricity.

Equations can be true or false.

TRUE $8 + 6 = 14$ $9 - 3 = 6$
FALSE $2 + 5 = 8$ $8 - 3 = 7$

1. True or false?

   a. $6 + 3 = 9$ **b.** $9 - 3 = 5$ **c.** $9 = 17 - 8$

2. Change the underlined numerals to make true sentences.

   a. Al has $\underline{7}$ eyes.   **b.** $9 = \underline{4} + 6$ **c.** $8 - 7 = \underline{3}$

EXERCISES

True or false?

1. $8 + 4 = 12$ **2.** $9 + 6 = 14$ **3.** $17 - 8 = 8$

4. $9 = 14 - 5$ **5.** $4 + 7 = 12$ **6.** $1 + 4 = 2 + 3$

7. $9 + 3 = 4 + 7$ **8.** $8 = 14 - 6$ **9.** $13 = 7 + 6$

Change the underlined numerals to make true sentences.

10. $4 + 8 = \underline{11}$ **11.** $3 + \underline{3} = 7$ **12.** $8 - 7 = \underline{2}$

13. $\underline{4} + 9 = 11$ **14.** $3 + 8 = 4 + \underline{9}$ **15.** $14 = 9 + \underline{7}$

OPEN SENTENCES

Some English sentences are neither true nor false.
        She made a famous American flag.
We can replace She to make the sentence true or false.

TRUE Betsy Ross made a famous American flag.
FALSE Minnie Mouse made a famous American flag.

1. Consider this sentence.

   He discovered America in 1492.

   a. Replace He to make it true.

   b. Replace He to make it false.

Open number sentences are neither true nor false.

$$8 + \square = 12 \qquad 9 - 7 = \triangle$$

Frames like $\square$ or $\triangle$ can be replaced. The replacements make true sentences or false sentences.

TRUE $8 + 4 = 12$ $9 - 7 = 2$
FALSE $8 + 5 = 12$ $9 - 7 = 4$

2. Consider $\square = 4 + 8$.

   a. Make it true.   **b.** Make it false.

3. Make true sentences. Use whole numbers.

   a. $7 + 6 = \square$ **b.** $9 - 3 = \triangle$ **c.** $\square = 7 - 3$

   d. $5 + \square = 12$ **e.** $\square - 3 = 11$ **f.** $8 - \square = 4$

4. Is each sentence true, false, or open? Write T, F, or O.

a. $6 + 7 = 12$ **b.** $6 + \square = 13$ **c.** $6 + 7 = 13$

Replace It to make true sentences; false sentences.

1. It has a long gray trunk.

2. It has a very long neck.

3. It has webbed feet and says quack.

Consider each open sentence. Make it true, then make it false.

4. $9 + \square = 12$ **5.** $\square + 4 = 12$ **6.** $6 + 6 = \square$

Make true sentences. Use whole numbers.

7. $8 + \square = 15$ **8.** $18 - 9 = \triangle$

9. $4 + 7 = \triangle$ **10.** $8 + 3 = \square + 6$

11. $3 + 8 = 7 + \square$ **12.** $7 + 3 = 2 + \triangle$

Are the sentences true, false, or open? Write T, F, or O.

13. $9 + 6 = 15$ **14.** $8 + \square = 15$

15. $15 - 8 = 7$ **16.** $14 - 8 = 5$

17. $5 + 3 = 8 + \square$ **18.** $12 - 6 = 6 + 6$

29

SENTENCES WITH TWO FRAMES

Look at these open sentences with two frames.

$$\square + \triangle = 4 \qquad\qquad \square + \square = 4$$

True Sentences   True sentences

$0 + 4 = 4 \quad 4 + 0 = 4$ $2 + 2 = 4$
$3 + 1 = 4 \quad 1 + 3 = 4$
$2 + 2 = 4$

The frames are differ-   The same frame ap-
ent. There are many   pears twice. The same
true sentences.   number must replace
                                 both frames.

1. Make true sentences.

  a. $\square + \triangle = 6$ **b.** $\square - \triangle = 2$

2. Make true sentences.

  a. $\square + \square = 6$ **b.** $\triangle + 0 = \triangle$

Make true sentences. Use whole numbers.

1. $\square + \triangle = 2$ **2.** $\square + \triangle = 5$ **3.** $\square + \square = 2$

4. $\triangle + \triangle = 0$ **5.** $\triangle + \triangle = 10$ **6.** $\square + \triangle = 8$

7. $2 + \square = \triangle$ **8.** $0 + \square = \square$ **9.** $\square + \triangle = 5$

10. $\square - 3 = \triangle$ ★**11.** $\triangle + \triangle = 50$ ★**12.** $8 - \square = \square$

READING MATH PROBLEMS

The annual Springvale Carnival opened in May. There were some booths for playing games and some booths for buying food. How many booths were there in all?

What is the problem asking?
How many booths were there in all?

What information is needed to solve the problem?
The number of game booths.
The number of food booths.

1. Carlita Sanchez went to the carnival on opening day. She spent part of her allowance. How much did Carlita have left?

   a. What is the problem asking?

   b. What information is needed to solve the problem?

2. There was a merry-go-round at the carnival. Some of the horses moved up and down. The other horses did not move at all. How many horses were there?

   a. What is the problem asking?

   b. What information is needed to solve the problem?

3. Carlita bought some cotton candy, a drink, and a hot dog. How much did she spend in all?

   a. What is the problem asking?

   b. What information is needed to solve the problem?

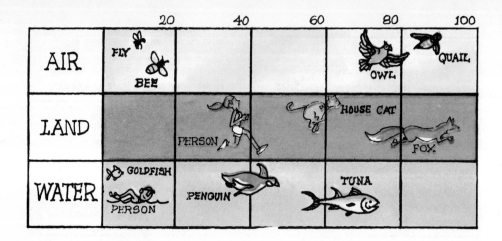

ANIMAL SPEEDS

1. A bee can go 15 kilometers an hour. A fly can travel 9 kilometers an hour. How much faster is the bee?

    a. What is the problem asking?

    b. What are the important facts?

    c. Would you add or subtract to solve the problem?

This number sentence fits the problem.

$$15 \quad - \quad 9 \quad = \quad \square$$

| bee's distance | fly's distance | difference in distance |

2. A man ran 9 kilometers. He then walked 6 kilometers. How many kilometers did he travel in all?

    a. What are the important facts?

    b. Would you add or subtract to solve the problem?

    c. Which number sentence fits the problem?
    $9 + 6 = \square$ $6 + \square = 9$ $9 - 6 = \square$

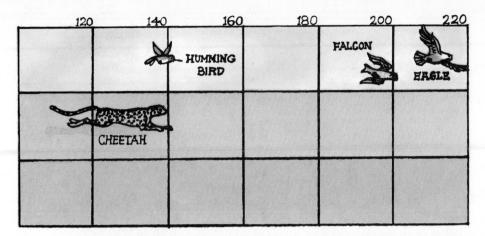

3. A woman is in a 20-kilometer race. She has gone 13 kilometers. How far does she have to go? Which **two** number sentences fit the problem?

$20 + 13 = \square$ $20 - 13 = \square$ $13 + \square = 20$

4. An eagle can fly about 220 kilometers an hour. A penguin can swim about 40 kilometers an hour. How much faster is the eagle? Which number sentence fits the problem?

$220 + 40 = \square$ $220 - 40 = \square$ $40 + 220 = \square$

5. An owl can fly 80 kilometers an hour. A quail can fly 10 kilometers an hour faster. How many kilometers an hour can a quail fly? Write a number sentence to fit the story. Do not solve.

6. A cheetah can run 130 kilometers an hour. A fox can run 90 kilometers an hour. How much faster is the cheetah? Write a number sentence that fits the story. Do not solve.

7. A goldfish can swim only 8 kilometers in an hour. A tuna is able to swim 30 kilometers in an hour. How much further can a tuna swim in an hour? Write a number sentence to fit the story. Do not solve.

ADDITION

Addition is related to joining sets.

$$8 \quad + \quad 5 = 13$$

Addends   Sum

1. **a.** Draw a picture to show a set of 7 being joined with a set of 6.

   b. Make true: $7 + 6 = \square$.

   c. Give the addends. Give the sum.

2. We can also show addition on a number line. Consider $9 + 3 = 12$.

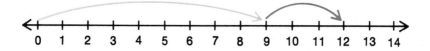

   a. Show $8 + 4$ on a number line.

   b. Make true: $8 + 4 = \square$.

   c. Give the addends. Give the sum.

3. Add.

   a. $3 + 4$ **b.** $1 + 7$ **c.** $2 + 5$

   d. $\begin{array}{r} 9 \\ +6 \\ \hline \end{array}$ **e.** $\begin{array}{r} 3 \\ +2 \\ \hline \end{array}$ **f.** $\begin{array}{r} 7 \\ +3 \\ \hline \end{array}$ **g.** $\begin{array}{r} 4 \\ +9 \\ \hline \end{array}$ **h.** $\begin{array}{r} 6 \\ +6 \\ \hline \end{array}$

4. Make true sentences. Use =, >, or <.

    a. $1 + 5 \equiv 3 + 3$ **b.** $7 + 6 \equiv 6 + 7$

    c. $3 + 4 \equiv 5 + 3$ **d.** $8 + 7 \equiv 9 + 5$

EXERCISES

Add.

1. $\begin{array}{r} 7 \\ +8 \\ \hline \end{array}$	**2.** $\begin{array}{r} 9 \\ +2 \\ \hline \end{array}$	**3.** $\begin{array}{r} 9 \\ +5 \\ \hline \end{array}$	**4.** $\begin{array}{r} 7 \\ +4 \\ \hline \end{array}$	**5.** $\begin{array}{r} 6 \\ +7 \\ \hline \end{array}$
6. $\begin{array}{r} 5 \\ +6 \\ \hline \end{array}$	**7.** $\begin{array}{r} 8 \\ +8 \\ \hline \end{array}$	**8.** $\begin{array}{r} 7 \\ +7 \\ \hline \end{array}$	**9.** $\begin{array}{r} 9 \\ +8 \\ \hline \end{array}$	**10.** $\begin{array}{r} 7 \\ +9 \\ \hline \end{array}$
11. $\begin{array}{r} 3 \\ +6 \\ \hline \end{array}$	**12.** $\begin{array}{r} 5 \\ +4 \\ \hline \end{array}$	**13.** $\begin{array}{r} 8 \\ +2 \\ \hline \end{array}$	**14.** $\begin{array}{r} 5 \\ +7 \\ \hline \end{array}$	**15.** $\begin{array}{r} 6 \\ +4 \\ \hline \end{array}$
16. $\begin{array}{r} 3 \\ +3 \\ \hline \end{array}$	**17.** $\begin{array}{r} 5 \\ +8 \\ \hline \end{array}$	**18.** $\begin{array}{r} 9 \\ +9 \\ \hline \end{array}$	**19.** $\begin{array}{r} 8 \\ +6 \\ \hline \end{array}$	**20.** $\begin{array}{r} 3 \\ +9 \\ \hline \end{array}$

Make true sentences. Use =, >, or <.

21. $4 + 8 \equiv 9 + 3$ **22.** $9 + 7 \equiv 5 + 8$

23. $8 + 8 \equiv 9 + 6$ **24.** $6 + 8 \equiv 9 + 7$

25. $9 + 2 \equiv 7 + 6$ **26.** $8 + 3 \equiv 4 + 7$

Write number sentences and make them true.

27. There are 7 apples and 4 pears. How many pieces of fruit are there in all?

28. Mary has 8 cents. She earned 5 cents more. How much does she have now?

PROPERTIES OF ADDITION

SKIP   CHIP   Number of Bananas
Skip, $3 + 2 = 5$
Chip, $2 + 3 = 5$
So $3 + 2 = 2 + 3$

Changing the order of the addends does not change the sum.
This is the **order property of addition.**

1. Find the sums. Do the work in the parentheses first.

   a. $(7 + 3) + 4 \, ; \, 7 + (3 + 4)$

   b. Are the sums the same?

   $(8 + 7) + 6 = 21$ and $8 + (7 + 6) = 21$,
   so $(8 + 7) + 6 = 8 + (7 + 6)$

Changing the grouping of the addends does not change the sum.
This is the **grouping property of addition.**

2. Complete.

   a. $4 + 3 = 7$, so $3 + 4 = $ _____ .

   b. $(4 + 2) + 6 = 12$, so $4 + (2 + 6) = $ _____ .

3. Add.

   a. $8 + 0$ **b.** $0 + 8$ **c.** $9 + 0$

   $7 + 0 = 7$ $98 + 0 = 98$
When we add 0 to a number, the sum is that number.
This is the **property of zero for addition.**

4. What properties are shown?

    a. $632 + 0 = 632$ **b.** $23 + 42 = 42 + 23$

    c. $(123 + 354) + 145 = 123 + (354 + 145)$

5. Make true sentences.

    a. $34 + 0 = \square$ **b.** $12 + 2 = 2 + \square$

What properties are shown?

1. $(87 + 36) + 19 = 87 + (36 + 19)$

2. $476 + 287 = 287 + 476$

3. $984 + 0 = 984$

Complete.

4. $7 + 8 = 15$, so $8 + 7 =$ _____

5. $9 + (4 + 3) = 16$, so $(9 + 4) + 3 =$ _____

6. $84 + 26 = 110$, so $26 + 84 =$ _____

7. $(310 + 42) + 10 = 362$, so $310 + (42 + 10) =$ _____

8. $357 + 293 = 650$, so $293 + 357 =$ _____

Make true sentences.

9. $9 + 8 = \square + 9$ **10.** $4 + 5 = 5 + \square$

11. $(3 + 5) + 8 = 3 + (5 + \square)$ **12.** $276 + 0 = \square$

37

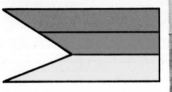
Race Time

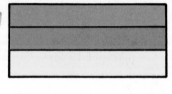

Add.

1. 2 2	**2.** 3 6	**3.** 7 8	**4.** 4 9	**5.** 1 8	**6.** 5 0
7. 8 4	**8.** 2 3	**9.** 5 6	**10.** 3 8	**11.** 7 2	**12.** 4 4
13. 9 1	**14.** 3 5	**15.** 4 7	**16.** 4 2	**17.** 3 3	**18.** 6 8
19. 2 0	**20.** 9 3	**21.** 4 5	**22.** 7 6	**23.** 2 6	**24.** 5 5
25. 6 9	**26.** 0 8	**27.** 6 6	**28.** 5 7	**29.** 1 4	**30.** 6 4
31. 8 2	**32.** 7 1	**33.** 4 3	**34.** 0 3	**35.** 7 3	**36.** 2 5
37. 5 8	**38.** 1 2	**39.** 8 9	**40.** 7 7	**41.** 9 5	**42.** 6 1
43. 1 1	**44.** 9 7	**45.** 0 6	**46.** 8 8	**47.** 1 3	**48.** 2 7
49. 9 9	**50.** 0 4	**51.** 5 1	**52.** 3 4	**53.** 6 5	**54.** 9 2
55. 3 9	**56.** 8 6	**57.** 5 9	**58.** 9 0	**59.** 2 8	**60.** 7 4

Subtraction is related to taking away part of a set.

$10 - 3 = 7$

difference

1. **a.** Draw a picture to show a set of 12. Show 5 being taken away.

   b. Make true: $12 - 5 = \square$.

2. We can also show subtraction on a number line. Consider $8 - 5 = 3$.

   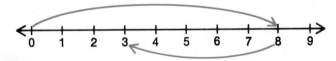

   a. Show $12 - 7$ on a number line.

   b. Make true: $12 - 7 = \square$.

3. Finding a difference is like finding a missing addend.

   $13 - 5 = \square$ $\square + 5 = 13$

   You know this   If you know this
   difference   missing addend

   Make true sentences.

   a. $16 - 9 = \square$ and $\square + 9 = 16$

   b. $14 - 8 = \square$ and $\square + 8 = 14$

4. Subtract.

    a. $13 - 5$ **b.** $14 - 6$ **c.** $17 - 8$

	d.	**e.**	**f.**	**g.**	**h.**
	7	8	13	7	10
	-6	-4	-8	-7	-6

Subtract.

	1.	**2.**	**3.**	**4.**	**5.**
	14	14	16	11	14
	-8	-5	-9	-6	-7

	6.	**7.**	**8.**	**9.**	**10.**
	11	18	12	11	8
	-8	-9	-3	-4	-7

	11.	**12.**	**13.**	**14.**	**15.**
	12	6	12	13	7
	-7	-2	-4	-4	-0

	16.	**17.**	**18.**	**19.**	**20.**
	13	11	15	16	15
	-9	-2	-6	-8	-8

	21.	**22.**	**23.**	**24.**	**25.**
	12	9	6	12	13
	-5	-4	-1	-6	-7

Write number sentences that fit these problems. Make them true.

26. Amy read 9 pages of a book with 18 pages. How many pages has she left to read?

27. Armando got 7 right on his spelling test. Ernesto got 9 right. How many more did Ernesto get right?

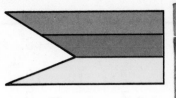

Race Time

Subtract.

1. 11 <u>2</u>	**2.** 9 <u>1</u>	**3.** 10 <u>6</u>	**4.** 8 <u>7</u>	**5.** 4 <u>4</u>	**6.** 13 <u>8</u>
7. 9 <u>3</u>	**8.** 8 <u>0</u>	**9.** 12 <u>3</u>	**10.** 18 <u>9</u>	**11.** 6 <u>2</u>	**12.** 11 <u>5</u>
13. 5 <u>4</u>	**14.** 6 <u>3</u>	**15.** 7 <u>6</u>	**16.** 14 <u>7</u>	**17.** 6 <u>0</u>	**18.** 15 <u>6</u>
19. 10 <u>8</u>	**20.** 12 <u>6</u>	**21.** 9 <u>4</u>	**22.** 5 <u>5</u>	**23.** 14 <u>6</u>	**24.** 8 <u>3</u>
25. 16 <u>9</u>	**26.** 3 <u>0</u>	**27.** 13 <u>9</u>	**28.** 10 <u>7</u>	**29.** 3 <u>1</u>	**30.** 12 <u>7</u>
31. 9 <u>7</u>	**32.** 13 <u>5</u>	**33.** 7 <u>7</u>	**34.** 8 <u>6</u>	**35.** 14 <u>5</u>	**36.** 11 <u>4</u>
37. 4 <u>2</u>	**38.** 17 <u>9</u>	**39.** 9 <u>2</u>	**40.** 12 <u>8</u>	**41.** 1 <u>0</u>	**42.** 7 <u>5</u>
43. 16 <u>8</u>	**44.** 2 <u>2</u>	**45.** 15 <u>7</u>	**46.** 4 <u>1</u>	**47.** 0 <u>0</u>	**48.** 13 <u>6</u>
49. 5 <u>3</u>	**50.** 11 <u>8</u>	**51.** 10 <u>5</u>	**52.** 7 <u>4</u>	**53.** 6 <u>1</u>	**54.** 9 <u>9</u>
55. 15 <u>9</u>	**56.** 10 <u>9</u>	**57.** 13 <u>7</u>	**58.** 2 <u>1</u>	**59.** 12 <u>4</u>	**60.** 8 <u>4</u>

Study these machines.

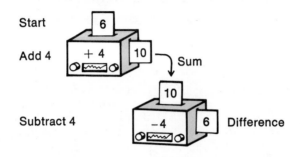

Addition and subtraction are **opposites.**
One undoes the other.

1. Look at these two machines.

   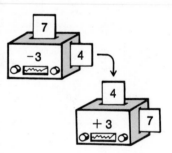

   a. Start with 7. Subtract 3. What is the difference?

   b. Add 3 to the difference. What is the sum?

2. Start with 8. Add 7. Subtract 7 from the sum. What do you get?

Add 5 to each. Then subtract 5 from the sum.

1. 1   **2.** 4   **3.** 8   **4.** 10   **5.** 25

Subtract 6 from each. Then add 6 to the difference.

6. 9   **7.** 6   **8.** 10   **9.** 15   **10.** 26

FLOW CHARTS

Directions given by flow charts are easy to follow. Here are directions to sharpen a pencil.

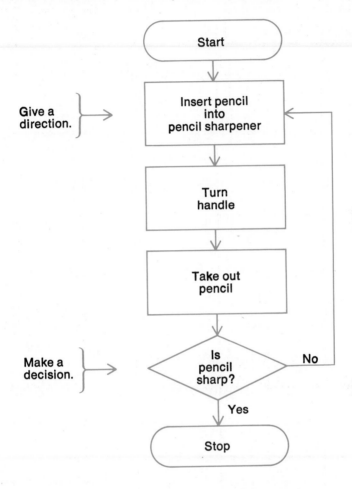

1. Draw the shape which gives a direction.

2. Draw the shape when a decision is made.

3. The decision is no in the flow chart above. What must you do now?

★4. Make a flow chart to show how you make toast.

Keeping Fit

Write expanded numerals.

Example   496 = 400 + 90 + 6

1. 36   **2.** 684   **3.** 752

4. 903   **5.** 3,698   **6.** 8,932

What is the value of each underlined digit?

Example   For 6,843,967: 800,000

7. 483   **8.** 567   **9.** 832

10. 3,946   **11.** 7,048   **12.** 2,967

13. 15,068   **14.** 37,947   **15.** 83,567

16. 347,893   **17.** 408,961   **18.** 747,663

19. 5,684,372   **20.** 57,348,627   **21.** 342,986,003

Write standard numerals.

22. Five hundred eighty-six

23. Seven thousand, five hundred seven

24. Eight million, nine hundred forty-seven thousand, three hundred fifty

25. Eighty thousand, six

Compare. Use =, >, or <.

26. 48 ≡ 84   **27.** 746 ≡ 738

28. 4,987 ≡ 2,999   **29.** 6,483 ≡ 6,472

AIR TRAFFIC CONTROLLERS

1. 8 jets.
7 helicopters.
How many in all?

2. 5 women controllers.
5 men controllers.
How many in all?

3. 8 planes.
7 take off.
How many are left?

4. 12 planes in air.
7 land.
How many still in air?

5. 13 controllers.
7 women.
How many men?

6. 7 planes in air.
6 on ground.
How many in all?

Brainteaser

1. Mr. Osborne is controlling □ planes. Miss Anderson is controlling △ planes. Together they control 10 planes. How many planes could each have? Give all possible answers.

2. Ms. Orr is controlling 2 more planes than Mr. Jones. Together they control 10 planes. How many does each control?

CHAPTER REVIEW

Which are equations? Which are inequalities? [26]

1. $7 = 4 + 3$ **2.** $8 > 4 + 3$ **3.** $9 + 9 < 12 + 7$

Are the sentences true, false, or open? Write T, F, or O. [27, 28]

4. $5 + 8 = \square$ **5.** $5 + 8 = 12$

6. $13 = 8 + 5$ **7.** $7 + 6 = 4 + 9$

Make true sentences. [28, 30]

8. $6 + 4 = \square + 7$ **9.** $\square = 12 - 7$

10. $\square + \triangle = 2$ **11.** $\square + \square = 2$

Add or subtract. [34, 39]

12. $\begin{array}{r} 8 \\ +7 \\ \hline \end{array}$ **13.** $\begin{array}{r} 16 \\ -\ 9 \\ \hline \end{array}$ **14.** $\begin{array}{r} 7 \\ +6 \\ \hline \end{array}$ **15.** $\begin{array}{r} 18 \\ -\ 9 \\ \hline \end{array}$ **16.** $\begin{array}{r} 8 \\ +0 \\ \hline \end{array}$

17. $\begin{array}{r} 12 \\ -\ 9 \\ \hline \end{array}$ **18.** $\begin{array}{r} 14 \\ -\ 8 \\ \hline \end{array}$ **19.** $\begin{array}{r} 9 \\ +9 \\ \hline \end{array}$ **20.** $\begin{array}{r} 9 \\ +6 \\ \hline \end{array}$ **21.** $\begin{array}{r} 15 \\ -\ 7 \\ \hline \end{array}$

What properties of addition are shown? [36]

22. $2 + 3 = 3 + 2$ **23.** $(1 + 2) + 3 = 1 + (2 + 3)$

Solve.

24. There were 9 girls and 5 boys in the room. How many children were there in all?

25. 15 planes on ground.
6 took off.
How many are left?

26. 9 men.
8 women.
How many in all?

46

CHAPTER TEST

Which are equations? Which are inequalities?

1. $7 + 6 > 6 + 6$ **2.** $9 + 7 = 8 + 8$

Are the sentences true, false, or open? Write T, F, or O.

3. $7 + 6 = 13$ **4.** $18 - 9 = 8$

5. $7 + 6 = 3 + 9$ **6.** $\square = 3 + 4$

Make true sentences.

7. $9 + 6 = \square + 8$ **8.** $\square = 14 - 9$

9. $\square + \triangle = 4$ **10.** $\square + \square = 16$

Add or subtract.

11.	7	**12.**	8	**13.**	4	**14.**	9
	$+7$		-5		$+9$		$+7$

15.	9	**16.**	8	**17.**	6	**18.**	12
	-7		$+6$		$+8$		-3

What properties of addition are shown?

19. $(8 + 7) + 6 = 8 + (7 + 6)$ **20.** $8 + 9 = 9 + 8$

Solve.

21. Ann sold Scout cookies. She sold 4 boxes on Monday and 8 boxes on Tuesday. How many boxes did she sell in all?

22. 17 planes.
8 took off.
How many are left?

23. 8 squirrels.
7 rabbits.
How many animals in all?

47

3 ADDING

ONE ADDEND LESS THAN TEN

Add	Expanded Form		Short Form
12 →	1 ten + 2		12
+ 7 →	7		+ 7
	1 ten + 9		19

1. Add.

14 → 1 ten + 4   14
+ 3 →   3   + 3

2. Sometimes we must regroup. Let's add 13 + 9.

Expanded Form

13 → 1 ten + 3
+ 9 →   9
    1 ten + 12
    1 ten + 1 ten + 2
    2 tens + 2
        22

Short Form

ADD ONES
  1
  1 3
+   9
    2

ADD TENS
  1
  1 3
+   9
  2 2

Copy and complete.

a.   25 → 2 tens + 5
    + 9 →   9
        2 tens + 14
        2 tens + ___ ten + 4
        ___ tens + 4
        ___

b.   1
        25
      + 9
        34
      5 + 9 = ___
      14 = ___ ten + ___
      How is 14 shown?

48

3. Add. Use the short form.

a. 23
  + 5

b. 44
  + 5

c. 23
  + 8

d. 49
  + 6

Add. Look for patterns.

1.   3   13   23   43   73
  +6   + 6   + 6   + 6   + 6

2.   4   14   24   64   84
  +7   + 7   + 7   + 7   + 7

Add.

3.   41   **4.**   65   **5.**   93   **6.**   14
  + 2   + 2   + 6   + 5

7.   23   **8.**   41   **9.**   65   **10.**   84
  + 8   + 9   + 6   + 9

11.   84   **12.**   36   **13.**   48   **14.**   36
  + 6   + 9   + 8   + 7

Solve these problems.

15. 17 cents for candy.
8 cents for gum.
How much in all?

16. 76 players.
3 more joined.
How many now?

17. 35 red apples.
9 green apples.
How many in all?

18. 24 bees.
8 ants.
How many insects?

49

ORDER AND GROUPING OF ADDENDS

We can add $2 + 3 + 5 + 8$ in different ways.

$(2 + 3) + 5 + 8 = 18$ $(3 + 5) + 2 + 8 = 18$
$(2 + 5) + 3 + 8 = 18$ $(3 + 8) + 2 + 5 = 18$
$(2 + 8) + 3 + 5 = 18$ $(5 + 8) + 2 + 3 = 18$

We can add any two numbers first. The final sum is the same. This is because of the order and grouping properties.

1. Find the sum. Add any two numbers first.

   a. $7 + 9 + 3$ **b.** $6 + 2 + 8 + 5$

2. Three children added $7 + 9 + 3 + 1$.

   Al   *Sharon*   *Marva*

Al	Sharon	Marva
7 ⟩16	7 ↑ 20	7 ⟩10
9	9 13	9 ⟩20
3 19	3 ⟩4	3 ⟩10
+1 ↓ 20	+1	+1

   a. Al added from top to bottom. What is his sum?

   b. Explain what Sharon did. What is her sum?

   c. Marva looked for tens. What is her sum?

3. Add.

   a. 9   **b.** 4   **c.** 9   **d.** 4   **e.** 6
           8   6   1   5   9
          +1   +1   2   6   4
                                          +8   +7   +1

Add.

1. 8 + 7 + 6
2. 9 + 4 + 7

3. 1 + 7 + 8 + 3
4. 3 + 7 + 9 + 4

5. 5 + 6 + 7 + 8
6. 1 + 2 + 3 + 4

7. 2 + 4 + 6 + 8
8. 1 + 3 + 5 + 7

9. 4 + 3 + 6 + 8
10. 5 + 7 + 4 + 3

Add.

11.	**12.**	**13.**	**14.**	**15.**
8	6	4	7	4
7	7	6	5	9
+6	+8	3	5	6
		+8	+3	+8

16.	**17.**	**18.**	★ **19.**	★ **20.**
3	8	9	8	3
9	6	9	7	6
6	7	9	8	4
+4	+5	+9	7	7
			+8	5
				+6

Brainteaser

Copy this triangle. Fill in the circles with 1, 2, 3, 7, 8, and 9 so that the sum of each side is 20. Use each digit only once.

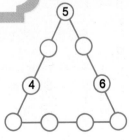

Let's add 164 + 325.

Expanded Form

164 →	1 hundred	+ 6 tens	+ 4
+ 325 →	3 hundreds	+ 2 tens	+ 5
	4 hundreds	+ 8 tens	+ 9

Short Form

ADD ONES
```
  16 4
+ 32 5
------
     9
```

ADD TENS
```
  1 6 4
+ 3 2 5
-------
    8 9
```

ADD HUNDREDS
```
  1 6 4
+ 3 2 5
-------
  4 8 9
```

1. Add 237 + 421.

  a. Use the expanded form.

  b. Use the short form.

2. Here is how we check addition.

ADD DOWN
```
  346
+ 413
-----
  759
```

ADD UP TO CHECK
```
  346
+ 413
-----
  759
```

Add. Use the short form.

a. 35
     + 24

b. 463
     + 225

c. 7,324
     + 1,463

d. 421
       245
     + 323

Add.

1.	23 +46	2.	48 +31	3.	73 +21	4.	45 +34
5.	231 +463	6.	784 +213	7.	724 +155	8.	706 +233
9.	1,348 + 451	10.	2,964 +3,014	11.	7,348 +1,421	12.	3,964 +2,023
13.	35 21 +41	14.	34 21 +20	15.	513 240 +124	16.	372 410 +215
17.	1,248 630 + 21	18.	2,124 3,351 +3,412	19.	4,431 3,232 +1,323	20.	5,524 344 +3,101

★ Find the missing digits.

21.	624 3? +1?1 797	22.	3,40? 2,1?2 + 31 5,?76	23.	1,?34 ?,43? +2,121 8,7?6	24.	2,4?3 1,062 +3,42? 6,?89

Solve these problems.

25. There are 433 children at Madison School and 324 children at Park School. How many children are at both schools?

26. There are 31 days in March, 30 days in April and 31 days in May. How many days in all for the 3 months?

53

STORY PROBLEMS

Some problems have extra information.

Al watched TV 45 minutes on Sunday, 30 minutes on Monday, and 50 minutes on Tuesday. How much TV did he watch on Sunday and Monday?

We do not need to know how much time he watched TV on Tuesday.

Some problems do not have enough information.

Pam has already baked 4 pies for her class party. How many more does she have to bake?

We need to know how many pies she had to bake in all.

Charles bought a kite for 75 cents. He bought a puzzle for 50 cents. He bought bubble gum for 14 cents. How much did he pay for the puzzle and bubble gum in all?

1. What information in the problem is not needed?

2. Solve the problem.

David had 8 red marbles and some blue marbles. How many marbles did he have in all?

3. Can you solve the problem?

4. What information is missing?

5. Make up the missing information and solve.

54

Solve. If there is not enough information, write "not enough information." If there is extra information, tell what it is.

1. There are 324 boys, 353 girls, and 51 teachers at the Sun Valley School. How many children are there in all?

2. There are 48 members in the Sunrise School band. How many are boys?

3. The band has 5 drums, 13 trumpets, and 2 bells. How many drums and trumpets are there?

4. The band practiced 15 hours in September, 14 hours in October, and 11 hours in November. How many hours did they practice in September and October?

5. Raye wants a new tuba. She has saved $12.45. How much more does she need before she can buy the tuba?

6. There are 105 students going to a football game by bus. Of these, 42 are football players, 6 are cheerleaders, and 4 are majorettes. How many football players and cheerleaders are going?

7. The school they are visiting is 48 kilometers away. How much farther do they have to go?

REGROUPING

Let's add 59 + 28 using the short form.

ADD ONES

$$
\begin{array}{r}
\overset{1}{5}9 \\
+28 \\
\hline
7
\end{array}
$$

ADD TENS

$$
\begin{array}{r}
\overset{1}{5}9 \\
+28 \\
\hline
87
\end{array}
$$

1. Look at 35 + 59.

   a. What is the sum of the ones?

   b. How is 14 shown?

   c. What is the sum of the tens?

$$
\begin{array}{r}
\overset{1}{3}5 \\
+59 \\
\hline
94
\end{array}
$$

2. Add.

   a. 49 +26 b. 75 +58 c. 47 +63 d. 29 +48

3. Here is an example with 3 addends. Complete.

   a. Add ones. 9 + 8 + 6 = ___

   b. 23 = ___ tens + ___

   c. How is 23 shown?

   d. Add tens. 2 + 4 + 2 + 1 = ___

$$
\begin{array}{r}
\overset{2}{4}9 \\
28 \\
+16 \\
\hline
93
\end{array}
$$

4. Add.

   a. 17 24 +38 b. 46 15 19 +26 c. 35 36 37 + 2 d. 56 19 2 + 7

56

Add.

1. 38 + 47	**2.** 64 + 29	**3.** 56 + 8	**4.** 47 + 23
5. 59 + 5	**6.** 37 + 57	**7.** 45 + 66	**8.** 88 + 49
9. 21 89 + 55	**10.** 43 76 + 76	**11.** 72 27 + 27	**12.** 95 35 + 92
13. 78 49 + 8	**14.** 21 63 + 8	**15.** 36 85 76 + 49	**16.** 37 67 7 + 67

ACTIVITY

Copy and complete the puzzle.

Across

a. 89
 + 58

c. 37
 + 29

e. 59
 + 28

f. 64
 + 59

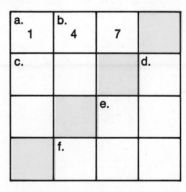

Down

a. 64
 39
 + 65

b. 18
 13
 + 15

d. 43
 46
 + 84

e. 25
 18
 + 39

57

ADDING HUNDREDS

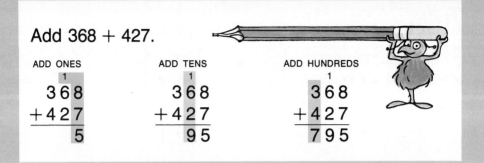

Add 368 + 427.

ADD ONES	ADD TENS	ADD HUNDREDS
1 368 +427 5	1 368 +427 95	1 368 +427 795

1. Look at 439 + 248.

   a. What is the sum of the ones?

   b. How is it shown?

   c. Add 475 + 219.

   $$\begin{array}{r}1\\439\\+248\\\hline687\end{array}$$

2. Sometimes we regroup the tens.

   a. What is the sum of the tens?

   b. How is it shown?

   c. Add 478 + 341.

   $$\begin{array}{r}1\\453\\+374\\\hline827\end{array}$$

3. Sometimes we regroup more than once.

ADD ONES	ADD TENS	ADD HUNDREDS
1 398 +476 4	1 1 398 +476 74	1 1 398 +476 874

Add.

a.   884
  + 138

b.   484
  + 376

c.   798
  589
  + 476

d.   198
  61
  389
  + 475

Add.

1.	416 + 327	**2.**	327 + 329	**3.**	728 + 36	**4.**	238 + 429
5.	771 + 185	**6.**	785 + 144	**7.**	325 + 381	**8.**	264 + 54
9.	628 + 197	**10.**	739 + 184	**11.**	253 + 487	**12.**	863 + 348
13.	937 + 368	**14.**	387 + 86	**15.**	627 + 84	**16.**	956 + 84
17.	248 324 + 135	**18.**	356 208 + 428	**19.**	543 271 + 162	**20.**	853 792 + 483
21.	968 437 253 + 94	**22.**	486 92 9 + 183	**23.**	995 8 489 + 42	**24.**	748 897 79 + 8

Solve these problems.

25. Jerri bowled 148, 139, and 164. What was her total score for the three games?

26. At a recent football game 249 student tickets were sold. There were 198 adult tickets sold. How many tickets were sold in all?

27. One of the highest scores ever recorded for a basketball game was 169 to 147. What was the total amount of scoring?

ADDING THOUSANDS

Here is how we add thousands.

ONES	TENS	HUNDREDS	THOUSANDS
1	1 1	1 1 1	1 1 1
4,7 3 6	4,7 3 6	4,7 3 6	4,7 3 6
+9,7 8 9	+9,7 8 9	+9,7 8 9	+9,7 8 9
5	2 5	5 2 5	1 4,5 2 5

1. Look at this example.

$$\begin{array}{r} {\scriptstyle 1\ 1\ 1} \\ 2{,}764 \\ +\ 9{,}287 \\ \hline 12{,}051 \end{array}$$

   a. What is the sum of the hundreds?
How is it shown?

   b. What is the sum of the thousands?

   c. To check, add up.

2. Add.

   a. $\begin{array}{r} 8{,}496 \\ +\ 5{,}684 \\ \hline \end{array}$
   b. $\begin{array}{r} 33{,}672 \\ +\ 7{,}399 \\ \hline \end{array}$
   c. $\begin{array}{r} 15{,}486 \\ 29{,}434 \\ +\ 2{,}941 \\ \hline \end{array}$

EXERCISES

Add.

1. $\begin{array}{r} 5{,}364 \\ +\ 1{,}438 \\ \hline \end{array}$
2. $\begin{array}{r} 7{,}836 \\ +\ 1{,}486 \\ \hline \end{array}$
3. $\begin{array}{r} 3{,}497 \\ +\ 2{,}874 \\ \hline \end{array}$
4. $\begin{array}{r} 8{,}679 \\ +\ 4{,}863 \\ \hline \end{array}$

5. $\begin{array}{r} 2{,}435 \\ +\ 4{,}698 \\ \hline \end{array}$
6. $\begin{array}{r} 6{,}409 \\ +\ 3{,}998 \\ \hline \end{array}$
7. $\begin{array}{r} 3{,}498 \\ +\ 4{,}584 \\ \hline \end{array}$
8. $\begin{array}{r} 7{,}486 \\ +\ 8{,}594 \\ \hline \end{array}$

9. $\begin{array}{r} 8{,}493 \\ +\ 2{,}746 \\ \hline \end{array}$
10. $\begin{array}{r} 9{,}387 \\ +\ 946 \\ \hline \end{array}$
11. $\begin{array}{r} 2{,}843 \\ +\ 972 \\ \hline \end{array}$
12. $\begin{array}{r} 7{,}890 \\ +\ 728 \\ \hline \end{array}$

13.	17,346 + 42,647	14.	55,346 + 12,780	15.	43,241 + 62,969
16.	79,386 + 57,975	17.	94,769 + 98,478	18.	23,671 + 84,783
19.	7,321 9,843 + 6,285	20.	4,989 7,385 + 6,941	21.	8,359 6,782 + 4,084
22.	54,672 83,798 + 78,436	23.	64,821 5,783 + 36,498	24.	85,468 29,391 + 37,483

Complete these chain reactions.

★ **25.**   9   → 18
         + 9   + 84   + 998   + 4,539
         ‾‾18‾‾   ‾‾5,639‾‾

★ **26.**   345
         + 829   + 8,971   + 86,432   + 48,211
         ‾‾‾‾   ‾‾144,788‾‾

Solve these problems.

27. The Lane City Post Office has 2 mail trucks. One truck picked up 32,190 letters and the other picked up 64,578. How many letters were picked up in all?

28. The Valetown Post Office sold 8,145 stamps in June; 11,605 in July; and 7,436 in August. How many stamps did they sell in all during the three months?

Add.

1.	36 + 3	**2.**	41 + 7	**3.**	68 + 8
4.	49 + 3	**5.**	9 9 7 +2	**6.**	6 9 4 +8

7. 41
+ 35   **8.** 72
+ 16   **9.** 49
+ 28   **10.** 74
+ 39

11. 314
+ 629   **12.** 478
+ 217   **13.** 428
+ 126   **14.** 391
+ 268

15. 497
+ 271   **16.** 486
+ 121   **17.** 498
+ 762   **18.** 749
+ 876

19. 984
+ 376   **20.** 7,941
+ 9,844   **21.** 8,273
+ 7,699   **22.** 14,392
+ 14,873

23. 78
96
+ 49   **24.** 238
476
+ 925   **25.** 4,287
9,649
+ 8,768   **26.** 37,982
45,694
+ 12,345

Brainteaser

A: 1
2
+3
——
6

B: 4
5
+6
——
15

C: 7
8
+9
——
24

Each of the columns above has a different sum. Move just one addend into another column. Each column should now have the same sum.

What properties are shown?

1. $8 + 7 = 7 + 8$

2. $7 + 0 = 7$

3. $(6 + 4) + 8 = 6 + (4 + 8)$

True or false?

4. $9 + 3 = 12$

5. $8 - 5 = 2$

6. $8 + 7 = 15$

7. $16 - 8 = 8$

8. $4 + 3 = 2 + 5$

9. $6 + 7 = 13$

10. $15 - 6 = 9$

11. $8 + 6 = 9 + 7$

Make true sentences.

12. $4 + 7 = \square$

13. $6 + \square = 11$

14. $15 - \square = 9$

15. $\triangle + 9 = 17$

16. $5 + \triangle = 6 + 4$

17. $7 + 4 = \square + 6$

18. $\triangle + \square = 8$

19. $\triangle + \triangle = 8$

20. $\square + 0 = \square$

21. $\square - 4 = \triangle$

What is the value of each underlined digit?

Example   For 8,463: 8,000

22. 694

23. 8,493

24. 7,682

25. 15,063

26. 35,688

27. 268,063

28. 2,453,287

29. 48,639,826

30. 747,804,006

MONEY NOTATION

We read each of these as "seventy-five cents."
75¢ $.75

We read this as "two dollars and seventy-five cents."
$2.75

1. Read these.

    a. 84¢   **b.** $.84   **c.** $.98   **d.** 98¢

    e. 6¢   **f.** $.06   **g.** 1¢   **h.** $.01

2. Name each of these in two ways.

    a. Forty-seven cents   **b.** Eleven cents

    c. Eight cents   **d.** Two cents

3. Read these.

    a. $9.86   **b.** $7.04   **c.** $19.87

    d. $29.08   **e.** $134.72   **f.** $2,133.05

4. Look at $2.75. What separates the dollars and cents?

5. We can think of $2.75 as 275¢.

Write each of these in two ways.

    a. Seven dollars and thirty-one cents.

    b. Six dollars and four cents.

    c. Three hundred forty-five cents.

6. Look at $45.85.

$45.85

Ones of cents (pennies)
Tens of cents (dimes)
Hundreds of cents (ones of dollars)
Tens of dollars

Look at $1,326.05. What digits are in these places?

a. Ones of Cents
b. Ones of dollars
c. Tens of cents
d. Tens of dollars
e. Hundreds of dollars
f. Thousands of dollars

EXERCISES

Write each in two ways.

1. Four cents
2. Thirteen cents

3. Fifty-eight cents
4. Seventy cents

5. Five dollars and forty-two cents

6. Three hundred eighty cents

7. One hundred one cents

8. Nine dollars and six cents

Look at $3,428.70. What digits are in these places?

9. Tens of cents
10. Tens of dollars

11. Ones of cents
12. Ones of dollars

13. Hundreds of dollars
14. Thousands of dollars

DOLLARS AND CENTS

We can add dollars and cents this way.

STEP 1	STEP 2	STEP 3
1	1 1	1 1
$ 3.9 8	$ 3.9 8	$ 3.9 8
+ 4.4 9	+ 4.4 9	+ 4.4 9
7	.4 7	$ 8.4 7

1. Look at $4.97 + $3.76 + $7.99.

    a. What is the sum of the ones of cents? How is it shown?

    b. What is the sum of the tens of cents? How is it shown?

    c. What is the sum of the dollars?

```
  2 2
$4.97
 3.76
+7.99
```

2. Add $6.98 + $2.49.

EXERCISES

Add.

1. $4.62 +8.76	**2.** $9.84 +3.49	**3.** $17.66 +22.48	**4.** $76.24 +98.29
5. $ .75 + .70	**6.** $ .86 + .99	**7.** $1.48 + .07	**8.** $12.49 + 3.46
9. $ 4.82 12.78 + 3.49	**10.** $ .75 .09 + .90	**11.** $ 3.43 9.86 + 10.89	**12.** $24.72 76.95 +42.80

STAGECOACHES

1. Passengers.
8 got on.
6 got off.
How many left?

2. Changing horses.
After 12 miles.
Again after 19 miles.
How far in all?

3. Travel.
72 miles Monday.
59 miles Tuesday.
How far in all?

4. Cost.
$12.35 to Boston.
$25.74 to Hartford.
How much in all?

5. 17 six-horse teams.
9 four-horse teams.
How many more six-
horse-teams?

6. 41 hours to New York.
499 hours from New
York to St. Louis.
How long to St. Louis?

7. Cost for Hodges family.
Parents: $8.78.
Children: $6.94.
How much in all?

8. Passengers.
1,787 in one year.
2,492 the next year.
How many in all?

9. 124 six-horse teams.
238 four-horse teams.
How many teams in all?

10. 47 drivers.
35 guards.
How many in all?

ROUNDING NUMBERS

An **exact** number is found by counting.
A **rounded** number tells **about** how many.

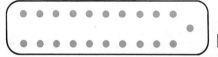

EXACT NUMBER 21
ROUNDED NUMBER 20

1. There were 54 children at the play.

   a. Do you think the number is exact or rounded?

   b. About how many were there? Choose one.
   About 40   About 50   About 60

2. Look at this part of the number line.

   a. Is 54 greater than 50?

   b. Is 54 less than 60?

   c. What number is halfway between 50 and 60?

   d. Is 54 closer to 50 or to 60?

   54 rounded to the nearest ten is 50.

3. Round to the nearest ten.

   a. 18

   b. 26

   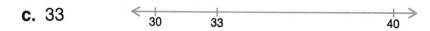

   c. 33

   d. 94

4. Is 35 closer to 30 or to 40?

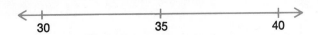

A number halfway between two numbers is rounded up to the greater number.

35 rounded to the nearest ten is 40.

5. Round to the nearest ten.

a. 25   **b.** 15   **c.** 85   **d.** 75   **e.** 45

EXERCISES

Do you think the number is exact or rounded?

1. There are 13 stripes on the American flag.

2. There are 90 beans in the jar.

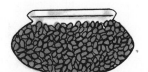

3. There are 30 days in April.

4. There are 29,000 people at the football game.

5. There are 300 parents at the school play.

Round to the nearest ten.

6. 41   **7.** 44   **8.** 45   **9.** 46   **10.** 48

11. 49   **12.** 93   **13.** 16   **14.** 81   **15.** 75

16. 13   **17.** 27   **18.** 62   **19.** 36   **20.** 54

★ **21.** 931 ★ **22.** 386 ★ **23.** 225 ★ **24.** 346 ★ **25.** 732

Shasta Dam in California is 602 feet high. We say it is 600 feet high, rounded to the nearest hundred feet.

1. Round to the nearest hundred.

   a. 328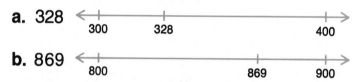
   300   328   400

   b. 869
   800   869   900

2. Is 750 closer to 700 or to 800?
   700   750   800

   750 rounded to the nearest hundred is 800.

3. Let's round thousands.

6,347 ↑	6,547 ↑	6,847 ↑
3 is less than 5. Round to 6,000	5 is halfway. Round to 7,000	8 is greater than 5. Round to 7,000.

   Round to the nearest thousand. Use the underlined digit to help you.

   a. 2,143   b. 5,642   c. 4,200   d. 4,500

4. Think of rounding $6.86 to the nearest dollar.

   a. How many cents in half a dollar?

   b. Is 86¢ more or less than half a dollar?

5. Round to the nearest dollar.

    a. $4.25   **b.** $6.48   **c.** $7.50   **d.** $1.89

EXERCISES

Round to the nearest hundred.

1. 237   **2.** 683   **3.** 450   **4.** 821

5. 119   **6.** 919   **7.** 770   **8.** 858

9. 250   **10.** 493   ★ **11.** 3,529   ★ **12.** 9,364

Round to the nearest thousand.

13. 3,964   **14.** 5,013   **15.** 3,199   **16.** 4,700

17. 4,500   **18.** 4,444   **19.** 5,555   **20.** 6,099

21. 8,732   **22.** 9,367   ★ **23.** 92,823   ★ **24.** 47,123

Round to the nearest dollar.

25. $1.19   **26.** $2.38   **27.** $7.63   **28.** $2.50

29. $9.26   **30.** $8.07   ★ **31.** $47.52   ★ **32.** $83.98

★ Find as many digits as you can to replace each □ to make a true sentence.

33. 4,□41 would be rounded to 4,000.

34. 2,□99 would be rounded to 3,000.

ESTIMATING SUMS

A woman who owns a parking lot kept this record.

NUMBER OF CARS PARKED THIS MONTH

Week	Exact Number	Rounded Number
1st	435	400
2nd	541	500
3rd	394	400
4th	550	600
Totals	1,920 Exact sum	1,900 Estimated sum

1. **a.** How were the numbers rounded?

   b. What is the difference between the estimated sum and the exact sum?

2. Estimate the sum by rounding each addend to the nearest **hundred.**

   a. 431 + 762   **b.** 349 + 301 + 731 + 178

3. Estimate the sum by rounding each addend to the nearest **ten.**

   a. 43 + 76   **b.** 78 + 43 + 75

4. **a.** Estimate the total cost of a skirt, a blouse, and a dress by rounding each to the nearest dollar.

   b. Find the exact cost.

Dresses	$4.98
Blouses	$3.79
Skirts	$5.14

Estimate the sum by rounding each addend to the nearest ten.

1. 72	**2.** 39	**3.** 83	**4.** 63
+48	52	91	+28
	+65	+27	

Estimate the sum by rounding each addend to the nearest hundred.

5. 364	**6.** 437	**7.** 346	**8.** 423
+743	361	821	613
	+721	+375	712
			+864

Estimate the sum by rounding each addend to the nearest dollar.

9. $4.25	**10.** $8.14	**11.** $6.24	**12.** $4.25
+4.79	9.28	2.98	7.84
	+7.84	+3.18	9.63
			+5.40

Solve these problems.

13. Four classes were going to a meeting. Class 1 had 32 pupils, class 2 had 29, class 3 had 33, and class 4 had 25. Estimate how many chairs will be needed to seat all the pupils.

14. George has $10. Estimate if he can buy a checker game for $1.98, a chess game for $2.75, and a pen set for $3.19.

73

Compare. Use =, <, or >.

1. 65 ≡ 79
2. 346 ≡ 281
3. 53 ≡ 52
4. 864 ≡ 863
5. 9,864 ≡ 9,742

Write standard numerals.

6. Four million, four

7. Four million, forty

8. Four million, four hundred

9. Four million, four thousand

ACTIVITY

Make a target like the one shown here.

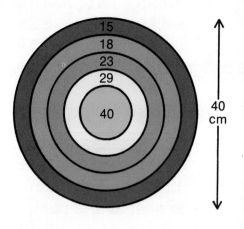

15
18
23
29
40

40 cm

1. Lay it on the floor. Each player gets 5 paper clips. Take turns dropping a paper clip on the target. Add the scores. The player with the highest score wins.

2. Play the game again. This time you should estimate the sum of your scores. See who wins.

★3. You get a score of exactly 100 using five paper clips. Where did the paper clips land?

TELEPHONE WORKERS

In a recent year telephone companies had 15,000 line-people, 31,000 cable splicers, and 4,000 helpers.

1. Find the total number of workers in these jobs.

2. Do you think these numbers are rounded or exact?

3. How many more cable splicers were there than linepeople?

Estimate the answer to each. Then find the exact answer.

4. A lineperson checked 25 kilometers of line on Monday, 32 on Tuesday, and 18 on Wednesday. How many kilometers of line were inspected in all?

5. A splicer connected 16 telephones in one building, 48 in another, and 41 in still another. How many telephones were connected in all?

6. A new telephone line was completed in 3 days. Crew A put in 78, 49, and 65 kilometers of line. Crew B put in 25, 79, and 81 kilometers of line. Which crew put in more line?

CHAPTER REVIEW

Add.

1. 56
[52] + 43

2. 876
[58] + 298

3. $.78
[66] + .04

4. $37.46
[66] + 98.28

5. 3,498
[52] + 2,401

6. 9,804
[60] + 6,189

7. 42,749
[60] + 63,240

8. 87,648
[60] + 99,999

9. 36
[56] 42
     + 27

10. 8,741
[60] 2,692
     + 3,411

11. $6.24
[66] 3.21
     + 4.39

12. 362
[58]   21
     + 46

Estimate the sum by rounding each addend to the nearest ten. [72]

13. 72 + 86

14. 48 + 72 + 35 + 71

Estimate the sum by rounding each addend to the nearest hundred. [72]

15. 346 + 287

16. 365 + 350 + 341

Round to the nearest thousand. [70]

17. 5,422

18. 3,550

Round to the nearest dollar. [70]

19. $6.58

20. $4.21

Solve these problems.

21. Jack bought a sweater for $6.49, gloves for $2.98, and shoes for $9.68. How much did he spend?

22. Jane drove 524 kilometers on Sunday, 412 kilometers on Monday, and 240 kilometers on Tuesday. How far did she drive the first two days?

76

CHAPTER TEST

Add.

1. 48 + 7	**2.** 51 + 33	**3.** 74 + 69	**4.** 733 + 118
5. 473 + 295	**6.** 4,982 + 7,395	**7.** 7,638 + 9,871	**8.** 51,624 + 19,352
9. 1,287 346 + 95	**10.** $.48 .09 + .55	**11.** $4.72 3.15 + 1.11	**12.** $48.75 + 39.64

Estimate the sum by rounding each addend to the nearest ten.

13. $89 + 26$ **14.** $43 + 75 + 31$

Estimate the sum by rounding each addend to the nearest hundred.

15. $624 + 295$ **16.** $455 + 210 + 333$

Round to the nearest thousand.

17. 3,966   **18.** 4,500

Round to the nearest dollar.

19. $7.62   **20.** $1.18

Solve these problems.

21. Joe drove 365 kilometers yesterday. Today he drove 346 kilometers. How far did he drive in all?

22. Elva bought a hot dog for $.40, cake for $.28, and juice for $.37. How much did she spend?

4 SUBTRACTING

Finding a difference is like finding a missing addend.

$$11 - 6 = \square \qquad\qquad \square + 6 = 11$$

difference   missing addend

1. Make true sentences: $15 - 9 = \square$ and $\square + 9 = 15$.

2. Is there a whole number answer for these sentences?

$$7 - 9 = \square \text{ and } \square + 9 = 7$$

3. Which do not have a whole number for the difference?

a.	b.	c.	d.	e.
9	12	8	12	8
−7	− 0	− 10	− 12	−9

EXERCISES

Subtract if you can. Use only whole numbers.

1.	2.	3.	4.	5.
6	8	5	15	16
−4	−5	−8	− 7	− 8

6.	7.	8.	9.	10.
3	9	4	7	14
− 11	−9	−8	−5	− 9

TENS, HUNDREDS, THOUSANDS

5 tens	6 hundreds	17 thousands
−4 tens	−1 hundred	− 8 thousands
1 ten	5 hundreds	9 thousands

50	600	17,000
−40	−100	− 8,000
10	500	9,000

1. Subtract.

a. 11 tens   110
   − 2 tens − 20

b. 9 thousands   9,000
  −5 thousands −5,000

2. Subtract.

a. 170   **b.** 1,700   **c.** 17,000   **d.** 15,000
  − 90   − 900   − 9,000   − 8,000

EXERCISES

Subtract.

1. 80   **2.** 800   **3.** 8,000   **4.** 18,000
  −30   −300   −3,000   − 9,000

5. 80   **6.** 120   **7.** 800   **8.** 900
  −20   − 90   −500   −100

9. 1,200   **10.** 9,000   **11.** 7,000   **12.** 14,000
  − 900   −2,000   −3,000   − 7,000

FORMS FOR SUBTRACTION

Expanded Form

$365 \rightarrow$ 3 hundreds + 6 tens + 5
$-124 \rightarrow$ 1 hundred + 2 tens + 4
2 hundreds + 4 tens + 1 = 241

Short Form

SUBTRACT ONES	SUBTRACT TENS	SUBTRACT HUNDREDS
365	365	365
−124	−124	−124
1	41	241

1. Subtract 75 − 21.

  a. Use the expanded form.

  b. Use the short form.

2. Subtract. Use the short form.

a.	76	**b.**	793	**c.**	487	**d.**	854
	− 14		− 371		− 86		−814

EXERCISES

Subtract. Use the short form.

1.	43	**2.**	63	**3.**	882	**4.**	647
	−21		−31		− 20		− 325

5.	863	**6.**	823	**7.**	4,547	**8.**	3,462
	−821		−711		− 3,223		− 412

CHECKING SUBTRACTION

This flow chart shows how to check subtraction.

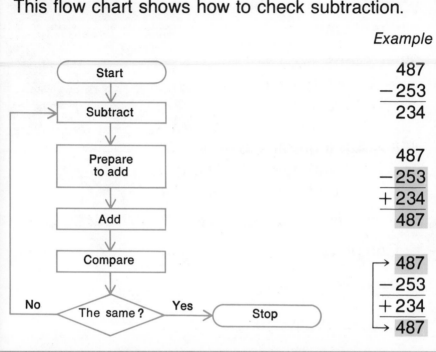

Example

```
   487
 − 253
   234
```

```
   487
 − 253
 + 234
   487
```

```
   487
 − 253
 + 234
   487
```

1. Ed checked his subtraction. He compared. The numbers were not the same. What should he do?

2. Subtract and check: 345 − 122.

Subtract and check.

| 1. | 87 − 7 | 2. | 75 − 70 | 3. | 235 − 114 | 4. | 378 − 76 |

| 5. | 749 − 245 | 6. | 5,487 − 4,172 | 7. | 2,943 − 232 | 8. | 4,999 − 11 |

RENAMING

We can name numbers in different ways.

$32 = 3 \text{ tens} + 2$
$\quad = 2 \text{ tens} + 1 \text{ ten} + 2$
$\quad = 2 \text{ tens} + 12$

$458 = 4 \text{ hundreds} + 5 \text{ tens} + 8$
$\quad = 3 \text{ hundreds} + 1 \text{ hundred} + 5 \text{ tens} + 8$
$\quad = 3 \text{ hundreds} + 15 \text{ tens} + 8$

1. Complete.

a. $49 = 4 \text{ tens} + \underline{\quad}$
$\quad = 3 \text{ tens} + 1 \text{ ten} + \underline{\quad}$
$\quad = 3 \text{ tens} + \underline{\quad}$

b. $783 = 7 \text{ hundreds} + \underline{\quad} \text{ tens} + 3$
$\quad = 6 \text{ hundreds} + 1 \text{ hundred} + \underline{\quad} \text{ tens} + 3$
$\quad = 6 \text{ hundreds} + \underline{\quad} \text{ tens} + 3$

c. $842 = 8 \text{ hundreds} + \underline{\quad} \text{ tens} + 2$
$\quad = 8 \text{ hundreds} + 3 \text{ tens} + \underline{\quad} \text{ ten} + 2$
$\quad = 8 \text{ hundreds} + 3 \text{ tens} + \underline{\quad}$

2. Complete.

a. $47 = 4 \text{ tens} + \underline{\quad}$
$\quad = 3 \text{ tens} + \underline{\quad}$

b. $537 = 5 \text{ hundreds} + \underline{\quad} \text{ tens} + 7$
$\quad = 4 \text{ hundreds} + \underline{\quad} \text{ tens} + 7$

c. $348 = 3 \text{ hundreds} + \underline{\quad} \text{ tens} + 8$
$\quad = 3 \text{ hundreds} + 3 \text{ tens} + \underline{\quad}$

Complete.

1. 75 = 7 tens + ___
  = 6 tens + 1 ten + ___
  = 6 tens + ___

2. 475 = 4 hundreds + ___ tens + 5
  = 3 hundreds + 1 hundred + ___ tens + 5
  = 3 hundreds + ___ tens + 5

3. 734 = 7 hundreds + 3 tens + ___
  = 7 hundreds + 2 tens + 1 ten + ___
  = 7 hundreds + 2 tens + ___

Complete.

4. 96 = 9 tens + ___
  = 8 tens + ___

5. 87 = 8 tens + ___
  = 7 tens + ___

6. 70 = 7 tens + ___
  = 6 tens + ___

7. 35 = 3 tens + ___
  = 2 tens + ___

8. 735 = 7 hundreds + ___ tens + 5
  = 6 hundreds + ___ tens + 5

9. 493 = 4 hundreds + 9 tens + ___
  = 4 hundreds + 8 tens + ___

10. 927 = 9 hundreds + ___ tens + 7
  = 8 hundreds + ___ tens + 7

11. 689 = 6 hundreds + ___ tens + 9
  = 5 hundreds + ___ tens + 9

83

Sometimes we must rename before subtracting.
Subtract 83 − 36.

Expanded Form

CAN'T SUBTRACT ONES   RENAME AND SUBTRACT

$$
\begin{array}{rclcl}
83 & \rightarrow & 8 \text{ tens} + 3 & \rightarrow & \overset{7}{\cancel{8}} \text{ tens} + \overset{13}{\cancel{3}} \\
-36 & \rightarrow & 3 \text{ tens} + 6 & \rightarrow & 3 \text{ tens} + 6 \\
\hline
& & & & 4 \text{ tens} + 7 = 47
\end{array}
$$

Short Form

CAN'T SUBTRACT ONES	RENAME	SUBTRACT ONES	SUBTRACT TENS
83 −36	7 13 8̸ 3̸ −36	7 13 8̸ 3̸ −36 —— 7	7 13 8̸ 3̸ −36 —— 4 7

1. Look at 74 − 38 in both forms.

   a. Why was 74 renamed?

   b. What is the new name for 74?

   $$74 \rightarrow \overset{6}{\cancel{7}} \text{ tens} + \overset{14}{4} \qquad \overset{6\ 14}{\cancel{7}\,4}$$
   $$-38 \rightarrow 3 \text{ tens} + 8 \qquad -38$$

   c. Complete both forms.

2. Let's subtract 438 − 219.

   $$438 \rightarrow 4 \text{ hundreds} + \overset{2}{\cancel{3}} \text{ tens} + \overset{18}{\cancel{8}} \qquad \overset{2\ 18}{4\,\cancel{3}\,\cancel{8}}$$
   $$-219 \rightarrow 2 \text{ hundreds} + 1 \text{ ten} + 9 \qquad -219$$

   a. Why was 438 renamed?

   b. What is the new name for 438?

   c. Complete both forms.

3. Subtract. Use the expanded and the short forms.

a.   64
     -28

b.   543
     -218

4. Subtract. Use the short form.

a.   34
     $-\ 9$

b.   50
     -27

c.   351
     $-\ 34$

d.   875
     -839

Subtract. Use the short form.

1.   53
     $-\ 7$

2.   64
     $-\ 8$

3.   56
     $-\ 9$

4.   60
     $-\ 4$

5.   86
     -38

6.   96
     -58

7.   64
     -59

8.   80
     -67

9.   72
     -63

10.   48
     -29

11.   90
     -65

12.   75
     -69

13.   765
     $-\ 39$

14.   425
     $-\ 18$

15.   276
     $-\ 37$

16.   425
     $-\ 9$

17.   574
     -207

18.   631
     -218

19.   397
     -348

20.   765
     -327

21.   765
     -336

22.   981
     -735

23.   648
     -619

24.   423
     -319

Solve this problem.

25. Jackie has read 76 pages of a 191-page book. How many pages does she have left to read?

Subtract 482 − 191.

Expanded Form

CAN'T SUBTRACT TENS
RENAME AND COMPLETE

$$
\begin{array}{ll}
482 & \rightarrow \quad \overset{3}{\cancel{4}} \text{ hundreds} + \overset{18}{\cancel{8}} \text{ tens} + 2 \\
-191 & \rightarrow \quad 1 \text{ hundred} + 9 \text{ tens} + 1 \\
\hline
& \quad 2 \text{ hundreds} + 9 \text{ tens} + 1 = 291
\end{array}
$$

Short Form

SUBTRACT ONES	CAN'T SUBTRACT TENS	RENAME	COMPLETE
		3 18	3 18
482	482	4̸8̸2	4̸8̸2
−191	−191	−191	−191
1	1	1	291

1. Let's do 638 − 453.

$$
\begin{array}{ll}
638 & \rightarrow \quad \overset{5}{\cancel{6}} \text{ hundreds} + \overset{13}{\cancel{3}} \text{ tens} + 8 \\
-453 & \rightarrow \quad 4 \text{ hundreds} + 5 \text{ tens} + 3 \\
\hline
\end{array}
$$

$$
\begin{array}{r}
\overset{5\ 13}{6\,3\,8} \\
-4\,5\,3 \\
\hline
\end{array}
$$

a. Why was 638 renamed?

b. What is the new name for 638?

c. Complete both subtractions.

2. Consider 4,638 − 1,927.

a. Why was 4,638 renamed?

b. What is the new name for 4,638?

c. Complete the subtraction.

$$
\begin{array}{r}
\overset{3\ 16}{4{,}6\,3\,8} \\
-1{,}9\,2\,7 \\
\hline
\end{array}
$$

3. Subtract. Use the short form.

a. 735	**b.** 648	**c.** 4,273	**d.** 6,285
−281	−573	−1,941	−6,094

Subtract.

1. 912	**2.** 476	**3.** 987	**4.** 428
−381	−195	−397	−209

5. 518	**6.** 729	**7.** 487	**8.** 941
−472	− 34	− 91	−803

9. 988	**10.** 949	**11.** 8,749	**12.** 7,386
−879	− 79	−8,380	−6,943

13. 9,284	**14.** 8,796	**15.** 6,487	**16.** 3,864
−6,147	−7,910	− 293	− 91

17. 3,849	**18.** 8,790	**19.** 6,395	**20.** 5,974
−2,050	−2,800	−3,286	−5,890

Solve these problems.

21. Mr. Elephant weighed 1,465 kilograms. He went on a diet and lost 372 kilograms. How much does he weigh now?

22. Allen the Anteater ate 5,926 ants on Monday and 3,784 ants on Tuesday. How many more ants did he eat on Monday than on Tuesday?

87

Sometimes we rename more than one time.

RENAME SUBTRACT ONES	RENAME SUBTRACT TENS	SUBTRACT HUNDREDS
2 14 5 3 4 − 2 5 8 6	12 4 2 14 5 3 4 − 2 5 8 7 6	12 4 2 14 5 3 4 − 2 5 8 2 7 6

1. Subtract.

a. 427
− 198

b. 760
− 278

c. 286
− 197

2. We can rename with thousands.

SUBTRACT ONES	SUBTRACT TENS	SUBTRACT HUNDREDS	SUBTRACT THOUSANDS
1 14 5,6 2 4 − 3,9 8 6 8	11 5 1 14 5,6 2 4 − 3,9 8 6 3 8	15 11 4 5 1 14 5,6 2 4 − 3,9 8 6 6 3 8	15 11 4 5 1 14 5,6 2 4 − 3,9 8 6 1,6 3 8

Subtract.

a. 7,853
− 4,995

b. 72,413
− 59,198

c. 83,274
− 28,495

Subtract.

1. 462
− 147

2. 835
− 778

3. 376
− 189

4. 480
− 195

5. 872
− 399

6. 487
− 88

7. 947
− 289

8. 586
− 297

9.	6,574 − 3,267	10.	8,326 −　667	11.	3,180 −　235	12.	7,835 − 6,576
13.	5,630 − 4,874	14.	7,683 −　479	15.	7,642 − 3,818	16.	6,842 − 3,971
17.	27,111 − 14,523	18.	53,425 − 31,869	19.	68,476 − 57,895		
20.	37,244 − 16,159	21.	46,487 − 29,678	★22.	8,424,826 − 2,937,939		

Solve these problems.

23. The first adding machine was invented in France in 1642. How many years ago was that?

24. The zipper was invented in 1891. How long ago was that?

25. The Mississippi River is about 3,860 miles long. The longest river is the Nile River in Africa. It is 4,145 miles long. How much longer is the Nile than the Mississippi?

Brainteaser

Find the differences. What pattern do you find for each row? Show three more subtractions that fit each pattern.

1.	765 − 567	987 − 789	321 − 123
2.	4,321 − 1,234	7,654 − 4,567	5,432 − 2,345

89

ELECTRICIANS

1. Had 1,871 meters of cable.
   Used 1,867 meters
   How much left?

2. Needs 72 meters of tubing.
   Has 29 meters.
   How much more needed?

3. Worked.
   40 hours.
   56 hours.
   39 hours.
   How many hours in all?

4. Workers.
   12 painters.
   6 welders.
   19 electricians.
   How many in all?

5. Hours worked.
   156 in April.
   209 in May.
   How many more in May?

6. Installed switches.
   31 Monday.
   28 Tuesday.
   How many in all?

7. Became an electrician in 1949.
   Retired this year.
   How many years in this career?

8. Spent.
   $27.80 on tools.
   $18.95 on work clothes.
   How much in all?

RENAMING: ZEROS

We can rename hundreds and thousands as tens.

$900 = 90$ tens $+ 0$ $8,003 = 800$ tens $+ 3$
    $= 89$ tens $+ 10$ $= 799$ tens $+ 13$

1. Copy and complete.

   a. $400 = 40$ tens $+ 0$
            $= 39$ tens $+$ ___

   b. $7,000 = 700$ tens $+ 0$
              $=$ ___ tens $+ 10$

2. Complete.

   a. $706 =$ ___ tens $+ 16$

   b. $4,007 =$ ___ tens $+ 17$

EXERCISES

Complete.

1. $300 =$ ___ tens $+ 0$
      $=$ ___ tens $+ 10$

2. $4,000 = 400$ tens $+$ ___
        $= 399$ tens $+$ ___

3. $400 = 39$ tens $+$ ___

4. $407 =$ ___ tens $+ 17$

5. $2,008 =$ ___ tens $+ 18$

Let's subtract 400 − 198.

Short Form

CAN'T SUBTRACT
ONES

```
  4 0 0
− 1 9 8
```

RENAME
```
39  10
4̶0̶ 0̸
− 1 9 8
```

SUBTRACT
```
39  10
4̶0̶ 0̸
− 1 9 8
  2 0 2
```

```
400
198
202T
```

1. Let's subtract 305 − 126.

   a. Why was 305 renamed?

   b. What is the new name for 305?

   c. Complete the subtraction and check.

```
   29 15
   3̶0̶5̶
 − 1 2 6
```

2. Here is an example with thousands.

   a. What is the new name for 6,003?

   b. Complete the subtraction and check.

```
   599  13
   6̶,0̶0̶3̶
 − 2,7 8 9
```

3. Subtract.

   a.
```
   5 0 0
 − 3 4 7
```
   b.
```
   9,0 0 8
 − 6,4 8 9
```
   c.
```
   4,0 0 0
 − 3,1 9 4
```

4. Sometimes we must rename twice.

CAN'T SUBTRACT
ONES
```
   8,0 4 0
 − 4,6 5 8
```

RENAME AND
SUBTRACT
```
     3 10
   8,0 4̶0̸
 − 4,6 5 8
       2
```

CAN'T SUBTRACT
TENS
```
     3 10
   8,0 4̶0̸
 − 4,6 5 8
       2
```

RENAME AND
SUBTRACT
```
      13
   79  3̶ 10
   8̶,0̶4̶0̸
 − 4,6 5 8
   3,3 8 2
```

92

Subtract. Use the short form.

a.   4,030
        − 2,145

b.   6,070
        − 1,486

c.   6,020
        − 844

d.   7,030
        − 1,478

Subtract.

1.   300
        − 225

2.   704
        − 399

3.   700
        − 643

4.   607
        − 239

5.   600
        − 473

6.   900
        − 372

7.   400
        − 297

8.   806
        − 229

9.   2,000
        − 1,398

10. 7,003
        − 2,586

11. 3,703
        − 1,997

12. 4,000
        − 3,247

13. 5,007
        − 3,284

14. 8,000
        − 7,463

15. 7,076
        − 5,984

16. 4,005
        − 2,876

17. 6,020
        − 2,395

18. 2,704
        − 1,347

19. 8,000
        − 7,645

20. 9,020
        − 4,083

21. 87,700
        − 43,847

22. 36,030
        − 22,928

23. 60,500
        − 39,743

★ Find the missing digits.

24. 9?,?04
        − 23,297
        ‾‾‾‾‾‾‾
         66,707

25. 60,?5?
        − 48,141
        ‾‾‾‾‾‾‾
         1?,915

26. 4?,0?3
        − 27,874
        ‾‾‾‾‾‾‾
         ?1,129

Solve this mini-problem.

27. 40,806 people at a football game.
32,649 adults.
How many children?

93

Subtract.

1.	70 − 30	**2.**	500 − 200	**3.**	9,000 − 3,000
4.	75 − 24	**5.**	83 − 71	**6.**	95 − 25
7.	73 − 9	**8.**	42 − 8	**9.**	35 − 6

10.	84 − 48	**11.**	461 − 39	**12.**	475 − 349	**13.**	428 − 193
14.	935 − 280	**15.**	4,132 − 1,811	**16.**	732 − 298	**17.**	464 − 398
18.	4,123 − 2,324	**19.**	7,942 − 6,988	**20.**	74,732 − 32,984	**21.**	91,191 − 72,445
22.	700 − 393	**23.**	805 − 218	**24.**	4,000 − 3,943	**25.**	45,003 − 33,498

ACTIVITY

Your number is 0. Follow the race track. Add or subtract the number of each car that you pass.

START +1,000 −732 +925 +6,458 −3,719 −353 +1,354 −4,929 FINISH

Is your number 4?

94

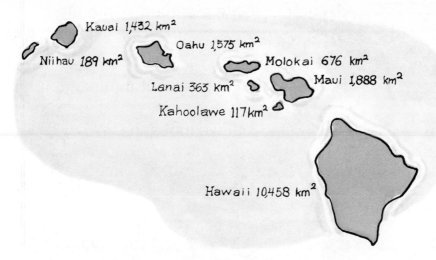

Kauai 1,432 km²

Niihau 189 km²

Oahu 1,575 km²

Molokai 676 km²

Lanai 363 km²

Maui 1,888 km²

Kahoolawe 117 km²

Hawaii 10,458 km²

HAWAII, OUR FIFTIETH STATE

1. The three largest islands in the state of Hawaii are Hawaii, Maui, and Oahu. What is the total area of these three islands in km²?

2. Hawaii is the largest of the islands. The capital city, Honolulu, is on the island of Oahu. How much larger is the island of Hawaii than the island of Oahu?

3. Captain Cook landed on the Hawaiian Islands in 1778. How long ago was this?

4. The State of Hawaii, called the Aloha State, became our fiftieth state in 1959. How long ago was this?

5. It is about 4,110 kilometers from New York City to San Francisco. It is about 3,850 kilometers from San Francisco to Honolulu. How far is it from New York to Honolulu by way of San Francisco?

6. Liliuokalini was the last queen of Hawaii. She left her throne in 1873. How many years ago was that?

Keeping Fit

Write standard numerals.

1. Six million

2. Thirty-eight thousand, forty

3. Five thousand, five

Compare. Use =, <, or >.

4. 63 ≡ 74

5. 47 ≡ 49

6. 583 ≡ 634

7. 324 ≡ 327

8. 8,743 ≡ 8,684

9. 2,532 ≡ 2,356

10. 4,864 ≡ 4,873

11. 7,432 ≡ 7,435

Round to the nearest ten.

12. 64
13. 38
14. 75
15. 91

Round to the nearest hundred.

16. 327
17. 467
18. 850
19. 784

Round to the nearest dollar.

20. $7.24
21. $3.05
22. $2.73
23. $4.53

Add.

24.
```
   98
 +74
```
25.
```
  650
 +729
```
26.
```
 8,496
+3,984
```
27.
```
 77,060
+25,948
```

28.
```
   7
   8
   5
  +7
```
29.
```
  72
  95
  65
 +48
```
30.
```
  348
  276
  398
 +496
```
31.
```
  285
  299
   84
 +947
```

DOLLARS AND CENTS

Charles has saved $4.85. He wants to buy a basketball that costs $9.49. How much more money does he need?

STEP 1	STEP 2	STEP 3
	8 14	8 14
$ 9.4 9	$ 9.4 9	$ 9.4 9
− 4.8 5	− 4.8 5	− 4.8 5
4	6 4	$ 4.6 4

He needs $4.64 more.

1. A green sleeping bag costs $12.95. A blue sleeping bag costs $14.50. Eric wants the green bag. How much less is the green bag than the blue bag?

2. Mrs. Lee bought 4 kilograms of meat for $13.94. She also bought 6 kilograms of fruit for $8.67. How much more did she spend for the meat?

3. Mr. Abrams saw a television set for $195.95. He bought it on sale a week later for $157.70. How much did he save?

4. Sarah paid $24.98 for a camera and $2.59 for a camera case. How much did she spend in all?

5. Mr. James bought a tie for $3.95. He gave the clerk $10. How much change should he receive?

6. Andrea bought a necklace for $2.99. How much change should she receive from a $20 bill?

MAKING CHANGE

Pretend you are a clerk. A man wants a hat for $5.49. He gives you a $20 bill. You give him change.

Give	Say
1 penny	$5.50
2 quarters	$5.75, $6.00
4 dollars	$7.00, $8.00, $9.00, $10.00
1 ten dollar bill	$20.00

1. A woman wants a scarf for $2.17. She gives you $5. What change would you give her?
Complete this list.

Give	Say
3 pennies	$2.18, $2.19, $2.20
1 nickel	$2.25
____	____, ____, ____
____	____, ____

2. A man wants a belt for $3.49. He gives you a $10 bill. Make a list to show what change you would give him.

3. In some stores the cash register tells the change to be returned.

This is how you would give $6.02.

Give	Say
1 five dollar bill	$5.00
1 one dollar bill	$6.00
2 pennies	$6.01, $6.02

98

List how you would return the change.

a. Owe $6.19
    Pay $10.00
    Change $3.81

b. Owe $7.21
    Pay $20.00
    Change $12.79

EXERCISES

Make a list to show what change you would return.

1. Shirt for $3.95
Given a $5 bill

2. Toy for $2.89
Given a $10 bill

3. Jacket for $16.48
Given a $20 bill

4. Hat for $3.98
Given a $20 bill

5. Wallet for $5.88
Given a $10 bill

6. Radio for $15.65
Given a $20.00 bill

List how you would return the change.

7. Owe $2.78
    Pay $10.00
    Change $7.22

8. Owe $7.45
    Pay $20.00
    Change $12.55

Solve these problems.

9. A man wants a coat that costs $12.94. He gives you a $20 bill. List how you would return the change.

★ **10.** A woman buys a purse for $6.98 and a hat for $2.54. She gives you a $20 bill. List how you would return the change.

99

Barbara had 81 cents. She bought a notebook for 29 cents. About how much did she have left?

Here is how we estimate:
Round to the nearest ten.
Estimate the difference.

$$\begin{array}{r} 80 \\ -30 \\ \hline 50 \end{array}$$

1. Ms. Reed has to drive 493 kilometers. She has already driven 213 kilometers. She has enough gas to go 200 more kilometers. Will she need more gas? Estimate to find out.

a. How were the numbers rounded?

b. Will she need more gas? Explain.

$$\begin{array}{r} 500 \\ -200 \\ \hline 300 \end{array}$$

2. Joan estimates to see if her answers are reasonable.

a. Is Joan's estimate close to her exact answer?

b. Correct the exact answer.

	Exact	Estimate
	4,036	4,000
	− 1,996	− 2,000
	3,040	2,000

EXERCISES

Estimate the differences by rounding.

1.	**2.**	**3.**	**4.**
73	265	395	$6.43
− 19	− 138	− 199	− 2.85

Estimate to find out which are incorrect. Correct them.

5.	**6.**	**7.**	**8.**
634	403	4,863	6,204
− 347	− 174	− 2,983	− 3,748
287	329	2,880	2,456

9.	10.	11.	12.
9,063	8,734	6,403	3,256
−4,784	−2,986	−2,874	−1,872
5,279	5,748	4,529	2,384

Solve these problems by estimating.

13. A farmer had 68 rows of corn. He picked 23 rows on Monday and the rest on Tuesday. About how many rows did he pick on Tuesday?

14. Nita wants a bicycle basket that costs $6.95. She has saved $4.18. Her father gave her $2.00. Does she have enough money now?

15. Carlos is on a 1,000 calorie a day diet. He had 618 calories for breakfast and lunch together. Can he have a dinner of 347 calories?

Keeping Fit

Make true sentences. Use =, <, or >.

1. $4 + 8 \equiv 9 + 2$ **2.** $7 + 4 \equiv 5 + 6$

3. $86 \equiv 67$ **4.** $534 \equiv 547$

5. $6,347 \equiv 7,219$ **6.** $8,746 \equiv 8,739$

Add.

7.	8.	9.	10.
95	428	$4.86	9,248
+63	+276	+7.85	+3,784

11.	12.	13.	14.
7	39	$3.98	3,287
8	48	2.76	946
4	76	4.95	484
+9	+49	+3.84	+ 48

CHAPTER REVIEW

Subtract.

1. 70
[79] − 40

2. 1,400
[79] − 500

3. 96
[80] − 45

4. 75
[80] − 23

5. 56
[84] − 29

6. 83
[84] − 68

7. 459
[86] − 285

8. 637
[86] − 594

9. 4,638
[88] − 2,749

10. 3,431
[88] − 2,753

11. 17,483
[88] − 14,587

12. 73,486
[88] − 57,898

13. 300
[92] − 135

14. 9,004
[92] − 7,385

15. 5,060
[92] − 2,484

16. 20,008
[92] − 14,689

17. $3.98
[97] − 2.76

18. $17.84
[97] − 9.98

19. $10.00
[97] − 8.76

20. $147.06
[97] − 98.47

Estimate the differences by rounding. [100]

21. 87
− 42

22. 526
− 394

23. 826
− 385

24. $9.48
− 3.24

Solve these problems.

25. The first Ferris wheel was built in 1893. How long ago was that?

26. A shirt costs $4.78. You give the clerk a $10 bill. How much change should you receive?

Brainteaser

How can you take 1 away from 19 and be left with 20?

102

CHAPTER TEST

Subtract.

1.	85 − 34	**2.**	1,700 − 800	**3.**	53 − 8	**4.**	624 − 195

5.	700 − 285	**6.**	4,182 − 3,731	**7.**	8,004 − 3,968	**8.**	$7.42 − 2.59

9.	$19.47 − 9.98	**10.**	$34.63 − 17.48	**11.**	17,476 − 3,989	**12.**	34,486 − 15,988

Estimate the differences by rounding.

13.	49 − 31	**14.**	827 − 586	**15.**	436 − 137	**16.**	$7.48 − 2.49

Solve these problems.

17. Babe Didrikson won 2 gold medals in the 1932 Olympic Games. How long ago was that?

18. A pair of jeans costs $9.48. You give the clerk a $20 bill. How much change should you receive?

Brainteaser

Digits: 0, 1, 2, 3, 4, 5, 6, 7, 8, 9

Make up an addition problem using all of the above digits once. No digit may be used more than once.

$$\begin{array}{r} ?\,?\,? \\ +\,?\,?\,? \\ \hline ?\,?\,?\,? \end{array}$$

5 GEOMETRY

POINTS AND PATHS

Look at this treasure map.

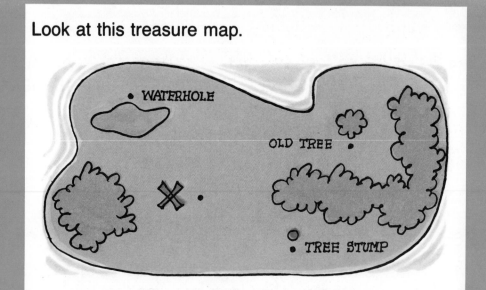

The treasure is marked with a **point.**
The point is named X.

1. Name three other points located on the map.

In geometry we think of a point as a location.
A point is pictured by a dot.
It is named with a capital letter.

Point A   • A

2. Name the points below.

•W   Y
                      •

3. Mark a point. Name it Q.

4. Some Scouts were hiking from the camp to the picnic ground. There are four paths they could take.

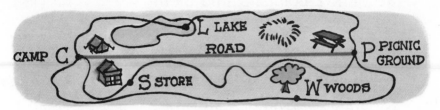

a. Point *C* is one endpoint. Name the other.

b. Trace the shortest path from *C* to *P* with your finger. What color is it?

The shortest path from *C* to *P* is a straight path.

EXERCISES

1. Name the points below.

R

• U

• S

T

2. Mark 2 points. Name them *O* and *P*.

3. Name the endpoints of these paths.

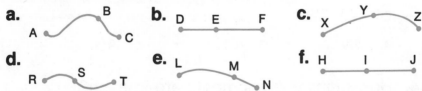

a. B / A / C

b. D E F

c. X Y Z

d. R S T

e. L M N

f. H I J

4. Which paths in Exercise 3 are straight paths?

5. Draw a picture of a path from your desk to a door. Name the endpoints *D* for desk and *E* for exit.

105

1. a. Mark 2 points. Name them *E* and *F*.

E F

b. Use your ruler. Draw a straight path from *E* to *F*.

E F

c. Draw three other paths from *E* to *F*.

E F

d. How many straight paths can you draw from *E* to *F*?

e. How many different paths could you draw from *E* to *F*?

We call a straight path between two endpoints a **line segment.** We name a segment like this: *EF*. It is read line segment *EF*.

E F

2. Give two names for this line segment.

X Y

3. Read these.

a. $\overline{MN}$ **b.** $\overline{NM}$ **c.** $\overline{AB}$

4. How many line segments are in each?

a. **b.** **c.**

5. Name 3 line segments.

106

Which are line segments?

1.

2.

3.

4. Draw a line segment. Label it $\overline{EF}$.

5. Give two names for this line segment.

How many line segments are in each?

6.    **7.**   **8.**

9.   **10.**    **11.**

12. Name 3 line segments.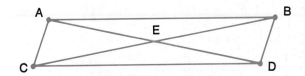

★ **13.** How many line segments can you find? Name them.

Brainteaser

Mark 6 points on your paper. How many different line segments can you draw connecting these points? Each line segment must connect 2 points.

RAYS

1. **a.** Draw a line segment. Name it $\overline{AB}$.

   b. Extend $\overline{AB}$ in one direction like this. How far could you extend it?

   c. Put an arrow on it like this. What does the arrow tell us?

   We call 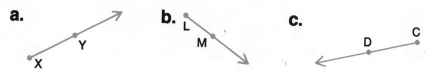 a ray.
   We name it $\overrightarrow{AB}$. The endpoint A is always named first.

2. Name each ray.

   a.   **b.**   **c.**

3. Look at these rays.

   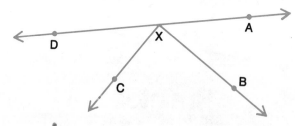

   a. Point to $\overrightarrow{XA}$.

   b. Point to $\overrightarrow{XD}$.

   c. Name two other rays.

108

Name each ray.

1.
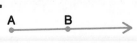
A   B

2.

M
L

3.

H
J

4.

E   D

5.
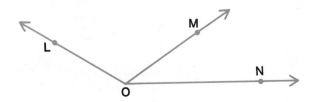
R
S

6.
O
P

Draw these.

7. Point *C*   **8.** $\overline{XY}$ **9.** $\overline{MN}$ **10.** $\overrightarrow{XY}$

11. $\overrightarrow{YX}$ **12.** $\overline{AB}$ **13.** $\overrightarrow{BA}$ **14.** $\overrightarrow{AB}$

15. Name three rays.

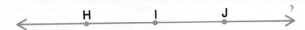

M
L
N
O

★**16.** Name as many rays as you can.

H   I   J

ACTIVITY

Look around your home and school for models of these figures. Make a display of your models.

1. Point   **2.** Path

3. Ray   **4.** Line segment

1. **a.** Draw $\overrightarrow{AB}$.

   b. Draw $\overrightarrow{AC}$. Use the same point A.

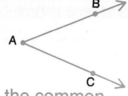

These two rays form an **angle.** We call the common point A the **vertex.** The two rays are called **sides.**

2. The name of this angle is angle *LMN* or angle *NML*. We write ∠ *LMN* or ∠ *NML*.

   a. Name the sides.

   b. Name the vertex.

   c. Where is the vertex named in ∠ *LMN*? in ∠ *NML*?

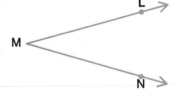

When we name an angle, the vertex is always in the middle.

∠ YXZ
∠ ZXY

3. Compare these angles.

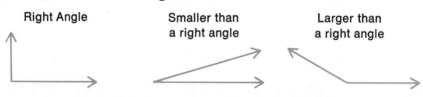

Right Angle   Smaller than a right angle   Larger than a right angle

   Which look like right angles?

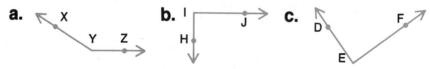

   a. X Y Z   **b.** I J H   **c.** D E F

4. Give 2 names for each angle in Items 3a–c.

Look at these angles.

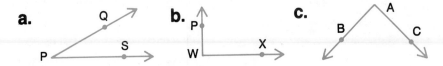

a. Q S P

b. P W X

c. A B C

1. Give two names for each angle.

2. Name the vertex of each angle.

3. Name the sides of each angle.

Which look like right angles?

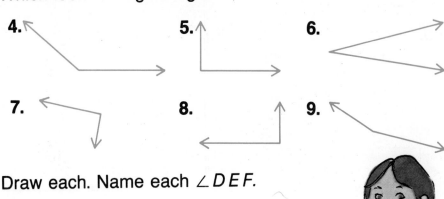

4.

5.

6.

7.

8.

9.

Draw each. Name each ∠DEF.

10. A right angle.

11. An angle smaller than a right angle.

12. An angle larger than a right angle.

★ 13. How many angles can you find? Name them.

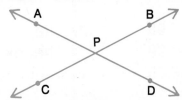

A B P C D

Write standard numerals.

1. 4 tens + 5 ones.

2. 1 hundred + 3 tens + 4 ones

3. 7 thousands + 5 tens

Compare. Use <, >, or =.

4.	73 ⬚ 64		**5.**	582 ⬚ 591
6.	804 ⬚ 703		**7.**	6,483 ⬚ 6,543
8.	9,746 ⬚ 8,437		**9.**	4,206 ⬚ 4,206

Add.

10.	43	**11.**	854	**12.**	2,949	**13.**	34,098
	+ 96		+ 397		+ 3,876		+ 27,784

14.	38	**15.**	153	**16.**	1,492	**17.**	8,492
	56		274		3,861		72
	+ 92		+ 86		+ 743		+ 851

Subtract.

18.	29	**19.**	93	**20.**	854	**21.**	$7.00
	− 12		− 27		− 199		− 2.84

22.	4,821	**23.**	6,004	**24.**	15,060	**25.**	53,478
	− 2,931		− 2,873		− 9,876		− 29,289

Round each to the nearest dollar. Estimate the total cost.

26. scarf $4.98
      gloves $7.29
      hat $6.75

27. tie $3.89
      handkerchief $1.19
      shirt $8.85

AUTO PARTS SALES

Use the chart to solve the problems below.

NUMBER OF AUTOMOBILE PARTS SOLD

Time	Mon.	Tues.	Wed.	Thurs.	Fri.
8 to 12	378	346	369	365	348
12 to 5	134	165	152	139	195

How many parts were sold on each of these days?

1. Monday   **2.** Wednesday   **3.** Friday

4. Were there more sales on Tuesday or Thursday?

5. Estimate the number of parts sold from 8 to 12 on Monday and Tuesday.

6. Estimate the number of parts sold from 12 to 5 on Wednesday, Thursday and Friday.

How many more parts were sold from 8 to 12 than 12 to 5 on each of these days?

7. Monday   **8.** Tuesday   **9.** Thursday

LINES

1. Mark two points, *K* and *L,* on your paper. Use the same points for each of these.

   a. Draw $\overrightarrow{KL}$.

   b. Draw $\overrightarrow{LK}$.

   c. What did you draw?

2. Which are lines?

   a.

   b.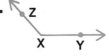

   c.

   d.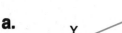

   e.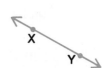

   f.

3. We can name 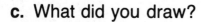 as $\overleftrightarrow{LM}$ or $\overleftrightarrow{ML}$. Name each line two ways.

   a.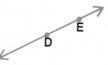

   b.

   c.

114

Which are lines?

1.

2.

3.

4.

5.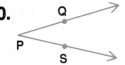

6.

Name these figures.

7.

8.

9.

10.

11. P •

12.

Draw these.

13. $\overrightarrow{QR}$

14. $\overline{AB}$

15. $\overline{CD}$

16. $\overleftrightarrow{PM}$

17. $\overline{ST}$

18. $\overleftrightarrow{GH}$

19. $\overleftrightarrow{KL}$

20. $\overrightarrow{OP}$

ACTIVITY

<u>O</u>   <u>M</u>   <u>G</u> <u>E</u>   <u>R</u>   <u>Y</u>   <u>E</u>   <u>T</u>

1. Name each segment in order from shortest to longest.

___   ___   ___   ___

Did the letters in your answers spell a word?

2. Make up a similar puzzle for your friends to solve.

1. a. Draw $\overleftrightarrow{EF}$.

   b. Draw $\overrightarrow{GH}$ so that it crosses $\overleftrightarrow{EF}$.

   c. Put a *Z* at the point where they cross.

If lines or line segments cross or touch, we say they **intersect**. They have a **common point**.

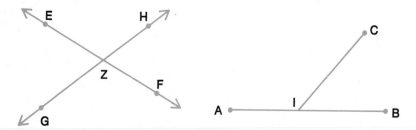

2. Draw two line segments that intersect.

   a. Name the common point *X*.

   b. Is there more than one common point?

   c. Try to draw two line segments that intersect at more than one point. Can you do it?

When two lines or line segments intersect, there is only one common point.

3. Look at these line segments.

   a. Do they intersect?

   b. Think of making them longer. Will they intersect?

4. Draw two line segments that will never intersect (no matter how long you make them).

Lines that will never intersect are **parallel**. Parallel segments will not intersect no matter how long you make them.

5. Which pairs look parallel?

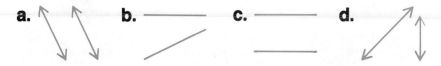

1. Draw two lines that intersect.

2. Draw two line segments that would intersect if you made them longer.

3. Draw two lines that are parallel.

What is the common point?

Which pairs look parallel?

12. Name some things that remind you of intersecting lines; of parallel lines.

117

CURVES

These paths are called **curves.**

curves

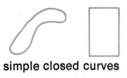

closed curves   simple closed curves

1. Trace this curve with your finger. Start at point A.

    a. Does it end at the same point it started?

    b. Does it cross itself?

2. Trace this curve. Start at point C.

    a. Does it end at the same point it started?

    b. Does it cross itself?

A **closed curve** ends where it starts.

3. Trace this figure. Start at A.

    a. Is it a closed curve?

    b. Does it cross itself?

118

A **simple closed curve** ends where it starts and does not cross or touch itself.

4. Which are curves? Which are closed curves? Which are simple closed curves?

a. b. c. d.

Which are curves? Which are closed curves? Which are simple closed curves?

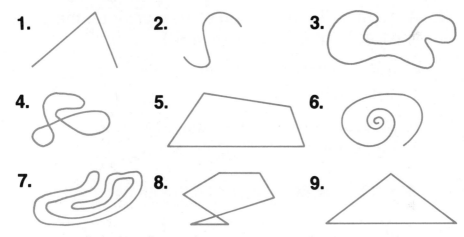

1. 2. 3.

4. 5. 6.

7. 8. 9.

Draw 2 pictures for each.

10. Simple closed curve.

11. Closed curve, but not a simple closed curve.

12. Curve, but not a closed curve.

★ 13. Print the capital letters of our alphabet. Which are closed curves? Which are simple closed curves?

119

1. a. Draw a point. Label it *A*.

b. Use your ruler. Draw 10 points all 1 cm from *A*.

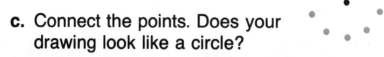

c. Connect the points. Does your drawing look like a circle?

A **circle** is a special simple closed curve. All points on a circle are the same distance from the center.

2. A segment from the center to a point on the circle is called a **radius** (plural — radii).

a. $\overline{LM}$ is a radius. Name the two other radii.

b. Measure each radius. How do the lengths compare?

Each radius of a circle has the same length.

3. Each segment through the center of a circle, with both endpoints on the circle, is called a **diameter.**

a. $\overline{AB}$ is a diameter. Name another diameter.

b. Measure radius $\overline{AX}$. Measure radius $\overline{XB}$. Add the lengths. Measure diameter $\overline{AB}$. How does its length compare with the sum of the two radii?

Look at this circle.

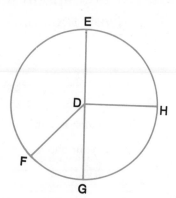

1. Name the center.

2. Name each radius.

3. Name a diameter.

4. How long is $\overline{FD}$?
   $\overline{DE}$? $\overline{DH}$? $\overline{DG}$? $\overline{EG}$?

The lengths of the radii of some circles are given below. What are the lengths of the diameters?

5. 3 cm   **6.** 4 cm   **7.** 8 in.   **8.** 2 in.

9. 7 cm   **10.** 6 cm   **11.** 9 in.   **12.** 12 in.

★ **13.** A diameter of a circle is 30 centimeters long. How long is a radius of the circle?

Keeping Fit

Add.

	1.	2.	3.	4.
	48	378	$12.58	23,487
	37	276	9.64	3,498
	65	498	+86.49	+ 468
	+24	+265		

Subtract.

	5.	6.	7.	8.
	47	478	3,498	$485.26
	−29	−299	−1,879	−149.77

121

DRAWING CIRCLES

1. Follow the steps in the flow chart to draw a circle with a given radius.

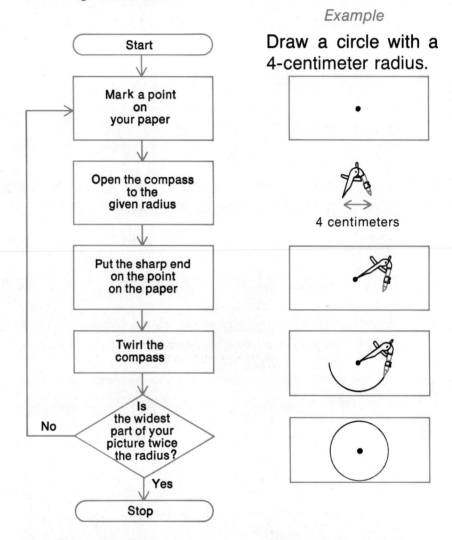

Example

Draw a circle with a 4-centimeter radius.

a. What did you measure to check your circle?

b. The widest part of your circle is not twice the radius. What should you do?

2. Draw a circle with a 3-cm radius; an 8-cm radius.

PROBLEM SOLVING

Use the chart to solve the problems.

FIRSTS IN TRANSPORTATION IN THE UNITED STATES			
Airplane	1903	Motorboat	1885
Automobile	1892	Motorcycle	1900
Bicycle	1819	Railroad Car	1825
Bus	1906	Steamboat	1763
Ferryboat	1811	Truck	1898

1. Which kind of transportation was used first? last?

2. How much older is the first truck than the first bus?

3. Which type of boat was first? How many years ago was it?

4. How many years ago was the first automobile?

5. Clara Barton organized the American Red Cross in 1881. Which kinds of transportation could she have used that year?

6. Which is older, the first airplane or the first bus?

7. How much older is the first bicycle than the first motorcycle?

8. Make up a problem using the facts in the chart.

CHAPTER REVIEW

Draw these.

1. $\overrightarrow{VW}$ **2.** $\angle ABC$ **3.** $\overline{RS}$ **4.** $\overleftrightarrow{PQ}$

[108]   [110]   [106]   [114]

5. A right angle *XYZ*

[110]

6. $\overline{CD}$ and $\overline{EF}$ as parallel line segments

[116]

7. $\overleftrightarrow{PQ}$ and $\overleftrightarrow{RS}$ as intersecting lines

[116]

8. A closed curve

[118]

Look at these pictures.

9. Name the endpoints of $\overline{AB}$.

[106]

10. Name the sides of $\angle EFG$.

[110]

11. Name the vertex of $\angle EFG$.

[110]

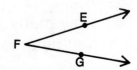

Solve this problem. [120]

12. The length of the radius of a circle is 3 centimeters. What is the length of the diameter?

For each figure, choose one of the names given below. You cannot use a name more than once.

13. [120]   **14.** [110]   **15.** [120]

16. [110]   **17.** [120]   **18.** [118]

| right angle |
| closed curve |
| circle |
| diameter |
| angle |
| radius |

CHAPTER TEST

Draw these.

1. Point *X*   **2.** $\overline{CD}$ **3.** $\overrightarrow{WV}$ **4.** ∠*EFG*

5. ∠*ABC* larger than a right angle

6. $\overleftrightarrow{AB}$ and $\overleftrightarrow{CD}$ as intersecting lines

7. $\overline{LM}$ and $\overline{NO}$ as parallel line segments

8. A simple closed curve

Look at these pictures.

9. Name the endpoints of $\overline{YZ}$.

10. Name the vertex of ∠*QRS*.

11. Name the sides of ∠*QRS*.

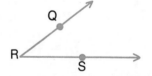

Solve this problem.

12. The length of the radius of a circle is 5 centimeters. What is the length of the diameter?

For each figure, choose one of the names given below. You cannot use a name more than once.

13.   **14.**   **15.**

| circle |
| closed curve |
| radius |
| angle |
| right angle |
| diameter |

16.   **17.**   **18.**

6 MULTIPLICATION AND DIVISION

MULTIPLICATION

Jenny has 4 packages of cookies.
Each package has 6 cookies.
How many cookies does she have in all?

Addition $6 + 6 + 6 + 6 = 24$
Multiplication $4 \times 6 = 24$

1. Write a multiplication sentence for each.

   a. $8 + 8 = 16$ **b.** $5 + 5 + 5 + 5 = 20$

2. The numbers we multiply are called **factors.**
   The answer is called the **product.**

$$4 \times 6 = 24$$
   factors   product

$$\begin{array}{r} 6 \\ \times 5 \\ \hline 30 \end{array}$$
   factors
   ← product

   Give the factors and product for each.

   a. $4 \times 9 = 36$ **b.** $49 = 7 \times 7$

3. Write an addition sentence to find each product.

   Example $2 \times 3 =$ ___ ; $3 + 3 = 6$; $2 \times 3 = 6$

   a. $2 \times 6 =$ ___ **b.** $3 \times 3 =$ ___ **c.** $4 \times 5 =$ ___

126

4. We can picture multiplication with arrays.

We can show
4 rows of 6

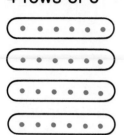

$4 \times 6 = 24$

We can show
5 rows of 3

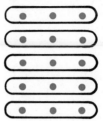

$5 \times 3 = 15$

Draw arrays. Find the products.

a. 6×3 **b.** 4×7 **c.** 3×2

EXERCISES

Write a multiplication sentence for each.

1. $8 + 8 + 8 + 8 = 32$ **2.** $7 + 7 + 7 = 21$

3. $2 + 2 + 2 + 2 + 2 = 10$ **4.** $6 + 6 + 6 + 6 = 24$

5. $4 + 4 + 4 + 4 = 16$ **6.** $5 + 5 + 5 + 5 = 20$

Write an addition sentence to find each product.

7. $2 \times 4 = $ ___ **8.** $5 \times 5 = $ ___ **9.** $5 \times 6 = $ ___

10. $3 \times 8 = $ ___ **11.** $6 \times 2 = $ ___ **12.** $4 \times 9 = $ ___

Draw an array for each. Find the product.

13. 8×3 **14.** 4×8 **15.** 2×8

16. 3×2 **17.** 6×6 **18.** 3×4

127

ORDER PROPERTY OF MULTIPLICATION

$2 \times 4 = 8$  $4 \times 2 = 8$

$$2 \times 4 = 4 \times 2$$

Changing the order of the factors does not change the product. This is called the **order property of multiplication.**

1. Make true sentences.

   a. $4 \times 9 = 36$, so $9 \times 4 = \square$

   b. $7 \times 6 = 42$, so $6 \times 7 = \square$

2. Make true: $2 \times 7 = 7 \times \square$.

EXERCISES

Make true sentences.

1. $8 \times 7 = 56$, so $7 \times 8 = \square$

2. $9 \times 6 = 54$, so $6 \times 9 = \square$

3. $9 \times 5 = 45$, so $5 \times 9 = \square$

4. $7 \times 9 = 63$, so $9 \times 7 = \square$

Make true sentences.

5. $3 \times 8 = 8 \times \square$ 6. $7 \times 3 = \square \times 7$

7. $4 \times 7 = \square \times 4$ 8. $6 \times 8 = 8 \times \square$

128

DIVISION

We find a **quotient** when we divide. Finding a quotient is like finding a missing factor.

$$6 \div 2 = \square \qquad \square \times 2 = 6$$

You know ↑   ↑ if you know this
this quotient   missing factor

1. Make true. Use multiplication to help you.

    a. $32 \div 4 = \square$ and $\square \times 4 = 32$

    b. $28 \div 7 = \square$ and $\square \times 7 = 28$

    c. $10 \div 2 = \square$ and $\square \times 2 = 10$

    > $5 \times 2 = 10$
    > $8 \times 4 = 32$
    > $4 \times 7 = 28$

2. Most multiplication sentences have two related division sentences. Some have only one sentence.

    Examples $2 \times 3 = 6$, so $6 \div 2 = 3$ and $6 \div 3 = 2$
    $5 \times 5 = 25$, so $25 \div 5 = 5$

    Make true sentences.

    a. $4 \times 5 = 20$, so $20 \div 4 = \square$ and $20 \div 5 = \triangle$

    b. $3 \times 3 = 9$, so $9 \div 3 = \square$

3. We can show division this way.
   There are 8 dots. Sets of 2 dots are circled.

    a. How many sets of 2 dots are circled?

    b. Find the quotient: $8 \div 2$.

4. **a.** Draw a picture to show $12 \div 6$.

    b. Find the quotient: $12 \div 6$.

Make true. Use multiplication to help you.

1. $16 \div 2 = \square$ and $\square \times 2 = 16$

2. $36 \div 9 = \square$ and $\square \times 9 = 36$

3. $56 \div 8 = \square$ and $\square \times 8 = 56$

4. $42 \div 7 = \square$ and $\square \times 7 = 42$

$$4 \times 9 = 36$$
$$7 \times 8 = 56$$
$$6 \times 7 = 42$$
$$8 \times 2 = 16$$

Make true sentences.

5. $4 \times 6 = 24$, so $24 \div 6 = \square$ and $24 \div 4 = \triangle$

6. $3 \times 8 = 24$, so $24 \div 8 = \square$ and $24 \div 3 = \triangle$

7. $4 \times 9 = 36$, so $36 \div 4 = \square$ and $36 \div 9 = \triangle$

8. $5 \times 3 = 15$, so $15 \div 5 = \square$ and $15 \div 3 = \triangle$

Write two related division sentences for each.

9. $3 \times 6 = 18$ **10.** $4 \times 8 = 32$

11. $7 \times 5 = 35$ **12.** $9 \times 8 = 72$

13. $6 \times 5 = 30$ **14.** $6 \times 7 = 42$

15. $4 \times 7 = 28$ **16.** $3 \times 4 = 12$

Draw dots. Circle sets of dots to find the quotient.

17. $12 \div 4$ **18.** $15 \div 3$

19. $9 \div 3$ **20.** $10 \div 5$

DIVISION AND SUBTRACTION

Consider $12 \div 4$.

```
  12
-  4
----
   8
-  4
----
   4
-  4
----
   0
```

3 fours were subtracted to get to 0.

$12 \div 4 = 3$

The **quotient** tells
the number of fours
subtracted.

1. Look at $24 \div 6$.

    a. How many sixes
    were subtracted?

    b. Complete.
    $24 \div 6 = $ _____

2. Find the quotient by subtraction.

    a. $8 \div 4$ **b.** $15 \div 5$

EXERCISES

Find each quotient by subtraction.

1. $8 \div 2$ **2.** $12 \div 2$ **3.** $12 \div 6$

4. $35 \div 7$ **5.** $20 \div 5$ **6.** $18 \div 6$

7. $10 \div 2$ **8.** $10 \div 5$ **9.** $20 \div 4$

10. $9 \div 3$ **11.** $14 \div 7$ ★ **12.** $18 \div 18$

Write expanded numerals.

Example $325 = 300 + 20 + 5$

1. 53   **2.** 89   **3.** 74

4. 136   **5.** 395   **6.** 652

What is the value of each underlined digit?

7. 87<u>6</u>   **8.** <u>6</u>07   **9.** 5,<u>8</u>07

10. 3<u>9</u>5,287   **11.** 4,<u>9</u>86,394   **12.** <u>1</u>7,982,279

Make true sentences. Use =, <, or >.

13. $8 + 6 \equiv 9 + 5$ **14.** $7 + 5 \equiv 6 + 8$

15. $546 \equiv 539$ **16.** $864 \equiv 732$

17. $8,493 \equiv 8,593$ **18.** $7,425 \equiv 7,436$

Add.

19. 48
      $+\ 37$

20. 128
      $+\ 338$

21. 4,286
      $+\ 3,117$

22. $69.28
      $+\ 38.76$

23. 49
      27
      86
      $+\ 49$

24. 348
      287
      396
      $+\ 481$

25. 241
      984
      396
      $+\ 874$

26. 281
      389
      21
      $+\ \ \ 7$

Subtract.

27. 49
      $-\ 32$

28. 75
      $-\ 26$

29. 684
      $-\ 238$

30. 700
      $-\ 498$

31. 6,291
      $-\ 3,064$

32. 8,006
      $-\ 3,948$

33. 18,712
      $-\ \ 9,993$

34. $27.48
      $-\ 18.97$

132

BARBERS

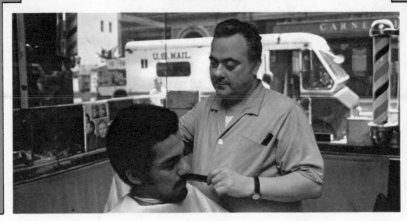

1. Mr. Gates can give 3 haircuts in an hour. How many can he give in 6 hours? Which number sentence fits the problem?

   $6 + 3 = \square$ $6 \times 3 = \square$ $6 \div 3 = \square$

2. Ms. Edwards charges 5 dollars for a haircut. She has received 30 dollars. How many haircuts has she given? Which number sentence fits the problem?

   $5 + 30 = \square$ $30 \times 5 = \square$ $30 \div 5 = \square$

3. There are 3 barbers in Mrs. Grosenick's shop. Each gave 15 haircuts one day. How many haircuts were given? Which number sentence fits the problem?

   $3 \times 15 = \square$ $15 \div 3 = \square$ $15 - 3 = \square$

4. Mr. Jackson bought a case of shampoo. There were 24 bottles in the case. There were 6 bottles in each row. How many rows were there? Which number sentence fits the problem?

   $6 \times 24 = \square$ $24 - 6 = \square$ $24 \div 6 = \square$

THE MULTIPLICATION TABLE

We can use a table like this to review the 100 multiplication facts. Make a copy of it. Save it and use it for the rest of this chapter.

X	0	1	2	3	4	5	6	7	8	9
0										
1										
2										
3										
4										
5										
6										
7										
8										
9										

1. We can show $2 \times 3 = 6$ in the table this way.

   a. Find 2 on the left.

   b. Find 3 on the top.

   c. Think of arrows going from each until they meet in a box.

   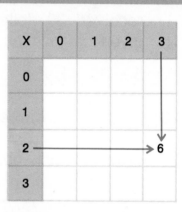

   d. We write the product 6 in that box.

2. a. Since $2 \times 3 = 6$, you know $3 \times 2 = 6$. Why?

   b. Show $3 \times 2 = 6$ on your table.

3. Show $5 \times 8 = 40$ on your table.

ZERO

2 sets with 0 members	0 sets with 2 members

$2 \times 0 = 0$	$0 \times 2 = 0$

1. Consider $4 \times 0 = 0$ and $0 \times 4 = 0$.

   a. Is 0 a factor of each?   **b.** Give the products.

2. $8 \times 0 = 0$, so $0 \times 8 = 0$. Tell why.

3. Multiply.

   a. 9   0   **b.** 0   3   **c.** 0   5
   $\times 0$ $\times 9$ $\times 3$ $\times 0$ $\times 5$ $\times 0$

   When zero is a factor, the product is zero.
   $0 \times 7 = 0$ $7 \times 0 = 0$

EXERCISES

Give the products. Write them in your table.

1. 0×0 2. 1×0 3. 0×1 4. 2×0

5. 0×2 6. 3×0 7. 0×3 8. 4×0

9. 0×4 10. 5×0 11. 0×5 12. 6×0

13. 0×6 14. 7×0 15. 0×7 16. 8×0

17. 0×8 18. 9×0 19. 0×9 ★ 20. 23×0

5 sets with 1 member	1 set with 5 members
$\boxed{X}$ $\boxed{X}$ $\boxed{X}$ $\boxed{X}$ $\boxed{X}$	$\boxed{X \quad X \quad X \quad X \quad X}$
$5 \times 1 = 5$	$1 \times 5 = 5$

1. Observe.

$$1 \times 1 = 1 \qquad 1 \times 1 = 1$$
$$2 \times 1 = 2 \qquad 1 \times 2 = 2$$
$$3 \times 1 = 3 \qquad 1 \times 3 = 3$$
$$4 \times 1 = 4 \qquad 1 \times 4 = 4$$

a. Is 1 a factor in each?

b. What are the products?

GEE WHIZ ! THOSE "ONES" ARE EASY!

When 1 is a factor, the product is the other factor.

$$9 \times 1 = 9 \qquad 1 \times 9 = 9$$

2. Look at $8 \div 1$.

$$8 \div 1 = \square \qquad \square \times 1 = 8$$

a. Give the missing factor. **b.** Give the quotient.

3. Divide.

a. $7 \div 1$ **b.** $6 \div 1$ **c.** $1 \div 1$

When a number is divided by 1, the quotient is that number.

$$9 \div 1 = 9$$

4. Look at $2 \div 2$.

$$2 \div 2 = \square \qquad \square \times 2 = 2$$

a. Give the missing factor.   b. Give the quotient.

5. Divide.

a. $4 \div 4$ b. $6 \div 6$ c. $7 \div 7$

When a number is divided by itself, the quotient is 1.

$$9 \div 9 = 1$$

EXERCISES

Multiply. Write the products in your multiplication table.

1. 1×1 **2.** 2×1 **3.** 1×2 **4.** 3×1

5. 1×3 **6.** 4×1 **7.** 1×4 **8.** 5×1

9. 1×5 **10.** 6×1 **11.** 1×6 **12.** 7×1

13. 1×7 **14.** 8×1 **15.** 1×8 **16.** 9×1

17. 1×9

Divide.

18. $9 \div 1$ **19.** $9 \div 9$ **20.** $8 \div 8$ **21.** $2 \div 1$

22. $1 \div 1$ **23.** $7 \div 7$ **24.** $6 \div 6$ **25.** $6 \div 1$

★ Compute.

26. $372 \div 372$ **27.** 1×21 **28.** 286×1

137

TWO

We can write 3 related sentences for $2 \times 5 = 10$.

$5 \times 2 = 10$ $10 \div 2 = 5$ and $10 \div 5 = 2$

order property   related divisions

1. Write an addition sentence to find each product.

    a. 2×3 **b.** 2×4 **c.** 2×6

    d. 2×7 **e.** 2×8 **f.** 2×9

2. Write 3 related sentences for each multiplication in Item 1.

EXERCISES

Multiply. Write the products in your multiplication table.

1. 2×2 **2.** 2×3 **3.** 3×2 **4.** 2×4

5. 4×2 **6.** 2×5 **7.** 5×2 **8.** 2×6

9. 6×2 **10.** 2×7 **11.** 7×2 **12.** 2×8

13. 8×2 **14.** 2×9 **15.** 9×2

Divide.

16. $12 \div 2$ **17.** $16 \div 2$ **18.** $18 \div 2$ **19.** $10 \div 2$

20. $4 \div 2$ **21.** $2 \div 2$ **22.** $0 \div 2$ **23.** $8 \div 2$

24. $6 \div 2$ **25.** $14 \div 2$ **26.** $12 \div 6$ **27.** $8 \div 4$

ODD AND EVEN NUMBERS

Even Numbers	Odd Numbers
0 = 2 × 0	1 = 2 × ?
2 = 2 × 1	3 = 2 × ?
4 = 2 × 2	5 = 2 × ?
6 = 2 × 3	7 = 2 × ?
8 = 2 × 4	9 = 2 × ?

An **even number** has 2 as a factor.

An **odd number** does not have 2 as a factor.

1. Study these even numbers: 14, 16, 18, 20, 22, 24.

    a. List the ones digits. Are they even or odd?

    b. Continue this list to 40: 24, 26, 28.

2. Study these odd numbers: 15, 17, 19, 21, 23, 25.

    a. List the ones digits. Are they even or odd?

    b. Continue this list to 41: 25, 27, 29.

EXERCISES

1. List the first 15 even numbers.

2. List the first 15 odd numbers.

Which are even? Which are odd? Write E or O.

3. 28 **4.** 37 **5.** 42 **6.** 60 **7.** 85

8. 29 **9.** 88 **10.** 100 **11.** 498 **12.** 1,000

In Multiplication	In Division
To find $3 \times 4 = 12$	$3 \times 4 = 12$, so
Think $4 + 4 + 4 = 12$	$12 \div 3 = 4 \qquad 12 \div 4 = 3$

1. Write an addition sentence to find each product.

    a. 3×5 **b.** 3×6 **c.** 3×7 **d.** 3×9

2. Use the order property to find these products.

    a. 5×3 **b.** 6×3 **c.** 7×3 **d.** 9×3

3. Write two division sentences for each.

    a. $6 \times 3 = 18$ **b.** $3 \times 8 = 24$ **c.** $9 \times 3 = 27$

4. We can write $21 \div 3 = 7$ as $3\overline{)21}$. Divide.

    a. $3\overline{)9}$ **b.** $5\overline{)15}$ **c.** $8\overline{)24}$ **d.** $3\overline{)12}$

EXERCISES

Multiply.

1.	**2.**	**3.**	**4.**	**5.**
9	3	8	3	4
$\times 3$	$\times 7$	$\times 3$	$\times 3$	$\times 3$

Divide.

6. $5\overline{)15}$ **7.** $7\overline{)21}$ **8.** $6\overline{)18}$ **9.** $3\overline{)24}$

10. Fill in the 3-facts on your multiplication table.

KEEPING THE TOWN CLEAN

1. The EZ Clean Club picked up roadside trash. They filled 4 trucks. Each truck held 2 metric tons. How many metric tons of trash did they collect?

2. In a clean-up drive 7 cents was paid for every kilogram of litter. Sara earned $3.48 collecting litter. She then bought a softball for $2.99. How much money did she have left?

3. *Sportsworld* gave a basketball to anyone collecting 4 kilograms of littered cans. A class collected 24 kilograms of cans. How many basketballs did they receive?

4. The *Ocean Weekly News* used to spend $70.64 a month on paper. Now they use recycled paper which costs $59.38 a month. How much do they save?

5. The litterbugs at Hill Elementary School were fined 2 cents for each time they littered. In April $7.32 was collected and in May $6.14 was collected. How much money was collected during the two months?

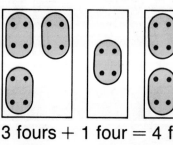

3 fours + 1 four = 4 fours
12 + 4 = 16

To find 4×4
Think $3 \times 4 = 12$
so $4 \times 4 = 12 + 4$
$= 16$

1. Complete.

a. $4 \times 4 = 16$
$5 \times 4 = 16 + \underline{}$
$= \underline{}$

b. $5 \times 4 = 20$
$6 \times 4 = 20 + \underline{}$
$= \underline{}$

2. Find the products.

a. 7×4 **b.** 8×4 **c.** 9×4

3. Make true sentences. Use the order property.

$6 \times 4 = \square$, so $4 \times 6 = \square$

4. We can use the 4-facts to find the 5-facts.

$4 \times 5 = 20$	$5 \times 5 = 25$	$6 \times 5 = 30$
$5 \times 5 = 20 + 5$	$6 \times 5 = 25 + 5$	$7 \times 5 = 30 + 5$
$= 25$	$= 30$	$= 35$

Complete.

a. $7 \times 5 = 35$
$8 \times 5 = 35 + \underline{}$
$= \underline{}$

b. $8 \times 5 = 40$
$9 \times 5 = 40 + \underline{}$
$= \underline{}$

5. Make true sentences. Use the order property.

$$6 \times 5 = \square, \text{ so } 5 \times 6 = \square$$

6. Write two division sentences for each.

a. $7 \times 4 = 28$ **b.** $5 \times 8 = 40$ **c.** $4 \times 9 = 36$

d. $4 \times 5 = 20$ **e.** $7 \times 5 = 35$ **f.** $5 \times 9 = 45$

EXERCISES

Multiply.

1. $\begin{array}{r} 4 \\ \times 4 \\ \hline \end{array}$ **2.** $\begin{array}{r} 5 \\ \times 5 \\ \hline \end{array}$ **3.** $\begin{array}{r} 8 \\ \times 4 \\ \hline \end{array}$ **4.** $\begin{array}{r} 4 \\ \times 7 \\ \hline \end{array}$ **5.** $\begin{array}{r} 9 \\ \times 5 \\ \hline \end{array}$

6. $\begin{array}{r} 5 \\ \times 7 \\ \hline \end{array}$ **7.** $\begin{array}{r} 4 \\ \times 9 \\ \hline \end{array}$ **8.** $\begin{array}{r} 6 \\ \times 4 \\ \hline \end{array}$ **9.** $\begin{array}{r} 5 \\ \times 4 \\ \hline \end{array}$ **10.** $\begin{array}{r} 8 \\ \times 5 \\ \hline \end{array}$

Divide.

11. $4\overline{)28}$ **12.** $5\overline{)20}$ **13.** $6\overline{)24}$ **14.** $9\overline{)45}$

15. $5\overline{)35}$ **16.** $4\overline{)32}$ **17.** $5\overline{)30}$ **18.** $9\overline{)36}$

Copy and complete each table by finding the rules.

19.

Input	Output
7	28
9	36
	32
	24
4	

20.

Input	Output
25	5
35	7
	6
	8
	9

21. Fill in the 4-facts and the 5-facts on your multiplication table.

143

MULTIPLICATION-ADDITION PROPERTY

Let's think of 2 rows of 7. We can rename 7 as $4 + 3$.

2 rows of $(4 + 3)$	(2 rows of 4) + (2 rows of 3)
$2 \times (4 + 3)$	$(2 \times 4) + (2 \times 3)$

So $2 \times (4 + 3) = (2 \times 4) + (2 \times 3)$

This is the **multiplication-addition property.**

1. We can also rename 7 as $5 + 2$.
   Make true: $2 \times (5 + 2) = (2 \times 5) + (2 \times \square)$.

2. Make true sentences.

   a. $2 \times (6 + 1) = (2 \times 6) + (2 \times \square)$

   b. $3 \times (2 + 4) = (3 \times \square) + (3 \times \triangle)$

3. Paula and José could not remember the answer to 5×6. Here is how they found it.

5×6	5×6
$5 \times (5 + 1)$	$5 \times (3 + 3)$
Paula $(5 \times 5) + (5 \times 1)$	José $(5 \times 3) + (5 \times 3)$
$25 + 5$	$15 + 15$
30	30

   a. How did they rename 6?

   b. What property did they use?

   c. Are their final products the same?

   d. Find 4×9 using their method.

144

Make true sentences.

1. $4 \times (3 + 6) = (4 \times 3) + (4 \times \square)$

2. $6 \times (2 + 3) = (6 \times \square) + (6 \times \triangle)$

Copy and complete.

3.
2×8
$2 \times (5 + 3)$
$(2 \times 5) + (2 \times \underline{\quad})$
$\underline{\quad} + \underline{\quad}$
$\underline{\quad}$

4.
3×9
$3 \times (6 + \underline{\quad})$
$(3 \times \underline{\quad}) + (3 \times \underline{\quad})$
$\underline{\quad} + \underline{\quad}$
$\underline{\quad}$

Multiply. Use the multiplication-addition property.

5. 9×5 **6.** 5×9 **7.** 8×4 **8.** 4×8

9. 4×6 **10.** 4×7 **11.** 5×4 **12.** 3×8

Keeping Fit

Add.

1. $\begin{array}{r} 24 \\ +38 \end{array}$ **2.** $\begin{array}{r} 73 \\ +47 \end{array}$ **3.** $\begin{array}{r} 403 \\ +297 \end{array}$ **4.** $\begin{array}{r} 189 \\ +253 \end{array}$

5. $\begin{array}{r} 8,463 \\ +1,987 \end{array}$ **6.** $\begin{array}{r} 3,847 \\ +9,286 \end{array}$ **7.** $\begin{array}{r} 7,488 \\ +3,294 \end{array}$ **8.** $\begin{array}{r} 34,814 \\ +68,328 \end{array}$

Subtract.

9. $\begin{array}{r} 82 \\ -49 \end{array}$ **10.** $\begin{array}{r} 73 \\ -64 \end{array}$ **11.** $\begin{array}{r} 647 \\ -398 \end{array}$ **12.** $\begin{array}{r} 705 \\ -358 \end{array}$

13. $\begin{array}{r} 6,843 \\ -2,938 \end{array}$ **14.** $\begin{array}{r} 9,003 \\ -8,494 \end{array}$ **15.** $\begin{array}{r} 8,362 \\ -4,783 \end{array}$ **16.** $\begin{array}{r} 34,060 \\ -23,482 \end{array}$

$$6 \times 6$$
$$6 \times (5 + 1)$$
$$(6 \times 5) + (6 \times 1)$$
$$30 + 6$$
$$36$$

I CAN FIND ANY PRODUCT WITH THE MULTIPLICATION-ADDITION PROPERTY.

1. Complete to find each product.

a.
$$6 \times 7$$
$$6 \times (6 + \underline{})$$
$$(6 \times 6) + (6 \times \underline{})$$
$$\underline{} + \underline{}$$
$$\underline{}$$

b.
$$6 \times 8$$
$$6 \times (7 + \underline{})$$
$$(6 \times \underline{}) + (6 \times \underline{})$$
$$\underline{} + \underline{}$$
$$\underline{}$$

2. Find 6×9. Use the multiplication-addition property.

3. Write two division sentences for each.

a. $6 \times 7 = 42$ **b.** $8 \times 6 = 48$ **c.** $6 \times 9 = 54$

4. Complete to find each product.

a.
$$7 \times 7$$
$$7 \times (6 + \underline{})$$
$$(7 \times 6) + (7 \times \underline{})$$
$$\underline{} + \underline{}$$
$$\underline{}$$

b.
$$7 \times 8$$
$$7 \times (7 + \underline{})$$
$$(7 \times \underline{}) + (7 \times \underline{})$$
$$\underline{} + \underline{}$$
$$\underline{}$$

$7 \times 8 = 56$, so $8 \times 7 = \underline{}$

5. Find 7×9. Use the multiplication-addition property.

6. Write two division sentences for $7 \times 8 = 56$;   for $9 \times 7 = 63$.

7. Multiply. Use the multiplication-addition property.

    a. 8 × 8   **b.** 8 × 9

8. Divide.

    a. 64 ÷ 8   **b.** 72 ÷ 8   **c.** 72 ÷ 9

Multiply.

1.	6	**2.**	7	**3.**	8	**4.**	7	**5.**	8
	×6		×7		×8		×6		×7

6.	9	**7.**	7	**8.**	8	**9.**	7	**10.**	8
	×6		×9		×9		×8		×6

Divide.

11. 6)42   **12.** 7)42   **13.** 8)48   **14.** 8)56

15. 9)54   **16.** 8)64   **17.** 9)72   **18.** 8)72

Copy and complete each table by finding the rules.

19.

Input	Output
9	54
7	42
	48
6	
	30
4	

20.

Input	Output
49	7
56	8
42	
	9
	5
21	

21. Fill in the 6-facts, the 7-facts and the 8-facts on your multiplication table.

$$9 \times 9$$
$$9 \times (8 + 1)$$
$$(9 \times 8) + (9 \times 1)$$
$$72 \quad + \quad 9$$
$$81$$

The multiplication table.

X	0	1	2	3	4	5	6	7	8	9
0	0	0	0	0	0	0	0	0	0	0
1	0	1	2	3	4	5	6	7	8	9
2	0	2	4	6	8	10	12	14	16	18
3	0	3	6	9	12	15	18	21	24	27
4	0	4	8	12	16	20	24	28	32	36
5	0	5	10	15	20	25	30	35	40	45
6	0	6	12	18	24	30	36	42	48	54
7	0	7	14	21	28	35	42	49	56	63
8	0	8	16	24	32	40	48	56	64	72
9	0	9	18	27	36	45	54	63	72	81

1. Write the product of 9×9 in your table.

2. Divide. $9\overline{)81}$

3. Nine is an interesting factor. Look at the factors and products.

   a. Compare the second factor to the tens digit in the product.

   Examples

   What did you find?

   b. Add the digits in each product.

   Examples $0 + 9$ $1 + 8$ $2 + 7$

   What did you find?

$9 \times 1 = 09$
$9 \times 2 = 18$
$9 \times 3 = 27$
$9 \times 4 = 36$
$9 \times 5 = 45$
$9 \times 6 = 54$
$9 \times 7 = 63$
$9 \times 8 = 72$
$9 \times 9 = 81$

4. Try 9×6 using what you found in Item 3. Complete.

Think: $6 - 1 = $ _____ and $5 + $ _____ $= 9$,

so $9 \times 6 = $ _____ .

5. Multiply.

    a. 9×8 **b.** 3×9 **c.** 9×5

6. Divide.

    a. $63 \div 9$ **b.** $45 \div 5$ **c.** $81 \div 9$

EXERCISES

Multiply.

1. $\begin{array}{r} 2 \\ \times 9 \\ \hline \end{array}$
  2. $\begin{array}{r} 9 \\ \times 4 \\ \hline \end{array}$
  3. $\begin{array}{r} 6 \\ \times 9 \\ \hline \end{array}$
  4. $\begin{array}{r} 9 \\ \times 8 \\ \hline \end{array}$
  5. $\begin{array}{r} 9 \\ \times 9 \\ \hline \end{array}$

Divide.

6. $9\overline{)18}$ **7.** $3\overline{)27}$ **8.** $9\overline{)36}$ **9.** $7\overline{)63}$

10. $9\overline{)9}$ **11.** $9\overline{)0}$ **12.** $9\overline{)63}$ **13.** $2\overline{)18}$

14. Copy and complete the puzzle.

Across	*Down*
a. 9×5	a. 7×6
c. 8×8	b. $93 - 36$
e. 3×9	c. 9×7
f. $24 + 14$	d. 6×8
g. 6×6	g. $19 + 18$
i. 8×7	h. $91 - 29$
k. 9×8	i. 9×6
l. 7×7	j. $47 + 22$

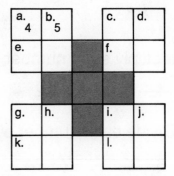

149

MULTIPLICATION AND DIVISION

Study these machines.

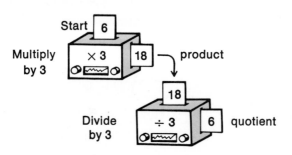

Multiplication and division are **opposites.**
One undoes the other.

1. Look at these two machines.

    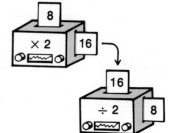

    a. Start with 8. Multiply by 2. What is the product?

    b. Divide the product by 2. What is the quotient?

2. Start with 15. Divide by 5. Multiply the quotient by 5. What do you get?

EXERCISES

Multiply each number by 6. Then divide the product by 6.

1. 1   **2.** 2   **3.** 4   **4.** 9   **5.** 8

Divide each number by 8. Then multiply the quotient by 8.

6. 32   **7.** 24   **8.** 40   **9.** 64   **10.** 56

SPINNER MATH

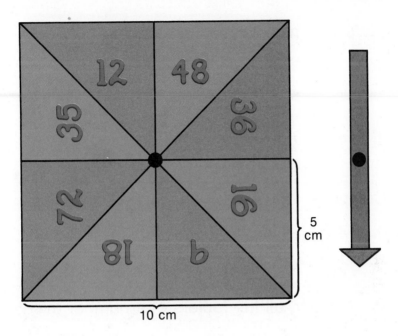

5 cm

10 cm

1. Draw this square and arrow on a piece of oaktag.

2. Mark the 8 sections as shown.

3. Write one product from the multiplication table in each section.

4. Cut out the square and arrow.

5. Attach the arrow to the center of the square with a brass fastener.

Play "Spinner Math".

Players: 2

How to play: The first player spins the arrow. When it stops the player names a pair of factors for the number it lands on. The other player then takes his or her turn.

Scoring: Score 2 points for a correct answer.

Winner: The first player to score 20 points.

151

FACTORS AND MULTIPLES

Study these multiplication sentences.

$$1 \times 12 = 12$$
$$2 \times 6 = 12$$
$$3 \times 4 = 12$$

1, 2, 3, 4, 6, and 12 are all factors of 12.

1. Complete.

   a. $1 \times$ ___ $= 20$, $2 \times$ ___ $= 20$, ___ $\times 5 = 20$

   b. The factors of 20: 1, 2, ___, ___, ___, ___.

2. We can find all the factors of a number this way.

   For 18, $1 \times 18 = 18$
                $2 \times 9 = 18$
            $\rightarrow 3 \times 6 = 18$
                $4 \times ? = 18$
                $5 \times ? = 18$
                $6 \times 3 = 18$, same as $3 \times 6 = 18$, stop!

All the factors of 18: 1, 2, 3, 6, 9, 18.

Find all the factors of each.

   a. 15   **b.** 9   **c.** 24   **d.** 7

3. We say 18 is a **multiple** of 3 because $3 \times 6 = 18$.

   a. Is 15 a multiple of 3? Show it with a multiplication sentence.

   b. Is 27 a multiple of 3? Show it.

   c. Is 11 a multiple of 3?

4. Is the first number a multiple of the second number?

    a. 36; 6   **b.** 49; 7   **c.** 23; 4

5. We can list the first 8 multiples of 4 this way.

Think:

$4 \times 1 =$	4		$4 \times 5 =$	20
$4 \times 2 =$	8		$4 \times 6 =$	24
$4 \times 3 =$	12		$4 \times 7 =$	28
$4 \times 4 =$	16		$4 \times 8 =$	32

Multiples of 4: 4, 8, 12, 16, 20, 24, 28, 32

List the first 8 multiples of each.

    a. 6   **b.** 9   **c.** 8

EXERCISES

Find all the factors of each.

1. 16   **2.** 10   **3.** 8   **4.** 13   **5.** 28

6. 27   **7.** 23   **8.** 6   **9.** 30   **10.** 36

Which of these are multiples of 8?

11. 24   **12.** 33   **13.** 64   **14.** 56   **15.** 47

Is the first number a multiple of the second number?

16. 45; 9   **17.** 56; 7   **18.** 15; 4   **19.** 81; 9

20. 43; 6   **21.** 32; 8   **22.** 35; 5   **23.** 48; 7

List the first 8 multiples of each.

24. 2   **25.** 7   **26.** 5   **27.** 3   **28.** 10

FUNNY STORIES

1. Willis Wertle's turtle, Myrtle, can waddle 9 feet an hour. How far can Willis Wertle's turtle, Myrtle, travel in 3 hours?

2. Frank Fogg's frog, Grogg, can leap 8 feet in one hop. How far can Fogg's Grogg hop in 7 leaps?

3. Sam Spake's snake, Jake, can sneak 6 feet a minute. How far can Spake's Jake sneak in 9 minutes?

4. Cathy Slatt's cat, Matt, caught three mice, thrice (three times). How many mice did Slatt's Matt catch?

5. Danny Cog's dog, Jog, ate 21 cans of food in 7 days. Jog ate the same number of cans each day. How many did he eat each day?

Dude: How do you count all those horses?
Cowboy: Easy. Just count the legs and divide by 4.

Find the number of horses.

6. 8 legs   7. 20 legs   8. 16 legs   9. 36 legs

We can write many mini-problems for a number sentence.

For $4 \times 5 = \square$, we can write:

4 baskets.	4 gogs.
5 apples in each.	5 plogs in each gog.
How many apples in all?	How many plogs in all?

1. Write two mini-problems for $7 \times 4 = \triangle$.

2. Write one mini-problem for each.

   a. $7 + 8 = \square$ **b.** $12 - 9 = \triangle$ **c.** $12 \div 3 = \triangledown$

Write one mini-problem for each.

1. $7 + 4 = \square$ **2.** $8 - 4 = \triangle$

3. $3 \times 2 = \triangledown$ **4.** $12 \div 4 = \square$

5. $9 - 9 = \square$ **6.** $3 + 12 = \square$

7. $3 \times 4 = \square$ ★ **8.** $9 + 6 + 3 = \triangle$

Brainteaser

Jerri has $\square$ marbles in each bag. She has twice as many bags as she has marbles in each bag. She has 32 marbles in all. How many marbles does she have in each bag?

CHAPTER REVIEW

Write a multiplication sentence for each. [126]

1. $4 + 4 = 8$ **2.** $3 + 3 + 3 = 9$ **3.** $6 + 6 + 6 = 18$

Write an addition sentence for each. [126]

4. $4 \times 9 = 36$ **5.** $5 \times 2 = 10$ **6.** $3 \times 8 = 24$

Write a related division sentence for each. [129]

7. $9 \times 6 = 54$ **8.** $7 \times 6 = 42$ **9.** $9 \times 1 = 9$

Which are even? Which are odd? Write E or O. [139]

10. 18   **11.** 43   **12.** 92

Make true sentences.

13. $9 \times 8 = 8 \times \square$ **14.** $56 \div 8 = \square$ and $\square \times 8 = 56$
[128]   [129]

15. $7 \times (3 + 2) = (7 \times 3) + (7 \times \square)$
[144]

Multiply.

16. 7	**17.** 5	**18.** 8	**19.** 9	**20.** 1
[146] $\times 9$	[142] $\times 4$	[146] $\times 6$	[135] $\times 0$	[136] $\times 2$

Divide.

21. $4\overline{)12}$ **22.** $8\overline{)8}$ **23.** $9\overline{)81}$ **24.** $4\overline{)32}$ **25.** $7\overline{)49}$
[140]   [136]   [148]   [142]   [146]

26. $8\overline{)40}$ **27.** $1\overline{)9}$ **28.** $7\overline{)35}$ **29.** $8\overline{)64}$ **30.** $5\overline{)45}$
[142]   [136]   [142]   [146]   [142]

Solve these mini-problems.

31. 24 cupcakes.   **32.** 5 children.
    3 for each child.   6 tickets sold by each.
    How many children?   How many tickets sold?

156

CHAPTER TEST

Write a multiplication sentence for each.

1. $7 + 7 + 7 = 21$ **2.** $9 + 9 = 18$ **3.** $2 + 2 = 4$

Write an addition sentence for each.

4. $2 \times 8 = 16$ **5.** $5 \times 6 = 30$ **6.** $3 \times 9 = 27$

Write a related division sentence for each.

7. $4 \times 6 = 24$ **8.** $7 \times 6 = 42$ **9.** $4 \times 5 = 20$

Which are even? Which are odd? Write E or O.

10. 26 **11.** 0 **12.** 99

Make true sentences.

13. $8 \times 6 = \square \times 8$

14. $36 \div 4 = \square$ and $\square \times 4 = 36$

15. $3 \times (4 + 5) = (3 \times \square) + (3 \times 5)$

Multiply.

16. $\begin{array}{r} 0 \\ \times 7 \\ \hline \end{array}$ **17.** $\begin{array}{r} 8 \\ \times 1 \\ \hline \end{array}$ **18.** $\begin{array}{r} 8 \\ \times 8 \\ \hline \end{array}$ **19.** $\begin{array}{r} 6 \\ \times 4 \\ \hline \end{array}$ **20.** $\begin{array}{r} 5 \\ \times 9 \\ \hline \end{array}$

Divide.

21. $1\overline{)6}$ **22.** $6\overline{)6}$ **23.** $9\overline{)63}$ **24.** $7\overline{)21}$ **25.** $7\overline{)42}$

Solve these mini-problems.

26. 9 boxes.
5 cookies in each.
How many cookies in all?

27. 18 pictures.
9 in each row.
How many rows?

7 MULTIPLYING

TENS, HUNDREDS, THOUSANDS

Look for patterns.

$4 \times 10 = 40$ $4 \times 100 = 400$
$18 \times 10 = 180$ $18 \times 100 = 1,800$
$126 \times 10 = 1,260$ $126 \times 100 = 12,600$

1. Multiply.

   a. 7×10 **b.** 18×10 **c.** 324×100

2. Study this pattern.

   $4 \times 1,000 = 4,000$
   $18 \times 1,000 = 18,000$
   $126 \times 1,000 = 126,000$

   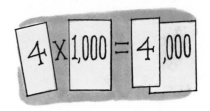

   Multiply.

   a. $2 \times 1,000$ **b.** $52 \times 1,000$ **c.** $483 \times 1,000$

3. Multiply. Use the order property to help you.

   a. 10×13 **b.** 100×3 **c.** $1,000 \times 265$

4. 40 is a **multiple** of 10 because $40 = 4 \times 10$.
   Make true sentences.

   a. $30 = 3 \times \square$ **b.** $60 = \square \times 10$ **c.** $90 = 9 \times \square$

5. 400 is a multiple of 100 because $400 = 4 \times 100$.
Make true sentences.

a. $200 = \square \times 100$ **b.** $500 = 5 \times \square$

6. 4,000 is a multiple of 1,000 because
$4,000 = 4 \times 1,000$. Make true sentences.

a. $6,000 = 6 \times \square$ **b.** $3,000 = 3 \times \square$

EXERCISES

Multiply.

1. 8×10

2. 14×10

3. 10×25

4. 347×10

5. 10×9

6. 10×247

7. 6×100

8. 100×3

9. 86×100

10. 256×100

11. 100×48

12. 100×691

13. $2 \times 1,000$

14. $1,000 \times 37$

15. $146 \times 1,000$

16. $29 \times 1,000$

17. $1,000 \times 6$

18. $1,000 \times 893$

Make true sentences.

19. $50 = 5 \times \square$

20. $80 = \square \times 10$

21. $700 = \square \times 100$

22. $600 = 6 \times \square$

23. $300 = 3 \times \square$

24. $9,000 = 9 \times \square$

25. $5,000 = \square \times 1,000$

26. $7,000 = \square \times 1,000$

★**27.** Show that 10,000 is a multiple of 1,000; of 100.

159

Race Time

Multiply.

1. 3 2	**2.** 5 4	**3.** 2 1	**4.** 6 5	**5.** 4 3	**6.** 1 7
7. 5 5	**8.** 1 0	**9.** 5 2	**10.** 2 9	**11.** 9 6	**12.** 0 8
13. 3 6	**14.** 5 9	**15.** 4 1	**16.** 3 7	**17.** 5 0	**18.** 9 9
19. 2 4	**20.** 7 6	**21.** 0 0	**22.** 8 7	**23.** 6 6	**24.** 9 8
25. 7 4	**26.** 1 1	**27.** 4 6	**28.** 8 8	**29.** 0 2	**30.** 6 3
31. 6 8	**32.** 3 5	**33.** 0 6	**34.** 2 2	**35.** 8 1	**36.** 7 2
37. 3 0	**38.** 6 1	**39.** 7 7	**40.** 8 5	**41.** 1 3	**42.** 5 7
43. 2 6	**44.** 9 4	**45.** 0 4	**46.** 9 2	**47.** 4 4	**48.** 8 3
49. 1 5	**50.** 2 8	**51.** 6 7	**52.** 3 9	**53.** 7 0	**54.** 5 1
55. 7 9	**56.** 4 8	**57.** 9 0	**58.** 3 3	**59.** 8 4	**60.** 1 9

PROBLEMS WITH MANY QUESTIONS

Jill saved $10.58. Jo saved $7.98. Sue saved $14.50.

1. How much more has Jill saved than Jo?

2. How much more has Sue saved than Jill?

3. How much have the 3 girls saved together?

4. Make up another question. Answer it.

Billy the busy beaver chews down trees. It took 145 chews for his first tree, 428 chews for his second tree, and 297 chews for his third tree.

5. How many chews did it take for all three trees?

6. How many more chews did it take for the second tree than for the first?

7. Make up another question. Answer it.

Carl the carrier pigeon receives birdseed for delivering messages. He earned 26 pieces of birdseed on Monday, 32 pieces on Tuesday, and 50 pieces on Wednesday.

8. How much more did he earn on Tuesday than on Monday?

9. How much did he earn on Monday and Tuesday?

10. Make up 2 more questions. Answer them.

THE GROUPING PROPERTY

$$(3 \times 2) \times 4 \qquad\qquad 3 \times (2 \times 4)$$
$$6 \times 4 \qquad\qquad\qquad 3 \times 8$$
$$24 \qquad\qquad\qquad\quad 24$$

$$(3 \times 2) \times 4 = 3 \times (2 \times 4)$$

We can change the grouping of the factors. We get the same product. This is the **grouping property of multiplication.**

1. Complete.

a. $(4 \times 2) \times 5 = \underline{} \times 5 \qquad 4 \times (2 \times 5) = 4 \times \underline{}$
$$= \underline{} \qquad\qquad\qquad\qquad = \underline{}$$

b. $(4 \times 2) \times 5 = 4 \times (2 \times \underline{})$

2. We can use the grouping property to find products.

$$6 \times 30 = 6 \times (3 \times 10) \qquad 3 \times 700 = 3 \times (7 \times 100)$$
$$= (6 \times 3) \times 10 \qquad\qquad\quad = (3 \times 7) \times 100$$
$$= 18 \times 10 \qquad\qquad\qquad = 21 \times 100$$
$$= 180 \qquad\qquad\qquad\quad = 2,100$$

Copy and complete.

a. $8 \times 400 = 8 \times (4 \times \underline{})$
$$= (8 \times 4) \times \underline{}$$
$$= \underline{} \times \underline{}$$
$$= \underline{}$$

b. $8 \times 4,000 = 8 \times (4 \times \underline{})$
$$= (8 \times 4) \times \underline{}$$
$$= \underline{} \times \underline{}$$
$$= \underline{}$$

3. Complete. Look for a pattern.

  a. $6 \times 70 = (6 \times 7) \times 10$
       $= \underline{}$

  b. $7 \times 800 = (7 \times 8) \times \underline{}$
       $= \underline{}$

  c. $4 \times 6{,}000 = (4 \times 6) \times \underline{}$
       $= \underline{}$

4. We can use the order property. Complete.

  a. $7 \times 80 = 560$, so $80 \times 7 = \underline{}$

  b. $9 \times 6{,}000 = 54{,}000$, so $6{,}000 \times 9 = \underline{}$

5. Multiply.

  a. 6×40 **b.** 700×4 **c.** $8 \times 5{,}000$

  d. 7×700 **e.** $6{,}000 \times 8$ **f.** 30×3

EXERCISES

Complete.

1. $(7 \times 1) \times 5 = 7 \times (1 \times \underline{})$

2. $8 \times (5 \times 3) = (8 \times 5) \times \underline{}$

Multiply.

  3. 4×30 **4.** 4×300 **5.** $4 \times 3{,}000$

  6. 70×4 **7.** 700×4 **8.** $7{,}000 \times 4$

  9. 6×80 **10.** 30×6 **11.** 400×2

12. 2×900 **13.** $4{,}000 \times 3$ **14.** $7 \times 3{,}000$

We get the same product with any order or grouping of factors. Look at $4 \times 2 \times 5 \times 2$.

$(4 \times 2) \times (5 \times 2)$
$8 \times 10 = 80$

$(4 \times 5) \times (2 \times 2)$
$20 \times 4 = 80$

$(2 \times 5) \times (2 \times 4)$
$10 \times 8 = 80$

$(2 \times 2) \times (5 \times 4)$
$4 \times 20 = 80$

We can use this to find products. Look at 40×30.

$40 \times 30 = (4 \times 10) \times (3 \times 10)$
$\qquad = (4 \times 3) \times (10 \times 10)$
$\qquad = 12 \times 100$
$\qquad = 1{,}200$

1. Copy and complete.

   a. $20 \times 30 = (2 \times \underline{\quad}) \times (3 \times \underline{\quad})$
$\qquad\qquad = (2 \times 3) \times (\underline{\quad} \times \underline{\quad})$
$\qquad\qquad = 6 \times \underline{\quad}$
$\qquad\qquad = \underline{\quad}$

   b. $400 \times 90 = (4 \times 100) \times (9 \times \underline{\quad})$
$\qquad\qquad = (4 \times 9) \times (100 \times \underline{\quad})$
$\qquad\qquad = \underline{\quad} \times \underline{\quad}$
$\qquad\qquad = \underline{\quad}$

   c. $60 \times 300 = (6 \times 10) \times (3 \times \underline{\quad})$
$\qquad\qquad = (6 \times 3) \times (\underline{\quad} \times \underline{\quad})$
$\qquad\qquad = \underline{\quad} \times \underline{\quad}$
$\qquad\qquad = \underline{\quad}$

2. We can use a short cut.

	Think	*Multiply*
30 × 60	3 × 10 6 × 10 18 × 100	30 × 60 1,800
300 × 60	3 × 100 6 × 10 18 × 1,000	300 × 60 18,000

Multiply.

a. 20
　　× 60

b. 70
　　× 80

c. 400
　　× 80

d. 600
　　× 30

EXERCISES

Multiply.

1. 90 × 40

2. 80 × 60

3. 50 × 50

4. 80 × 300

5. 30 × 800

6. 70 × 300

7. 60
　　× 60

8. 40
　　× 40

9. 20
　　× 80

10. 700
　　× 90

11. 800
　　× 20

12. 700
　　× 10

★ **13.** 600
　　× 700

★ **14.** 800
　　× 900

Solve this problem.

15. Mr. and Mrs. Gray Eagle ride bikes for fun and exercise. They ride 10 kilometers each day. How far do they ride in 30 days?

FINDING PRODUCTS

The multiplication-addition property helps us find products. Look
at 3 × 12.

$3 \times 12 = 3 \times (10 + 2)$
$= (3 \times 10) + (3 \times 2)$
$= 30 + 6$
$= 36$

1. Copy and complete.

   a. $4 \times 18 = 4 \times (10 + \underline{})$
   $= (4 \times \underline{}) + (4 \times \underline{})$
   $= \underline{} + \underline{}$
   $= \underline{}$

   b. $30 \times 12 = 30 \times (10 + \underline{})$
   $= (30 \times \underline{}) + (30 \times \underline{})$
   $= \underline{} + \underline{}$
   $= \underline{}$

2. We can use the multiplication-addition property with
   three addends. Complete.

   a. $3 \times 345 = 3 \times (300 + 40 + 5)$
   $= (3 \times 300) + (3 \times 40) + (3 \times \underline{})$
   $= 900 + \underline{} + \underline{}$
   $= \underline{}$

   b. $20 \times 214 = 20 \times (200 + \underline{} + \underline{})$
   $= (20 \times 200) + (20 \times 10) + (20 \times 4)$
   $= \underline{} + \underline{} + \underline{}$
   $= \underline{}$

3. Multiply.

    a. 3×31 **b.** 4×512

    c. 60×71 **d.** 30×352

Copy and complete.

1. $4 \times 16 = 4 \times (10 + \underline{})$
          $= (4 \times 10) + (4 \times \underline{})$
          $= \underline{} + \underline{}$
          $= \underline{}$

2. $7 \times 321 = 7 \times (\underline{} + \underline{} + \underline{})$
           $= (7 \times \underline{}) + (7 \times \underline{}) + (7 \times \underline{})$
           $= \underline{} + \underline{} + \underline{}$
           $= \underline{}$

3. $60 \times 21 = 60 \times (20 + \underline{})$
           $= (60 \times \underline{}) + (60 \times \underline{})$
           $= \underline{} + \underline{}$
           $= \underline{}$

4. $20 \times 643 = 20 \times (\underline{} + \underline{} + \underline{})$
           $= (20 \times \underline{}) + (20 \times \underline{}) + (20 \times \underline{})$
           $= \underline{} + \underline{} + \underline{}$
           $= \underline{}$

Multiply.

    5. 7×37 **6.** 3×23 **7.** 8×247

    8. 50×23 **9.** 70×921 ★ **10.** $90 \times 5,632$

FORMS FOR MULTIPLYING

Here are three forms for multiplying 3×23.

Expanded Forms

$$3 \times 23 = 3 \times (20 + 3)$$
$$= (3 \times 20) + (3 \times 3)$$
$$= 60 + 9$$
$$= 69$$

```
   23
  × 3
    9  (3 × 3)
   60  (3 × 20)
   69
```

Short Form

MULTIPLY ONES
```
  23
 × 3
   9
```

MULTIPLY TENS
```
  23
 × 3
  69
```

1. Complete.

a.
```
   31
  × 4
    4  (4 × ___)
  120  (4 × ___)
  124
```

b.
```
   62
  × 3
    6  ( ___ × ___)
  180  ( ___ × ___)
  186
```

2. Consider 2×93 in the short form. Complete.

a. Multiply ones. $2 \times 3 =$ ___

b. Multiply tens. 2×9 tens $=$ ___ tens

```
   93
  × 2
  186
```

3. Multiply. Use the short form.

a.
```
  24
 × 2
```

b.
```
  71
 × 8
```

c.
```
  90
 × 3
```

d.
```
  54
 × 2
```

4. We can use the short form with hundreds.

MULTIPLY ONES	MULTIPLY TENS	MULTIPLY HUNDREDS
2 4 **3**	2 **4** 3	**2** 4 3
× **2**	× **2**	× **2**
6	**8** 6	**4** 8 6

Multiply.

a. 522
  × 3

b. 914
  × 2

c. 321
  × 4

Multiply.

1. 42
  × 2

2. 31
  × 3

3. 12
  × 3

4. 12
  × 4

5. 22
  × 4

6. 40
  × 2

7. 31
  × 8

8. 62
  × 4

9. 51
  × 7

10. 72
  × 4

11. 412
  × 2

12. 322
  × 3

13. 123
  × 3

14. 421
  × 4

15. 514
  × 2

16. 311
  × 8

17. 432
  × 3

18. 723
  × 3

19. 634
  × 2

20. 911
  × 9

Solve these mini-problems.

21. 23 kilograms in one block. 3 cement blocks. How many kilograms?

22. 61 apples in one basket. 9 baskets. How many apples?

169

For 946,758,321 give the value of these digits.

Example   For 4:   40,000,000

1. 3   **2.** 5   **3.** 7   **4.** 9

5. 1   **6.** 2   **7.** 8   **8.** 6

Write expanded numerals.

Example   532 = 500 + 30 + 2

9. 49   **10.** 286   **11.** 743   **12.** 7,059

Make true sentences.

13. □ × 8 = 56   **14.** 4 × 3 = 3 × □   **15.** 7 × □ = 49

16. 36 ÷ □ = 6   **17.** 8 + (7 + 3) = □   **18.** 15 − △ = 6

Add.

19.　49
　　　28
　+ 34

20.　198
　　　274
　+ 368

21.　4,128
　　　3,927
　+ 6,485

22.　$1.98
　　　2.76
　+ 3.94

Subtract.

23.　78
　− 29

24.　471
　− 265

25.　400
　− 198

26.　$12.75
　− 9.87

Multiply.

27.　8
　×6

28.　9
　×7

29.　6
　×9

30.　7
　×7

31.　4
　×9

Divide.

32. 7)42   **33.** 6)30   **34.** 6)42   **35.** 5)45

NURSERY RHYME PROBLEMS

1. Peter Piper picked a peck of pickled peppers. It took 3 hours. How long would it take to pick these?

   a. 7 pecks   **b.** 22 pecks

2. Mary had a little lamb.
Its fleece was white as snow.
Its fleece was 82 cents a pound.
How much would Mary get for 4 pounds?

3. Little Bo-Peep had 128 sheep.
She lost some. She now has 79.
How many did she lose?

4. There was an old woman I've heard tell.
She went to market her eggs to sell.
She sold 3 dozen at 53 cents a dozen.
How much money did she get?

5. Hickory dickory dock.
The mouse ran up the
8-foot tall clock.
The clock struck one,
and down he did run.
How far did he run?

6. Humpty-dumpty sat on a wall.
Humpty-dumpty had a great fall.
245 horses and 352 men couldn't put Humpty together again.
How many more men than horses?

Sometimes we have to regroup in multiplication.

Expanded Form

MULTIPLY ONES	MULTIPLY TENS	ADD
24	24	24
× 3	× 3	× 3
12 (3 × 4)	12	12
	60 (3 × 20)	60
		72

Short Form

MULTIPLY ONES
```
  1
  24
× 3
   2
```

MULTIPLY TENS
```
  1
  24
× 3
  72
```

1. Complete.

a.
```
   73
 × 5
   15  ( 5 × ___ )
  350  ( ___ × ___ )
  365
```

b.
```
   68
 × 4
   32  ( ___ × ___ )
  240  ( ___ × ___ )
  272
```

2. Let's try 5 × 73 in the short form.

a. Multiply ones. 5 × 3 = ___

b. Rename. 15 = ___ ten + ___

c. How is 15 shown?

d. Multiply tens. 5 × 7 tens = ___ tens

e. Add 1 ten. 35 + 1 = ___

```
  1
  73
× 5
   5
```

```
  1
  73
× 5
 365
```

3. Multiply.

a. 27	**b.** 34	**c.** 47	**d.** 78
× 3	× 4	× 5	× 9

Multiply.

1. 37	**2.** 28	**3.** 56	**4.** 59	**5.** 45
× 3	× 4	× 5	× 3	× 7

6. 63	**7.** 48	**8.** 53	**9.** 54	**10.** 86
× 4	× 6	× 7	× 3	× 5

11. 83	**12.** 94	**13.** 39	**14.** 35	**15.** 68
× 4	× 3	× 6	× 7	× 8

Solve these mini-problems.

16. 16 ounces in one pound.
9 pounds.
How many ounces?

★**17.** 6 cans in a carton.
4 cartons in a case.
5 cases.
How many cans in all?

Brainteaser

Unscramble the phrases to make new words.

dad	we tic	cat for
till up my	carts tub	net
i son vidi	hi get	rum ben

173

Let's multiply hundreds.

ONES	TENS	HUNDREDS
2	2	2
5 1 8	5 1 8	5 1 8
× 3	× 3	× 3
4	5 4	1,5 5 4

Sometimes we regroup the tens.

ONES	TENS	HUNDREDS
	2	2
5 7 2	5 7 2	5 7 2
× 3	× 3	× 3
6	1 6	1,7 1 6

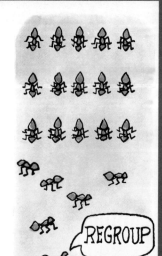

REGROUP

1. Consider 7 × 814. Complete.

   a. Multiply ones. 7 × 4 = ___
      How is 28 shown?

   $$\begin{array}{r} 2 \\ 814 \\ \times 7 \\ \hline 98 \end{array}$$

   b. Multiply tens. 7 × 1 = ___
      Add 2 tens. 7 + 2 = ___

   c. Complete the example.

2. We can multiply thousands.

   a. Multiply ones. 4 × 2 = ___

   $$\begin{array}{r} 2 \\ 3{,}152 \\ \times 4 \\ \hline 08 \end{array}$$

   b. Multiply tens. 4 × 5 = ___
      How is 20 shown?

   c. Multiply hundreds. 4 × 1 = ___
      Add 2 hundreds. 4 + 2 = ___

   $$\begin{array}{r} 2 \\ 3{,}152 \\ \times 4 \\ \hline 608 \end{array}$$

   d. Complete the example.

3. Multiply.

   a. 217
      × 4

   b. 308
      × 6

   c. 1,131
      × 7

   d. 4,823
      × 3

EXERCISES

Multiply.

1. 319 × 3	**2.** 425 × 3	**3.** 781 × 4	**4.** 980 × 9
5. 728 × 2	**6.** 403 × 5	**7.** 728 × 3	**8.** 416 × 4
9. 792 × 3	**10.** 932 × 4	**11.** 4,141 × 7	**12.** 8,253 × 3
13. 8,108 × 9	**14.** 5,843 × 2	**15.** 6,072 × 4	**16.** 2,437 × 2
17. 9,006 × 5	**18.** 3,721 × 4	**19.** 4,382 × 2	**20.** 7,018 × 4

Brainteaser

Change each letter to a number. All of the same letters must be changed to the same number. All different letters must be different numbers.

1.   P
      P
  + P
  ───
  UP

2.   OF
      OF
      OF
  + OF
  ────
  TO

3.   HA
  + A
  ────
  AH

REGROUPING MORE THAN ONCE

Bob sold 4 rolls of tickets at a carnival. Each roll had 749 tickets. How many tickets did he sell?

ONES	TENS	HUNDREDS
3	1 3	1 3
749	749	749
×4	×4	×4
6	96	2,996

TICKETS

1. Copy and complete.

a.
```
  3 5
  348
  ×7
  36
```

b.
```
  7 6
  798
  ×8
   4
```

c.
```
  8 4
  395
  ×9
   5
```

2. Here we regroup thousands.

ONES	TENS	HUNDREDS	THOUSANDS
3	3 3	4 3 3	4 3 3
4,756	4,756	4,756	4,756
×6	×6	×6	×6
6	36	536	28,536

Multiply.

a.
```
2,784
 ×7
```

b.
```
7,948
 ×9
```

c.
```
3,435
 ×5
```

d.
```
7,847
 ×4
```

3. We can multiply using money.

STEP 1	STEP 2	STEP 3	STEP 4
3	3 3	3 3	3 3
$ 4.98	$ 4.98	$ 4.98	$ 4.98
×4	×4	×4	×4
2	92	1992	$ 19.92

What was done in Step 4?

4. Multiply.

a. $2.29
  × 2

b. $.78
  × 8

c. $.07
  × 9

d. $25.49
   × 4

Multiply.

1. 245
 × 3

2. 337
 × 8

3. 369
 × 3

4. 737
 × 8

5. 578
 × 8

6. 865
 × 4

7. 945
 × 2

8. 493
 × 7

9. 1,395
  × 9

10. 4,756
  × 6

11. 1,369
  × 4

12. 7,457
  × 3

13. 9,872
  × 7

14. 7,777
  × 5

15. 2,436
  × 9

16. 8,467
  × 6

17. $.56
  × 6

18. $.76
  × 5

19. $.08
  × 6

20. $4.05
  × 4

21. $3.77
  × 3

22. $10.72
   × 9

23. $39.95
   × 2

★**24.** $384.39
    × 8

Solve these problems.

25. Jack earns $1.25 an hour for mowing lawns. How much would he earn in 8 hours?

26. Lisa bought 4 records. Each record cost $4.39. How much did she spend?

177

PICTURE PROBLEMS

Solve these picture problems.

1. How many more cars?

2. Popsicles.
15¢ each.
Total cost?

3. Crayons.
Shared equally.
How many for each?

4. How many pots and
pans in all?

5. How much change?

6. How many rows of 4
can you make?

7. Dinner at 6:45.
How much more time?

★**8.** Bakery.
Total cost?

Round to the nearest ten.

1. 34   **2.** 56   **3.** 91

4. 17   **5.** 85   **6.** 63

7. 48   **8.** 74   **9.** 25

Round to the nearest hundred.

10. 329   **11.** 874   **12.** 450   **13.** 926

14. 211   **15.** 753   **16.** 666   **17.** 543

Round to the nearest dollar.

18. $3.47   **19.** $9.04   **20.** $5.52   **21.** $8.75

22. $1.98   **23.** $6.32   **24.** $4.50   **25.** $7.29

Make true sentences. Use $=$, $<$, or $>$.

26. $9 + 7 \equiv 6 + 8$ **27.** $5 + 7 \equiv 6 + 6$

28. $87 \equiv 84$ **29.** $752 \equiv 893$

30. $447 \equiv 443$ **31.** $652 \equiv 651$

32. $8,604 \equiv 8,640$ **33.** $4,876 \equiv 4,867$

Add.

34. $\begin{array}{r} 48 \\ + 29 \\ \hline \end{array}$ **35.** $\begin{array}{r} 847 \\ + 193 \\ \hline \end{array}$ **36.** $\begin{array}{r} 3,743 \\ + 7,298 \\ \hline \end{array}$ **37.** $\begin{array}{r} 9,864 \\ + 8,439 \\ \hline \end{array}$

Subtract.

38. $\begin{array}{r} 486 \\ - 294 \\ \hline \end{array}$ **39.** $\begin{array}{r} 707 \\ - 348 \\ \hline \end{array}$ **40.** $\begin{array}{r} 8,643 \\ - 7,892 \\ \hline \end{array}$ **41.** $\begin{array}{r} 7,408 \\ - 3,949 \\ \hline \end{array}$

ESTIMATING PRODUCTS

Jim wants to buy 4 turtles. He has $4.00. Estimate if he has enough money.

Round $.89 to $.90.

Estimated Product

$$\begin{array}{r} \$ \ .90 \\ \times 4 \\ \hline \$3.60 \end{array}$$

1. Complete.

   a. To estimate 7 × 91, think 7 × 90 = ___ .

   b. To estimate 4 × $.75, think 4 × $.80 = ___ .

2. Estimate each product. Round the greater factor to the nearest ten.

   a. 72
   × 6

   b. $.43
   × 9

   c. $.78
   × 4

   d. 35
   × 6

3. Complete.

   a. To estimate 5 × 295, think 5 × 300 = ___ .

   b. To estimate 7 × 450, think 7 × ___ = ___ .

   c. To estimate 6 × $8.31, think 6 × ___ = ___ .

4. Estimate each product. Round the greater factor to the nearest hundred or dollar.

   a. 486
   × 5

   b. $7.21
   × 4

   c. 653
   × 6

   d. $6.85
   × 7

Estimate each product. Round the greater factor to the nearest ten.

1. 21
×7

2. 63
×9

3. $.28
×8

4. 55
×5

5. 49
×3

6. $.84
×6

7. 35
×2

8. 77
×9

Estimate each product. Round the greater factor to the nearest hundred or dollar.

9. 785
×6

10. 433
×5

11. 850
×4

12. $2.13
×2

13. 927
×4

14. $3.72
×8

15. $6.34
×3

16. 251
×2

Solve these problems.

17. A plane travels 428 kilometers per hour. Estimate how far it will travel in 7 hours.

18. A peanut factory packs 12 bags of peanuts in a carton. Estimate the number of bags in 9 cartons.

Estimate these costs.

19. 4 kilograms of hamburger

20. a 2-kilogram chicken

21. a 3-kilogram ham

22. 2 kilograms of pork chops

★ **23.** a $2\frac{1}{2}$-kilogram chicken

HAMBURGER
$1.91 a kilogram

HAM
$2.42
a kilogram

PORK CHOPS
$3.42
a kilogram

CHICKEN
$1.25
a kilogram

USING MULTIPLES OF TEN

We can use the group-
ing property.

$32 \times 20 = 32 \times (2 \times 10)$
$= (32 \times 2) \times 10$
$= 64 \times 10$
$= 640$

1. Copy and complete.

$24 \times 30 = 24 \times (3 \times \underline{})$
$= (24 \times 3) \times \underline{}$
$= 72 \times \underline{}$
$= \underline{}$

2. Multiply. Look for a pattern.

a. 26	26	**b.** 49	49	**c.** 952	952
$\times 3$	$\times 30$	$\times 7$	$\times 70$	$\times 6$	$\times 60$

EXERCISES

Multiply.

1. 74	**2.** 86	**3.** 97	**4.** 48
$\times 20$	$\times 30$	$\times 40$	$\times 50$

5. 92	**6.** 34	**7.** 684	**8.** 973
$\times 60$	$\times 40$	$\times 70$	$\times 80$

9. 441	**10.** 585	**11.** 843	**12.** 759
$\times 90$	$\times 60$	$\times 20$	$\times 80$

MULTIPLYING TENS AND ONES

There are 43 dozen pens on the store shelf. How many pens are there?

ONE DOZEN

MULTIPLY
ONES

```
  4 3
× 1 2
  8 6
```

MULTIPLY
TENS

```
  4 3
× 1 2
  8 6
4 3 0
```

ADD

```
  4 3
× 1 2
  8 6
4 3 0
5 1 6
```

1. Look at 38 × 42. Complete.

   a. Multiply ones.
      2 × 38 = ___

   b. Multiply tens.
      40 × 38 = ___

   c. Add. 76 + 1,520 = ___
      Give the product.

```
   38
 × 42
   76
```

```
   38
 × 42
   76
 1520
```

2. Copy and complete.

   a.
   ```
     48
   × 26
    288
    960
   ```

   b.
   ```
     63
   × 94
    252
   5670
   ```

   c.
   ```
     85
   × 57
    595
   ____
   ```

   d.
   ```
     57
   × 38
    456
   ____
   ```

3. Multiply.

   a.
   ```
     77
   × 21
   ```

   b.
   ```
     37
   × 46
   ```

   c.
   ```
     85
   × 78
   ```

   d.
   ```
   $.79
   × 94
   ```

183

Multiply.

1. 43
    × 34

2. 37
    × 24

3. 63
    × 24

4. 71
    × 24

5. 36
    × 27

6. 82
    × 18

7. 45
    × 22

8. 48
    × 33

9. 67
    × 44

10. 92
    × 86

11. 49
    × 49

12. 86
    × 67

13. $.59
    × 47

14. $.96
    × 34

15. $.83
    × 94

16. $.45
    × 26

Which are incorrect? Correct them.

17. 38
    × 57
    2,166

18. 29
    × 93
    2,677

19. 47
    × 35
    1,375

20. 85
    × 17
    1,445

21. 76
    × 32
    2,332

22. 95
    × 27
    2,565

23. 52
    × 13
    566

24. 44
    × 55
    2,420

Solve these problems.

25. The stadium at Phelps High School has 32 rows of seats. There are 85 seats in a row. How many seats are there in all?

26. At one game 43 cases of root beer were sold. Each case had 24 cans. How many cans were sold in all?

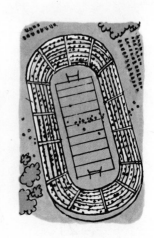

EXTENDING MULTIPLICATION

Let's multiply 437 × 27.

ONES	TENS	ADD
437	437	437
×27	×27	×27
3059	3059	3059
	8740	8740
		11799, or 11,799

1. Look at 48 × 927. Find the product.

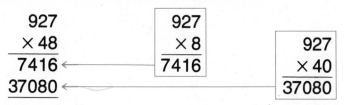

$$\begin{array}{r} 927 \\ \times 48 \\ \hline 7416 \\ 37080 \\ \hline \end{array}$$

$$\begin{array}{r} 927 \\ \times 8 \\ \hline 7416 \end{array}$$

$$\begin{array}{r} 927 \\ \times 40 \\ \hline 37080 \end{array}$$

2. Multiply.

a. 473
×22

b. 876
×98

c. 705
×28

d. $7.40
×87

EXERCISES

Multiply.

1. 498
×24

2. 786
×33

3. 499
×48

4. 999
×88

5. 470
×83

6. 907
×46

7. 818
×37

8. 666
×66

9. $4.88
×12

10. $3.49
×18

11. $6.07
×53

★ **12.** $9.74
×763

Multiply.

1. 32 × 3	2. 71 × 8	3. 53 × 7
4. 86 × 6	5. 94 × 7	6. 314 × 4
7. 827 × 2	8. 908 × 5	9. 761 × 4
10. 492 × 3	11. 870 × 9	12. 948 × 4
13. 695 × 8		
14. 376 × 9	15. 4,291 × 7	16. 8,948 × 6
17. 4,973 × 8		
18. 48 × 30	19. 72 × 60	20. 97 × 84
21. 62 × 93		
22. 83 × 76	23. 421 × 15	24. 863 × 95
25. 807 × 98		

ACTIVITY

Make a large square like the one below. Cut out 4 circles, 4 diamonds, 4 triangles, and 4 squares. Number each shape 1, 2, 3, and 4 as shown below. Place the circles on the large square as shown. Place the other figures on the large square.

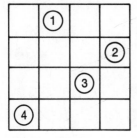

No similar shapes or numbers may be in the same row, column, or diagonal.

PHARMACISTS

Mr. Fields had two orders filled at the pharmacy. One cost $6.78 and the other cost $8.19.

1. Estimate the total cost.

2. Find the exact cost of the orders.

3. Was your estimate close to the exact cost?

Ms. Craig is a pharmacist. This table shows the number of prescriptions she filled in one week.

4. How many more did she fill on Monday than Tuesday?

5. Find the total number that she filled on Thursday and Friday.

★ 6. Estimate the total number filled that week.

7. Mrs. Harris bought some aspirin and cough medicine. How much did she spend?

Day	Number
Mon	236
Tues	187
Wed	98
Thurs	378
Fri	250

CHAPTER REVIEW

Multiply.

1. 9 × 10
[158]

2. 8 × 100
[158]

3. 6 × 1,000
[158]

4. 78 × 10
[158]

5. 8 × 40
[162]

6. 40 × 80
[164]

7. 800 × 70
[164]

8. 600 × 4
[162]

9. 8 × 7 × 2
[162]

Estimate each product. Round the greater factor to the nearest hundred or dollar. [180]

10. 4 × 317

11. $2.85 × 7

Multiply.

12.   80
[164] × 70

13.   43
[168] × 3

14.   86
[172] × 5

15. 928
[174] × 3

16. 804
[174] × 9

17. 271
[174] × 4

18. 498
[176] × 5

19. 4,562
[176]   × 8

20. 4,006
[174]   × 8

21. $47.95
[176]   × 8

22. 378
[182] × 70

23.   49
[183] × 33

24.   86
[183] × 42

25.   37
[183] × 48

26. 376
[185] × 48

27. 928
[185] × 42

Solve these problems.

The MacDonalds had a large farm. They had 128 cows, 364 sheep, and 265 chickens.

28. How many animals did they have in all?

29. How many more sheep did they have than chickens?

30. How many more sheep did they have than cows?

188

CHAPTER TEST

Multiply.

1. 5 × 10

2. 7 × 100

3. 5 × 1,000

4. 35 × 100

5. 2 × 40

6. 900 × 5

7. 30 × 60

8. 80 × 600

9. 6 × 9 × 10

Estimate each product. Round the greater factor to the nearest ten.

10. 5 × 79

11. $.55 × 4

Multiply.

12. 90
     × 30

13. 23
     × 2

14. 93
     × 8

15. 76
     × 5

16. 917
     × 4

17. 304
     × 5

18. 371
     × 8

19. 499
     × 8

20. 7,138
      × 8

21. 4,637
      × 9

22. 6,006
      × 6

23. $24.75
       × 3

24. 49
     × 84

25. 65
     × 36

26. 478
     × 34

27. 999
     × 76

Solve these problems.

Jack picked beans from his beanstalk. He picked 428 beans in May, 746 in June, and 625 in July.

28. How many beans did he pick in those 3 months?

29. How many more did he pick in June than in May?

8 DIVISION

DIVIDING TENS AND HUNDREDS

We divide to find a quotient.

$200 \div 4 = \square$ $\square \times 4 = 200$

quotient   missing factor

I CAN DO IT THIS WAY!

$$4\overline{)200} = 50$$

1. Make true. Look for a pattern.

   a. $\square \times 2 = 6$ $6 \div 2 = \square$ $2\overline{)6}$

        $\square \times 2 = 60$ $60 \div 2 = \square$ $2\overline{)60}$

        $\square \times 2 = 600$ $600 \div 2 = \square$ $2\overline{)600}$

   b. $\square \times 8 = 32$ $32 \div 8 = \square$ $8\overline{)32}$

        $\square \times 8 = 320$ $320 \div 8 = \square$ $8\overline{)320}$

        $\square \times 8 = 3,200$ $3,200 \div 8 = \square$ $8\overline{)3,200}$

2. Divide.

   a. $5\overline{)250}$ **b.** $7\overline{)2,800}$ **c.** $6\overline{)4,200}$

EXERCISES

Divide.

1. $9\overline{)540}$ **2.** $6\overline{)540}$ **3.** $8\overline{)240}$ **4.** $7\overline{)210}$

5. $3\overline{)2,400}$ **6.** $6\overline{)2,400}$ **7.** $4\overline{)240}$ **8.** $6\overline{)1,200}$

9. $7\overline{)350}$ **10.** $7\overline{)3,500}$ **11.** $6\overline{)1,800}$ **12.** $7\overline{)4,900}$

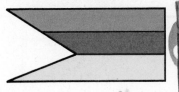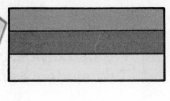

Race Time

Divide.

1. $3\overline{)9}$ 2. $6\overline{)6}$ 3. $6\overline{)48}$ 4. $1\overline{)3}$

5. $6\overline{)54}$ 6. $5\overline{)10}$ 7. $5\overline{)15}$ 8. $1\overline{)7}$

9. $4\overline{)28}$ 10. $8\overline{)64}$ 11. $5\overline{)25}$ 12. $3\overline{)27}$

13. $9\overline{)45}$ 14. $4\overline{)32}$ 15. $7\overline{)7}$ 16. $8\overline{)24}$

17. $1\overline{)0}$ 18. $7\overline{)28}$ 19. $4\overline{)24}$ 20. $9\overline{)72}$

21. $3\overline{)6}$ 22. $9\overline{)18}$ 23. $2\overline{)2}$ 24. $1\overline{)4}$

25. $9\overline{)81}$ 26. $8\overline{)40}$ 27. $9\overline{)0}$ 28. $4\overline{)36}$

29. $2\overline{)16}$ 30. $1\overline{)8}$ 31. $7\overline{)56}$ 32. $4\overline{)4}$

33. $8\overline{)56}$ 34. $3\overline{)18}$ 35. $1\overline{)1}$ 36. $5\overline{)0}$

37. $7\overline{)49}$ 38. $9\overline{)9}$ 39. $4\overline{)16}$ 40. $3\overline{)24}$

41. $5\overline{)20}$ 42. $1\overline{)9}$ 43. $9\overline{)27}$ 44. $5\overline{)5}$

45. $7\overline{)35}$ 46. $6\overline{)30}$ 47. $7\overline{)42}$ 48. $9\overline{)63}$

49. $3\overline{)3}$ 50. $4\overline{)12}$ 51. $2\overline{)12}$ 52. $8\overline{)8}$

53. $2\overline{)14}$ 54. $6\overline{)36}$ 55. $9\overline{)54}$ 56. $7\overline{)21}$

191

SUBTRACTION AND DIVISION

We can divide by subtracting.
Two students showed $72 \div 6$.

George

$$6 \overline{)72}$$
-30 (5×6)
$\overline{\quad 42}$
-30 (5×6)
$\overline{\quad 12}$
-12 (2×6)
$\overline{\quad 0} \quad 12$

Mary

$$6 \overline{)72}$$
-60 (10×6)
$\overline{\quad 12}$
-12 (2×6)
$\overline{\quad 0} \quad 12$

There are 12 sixes in 72: $72 \div 6 = 12$.
We can check by multiplying: $12 \times 6 = 72$.

1. a. How many 6's did George subtract the first time? The second time? The third time?

   b. How many 6's did George subtract in all?

2. How many 6's did Mary subtract the first time? The second time? How many in all?

3. Divide and check.

   a. $7 \overline{)91}$ b. $4 \overline{)92}$

4. Let's try $75 \div 25$.

   a. How many 25's were subtracted the first time?

   b. How many the second time?

   c. How many in all?

$$25 \overline{)75}$$
-25 (1×25)
$\overline{\quad 50}$
-50 (2×25)
$\overline{\quad 0} \quad 3$

5. Divide and check.

    a. 24$\overline{)48}$ **b.** 12$\overline{)48}$

Divide.

1. 2$\overline{)84}$ **2.** 3$\overline{)84}$ **3.** 4$\overline{)84}$ **4.** 6$\overline{)84}$

5. 7$\overline{)84}$ **6.** 3$\overline{)96}$ **7.** 8$\overline{)96}$ **8.** 5$\overline{)120}$

9. 12$\overline{)36}$ **10.** 15$\overline{)60}$ **11.** 12$\overline{)60}$ **12.** 20$\overline{)120}$

Write standard numerals.

Keeping Fit

1. 8 hundreds + 7 tens + 6

2. 9,000 + 700 + 6

3. Twenty-nine thousand, eighty-four

Compare. Use =, >, or <.

4. 904 $\equiv$ 899   **5.** 768 $\equiv$ 786

6. 5,583 $\equiv$ 4,583   **7.** 7,329 $\equiv$ 7,392

Draw these.

8. $\overline{AB}$ **9.** $\overrightarrow{AB}$ **10.** $\overrightarrow{BA}$ **11.** $\overleftrightarrow{AB}$ **12.** $\angle ABC$

13. Two parallel lines.

14. Two intersecting lines with a common point *R*.

There are three steps in dividing.
  (1) Estimate   (2) Multiply   (3) Subtract

Repeat the steps as needed. Consider 96 ÷ 8.

Estimate	Multiply	Subtract
10 8)96	10 8)96 80	10 8)96 80 16
2 10 8)96 80 16	2 10 8)96 80 16 16	12 ← quotient 2 10 8)96 80 16 16 0

1. Look at 138 ÷ 6.

  a. What was estimated?
    Multiply. 20 × 6 = ____
    Subtract. 138 − 120 = ____

$$\begin{array}{r} 20 \\ 6\overline{)138} \\ 120 \\ \hline 18 \end{array}$$

  b. What was estimated?
    Multiply. 3 × 6 = ____
    Subtract. 18 − 18 = ____
    Add the estimates. 20 + 3 = ____

  c. Check. 23 × 6 = ____

$$\begin{array}{r} 23 \\ 3 \\ 20 \\ 6\overline{)138} \\ 120 \\ \hline 18 \\ 18 \\ \hline 0 \end{array}$$

2. Two students divided 78 by 6.

```
            13
             4
             5
             4                    13
 Jo    6)78            Janet       3
            24 (4 × 6)            10          Check
            54              6)78               13
            30 (5 × 6)      60 (10 × 6)       × 6
            24              18                 78
            24 (4 × 6)      18 (3 × 6)
             0               0
```

a. What did Jo estimate the first time? The second time? The third time? How many 6's in all?

b. What did Janet estimate the first time? The second time? How many 6's in all?

3. Divide and check.

a. $9)\overline{108}$ **b.** $6)\overline{108}$ **c.** $4)\overline{108}$ **d.** $3)\overline{108}$

EXERCISES

Divide.

1. $6)\overline{66}$ **2.** $3)\overline{66}$ **3.** $2)\overline{66}$ **4.** $6)\overline{96}$

5. $7)\overline{84}$ **6.** $4)\overline{64}$ **7.** $9)\overline{99}$ **8.** $5)\overline{95}$

9. $3)\overline{63}$ **10.** $3)\overline{96}$ **11.** $3)\overline{84}$ **12.** $4)\overline{128}$

13. $7)\overline{161}$ **14.** $6)\overline{150}$ **15.** $4)\overline{76}$ **16.** $8)\overline{144}$

17. $9)\overline{243}$ **18.** $6)\overline{144}$ **19.** $5)\overline{130}$ **20.** $7)\overline{189}$

195

The multiples of 10 are:

10, 20, 30, 40, 50, 60, 70, 80, 90, . . .

Estimating with multiples of 10 makes dividing easier. Let's compare two ways to do 126 ÷ 2.

Kathy

```
    63
     3
    10
    50
2)126
   100
    26
    20
     6
     6
     0
```

Lisa

```
    63
     3
    60
2)126
   120
     6
     6
     0
```

ONE FOR YOU
AND
ONE FOR ME

1. **a.** Which multiple of 10 did Kathy choose first? Second?

   b. Which multiple of 10 did Lisa choose first?

2. Let's find the best multiple of 10 for 252 ÷ 6.

```
     30              40              50
6)252           6)252           6)252
  180             240             300
```

   a. Why is 30 too small?

   b. Why is 50 too large?

   c. Which multiple of 10 is the best?

3. Consider $7\overline{)476}$. Let's estimate.

    a. Try 60. Is 60 a good estimate?

    b. Try 70. Is 70 a good estimate?

    c. Which multiple of 10 is best?

4. Find the best multiple of 10 for the first estimate.

    a. $5\overline{)435}$ **b.** $8\overline{)232}$ **c.** $8\overline{)248}$ **d.** $9\overline{)738}$

EXERCISES

Find the best multiple of 10 for the first estimate.

1. $2\overline{)82}$ **2.** $6\overline{)342}$ **3.** $4\overline{)296}$ **4.** $8\overline{)416}$

5. $5\overline{)215}$ **6.** $9\overline{)756}$ **7.** $3\overline{)192}$ **8.** $7\overline{)427}$

9. $6\overline{)534}$ **10.** $4\overline{)208}$ **11.** $8\overline{)536}$ **12.** $7\overline{)392}$

13. $5\overline{)425}$ **14.** $3\overline{)282}$ **15.** $9\overline{)468}$ **16.** $8\overline{)592}$

Keeping Fit

Add.

1. 39 $+48$	**2.** 472 $+824$	**3.** 4,987 $+3,974$	**4.** 9,846 $+3,427$

Subtract.

5. 48 -19	**6.** 652 -498	**7.** 408 -399	**8.** 5,748 $-3,839$

Multiply.

9. 728 $\times 6$	**10.** 2,347 $\times 5$	**11.** 47 $\times 85$	**12.** 367 $\times 48$

DIVIDING TENS AND ONES

Here is how we divide $282 \div 6$.

Step 1: Is the quotient greater than 1? 10? 100?

$$\begin{array}{r} 1 \\ 6\overline{)282} \\ 6 \end{array} \qquad \begin{array}{r} 10 \\ 6\overline{)282} \\ 60 \end{array} \qquad \begin{array}{r} 100 \\ 6\overline{)282} \\ 600 \end{array}$$

The quotient is between 10 and 100.

Step 2: Find the best multiple of 10.

$$\begin{array}{r} 30 \\ 6\overline{)282} \\ 180 \end{array} \qquad \begin{array}{r} 40 \\ 6\overline{)282} \\ 240 \end{array} \qquad \begin{array}{r} 50 \\ 6\overline{)282} \\ 300 \end{array} \qquad\qquad \begin{array}{r} 47 \\ 7 \\ 40 \\ 6\overline{)282} \\ 240 \\ 42 \\ 42 \\ 0 \end{array}$$

too small   too large

40 is the best estimate.

Step 3: $42 \div 6 = 7$.

---

1. Let's try $7\overline{)455}$.

   a. Is the quotient greater than 1? 10? 100?

$$\begin{array}{r} 1 \\ 7\overline{)455} \\ 7 \end{array} \qquad \begin{array}{r} 10 \\ 7\overline{)455} \\ 70 \end{array} \qquad \begin{array}{r} 100 \\ 7\overline{)455} \\ 700 \end{array}$$

   b. Which multiple of 10 is the best?

$$\begin{array}{r} 60 \\ 7\overline{)455} \\ 420 \end{array} \qquad \begin{array}{r} 70 \\ 7\overline{)455} \\ 490 \end{array} \qquad \begin{array}{r} 80 \\ 7\overline{)455} \\ 560 \end{array}$$

   c. Complete the division. Check.

2. Divide and check.

    a. 3)$\overline{132}$ **b.** 4)$\overline{132}$ **c.** 6)$\overline{132}$ **d.** 2)$\overline{132}$

Divide.

  1. 2)$\overline{126}$ **2.** 3)$\overline{126}$ **3.** 6)$\overline{126}$ **4.** 9)$\overline{126}$

  5. 7)$\overline{364}$ **6.** 8)$\overline{504}$ **7.** 7)$\overline{441}$ **8.** 2)$\overline{112}$

  9. 7)$\overline{567}$ **10.** 4)$\overline{328}$ **11.** 8)$\overline{736}$ **12.** 9)$\overline{837}$

13. 6)$\overline{432}$ **14.** 7)$\overline{616}$ **15.** 8)$\overline{616}$ **16.** 4)$\overline{352}$

17. 4)$\overline{356}$ **18.** 2)$\overline{174}$ **19.** 3)$\overline{174}$ **20.** 5)$\overline{380}$

21. 9)$\overline{414}$ **22.** 7)$\overline{434}$ **23.** 5)$\overline{365}$ **24.** 4)$\overline{312}$

25. 3)$\overline{264}$ **26.** 8)$\overline{744}$ **27.** 6)$\overline{468}$ **28.** 7)$\overline{532}$

Solve these mini-problems.

29. Worked 248 hours.
8 hours a day.
How many days?

30. 294 jars of jelly.
6 jars in a carton.
How many cartons?

31. 96 quarts of milk.
4 quarts per gallon.
How many gallons?

32. 95 marchers in a band.
5 marchers in a row.
How many rows?

33. 348 passengers.
4 planes each holding the same
number of passengers.
How many passengers per plane?

We can use multiples of 100. Look at $4\overline{)2{,}744}$.

Step 1: Is the quotient greater than 10? 100? 1,000?

$$\begin{array}{r} 10 \\ 4\overline{)2{,}744} \\ \underline{40} \end{array} \qquad \begin{array}{r} 100 \\ 4\overline{)2{,}744} \\ \underline{400} \end{array} \qquad \begin{array}{r} 1{,}000 \\ 4\overline{)2{,}744} \\ \underline{4{,}000} \end{array}$$

The quotient is between 100 and 1,000.

Step 2: Find the best multiple of 100.

$$\begin{array}{r} 500 \\ 4\overline{)2{,}744} \\ \underline{2{,}000} \end{array} \qquad \begin{array}{r} \boxed{600} \\ 4\overline{)2{,}744} \\ 2{,}400 \end{array} \qquad \begin{array}{r} 700 \\ 4\overline{)2{,}744} \\ \underline{2{,}800} \end{array}$$

too small   too large

Step 3: Find the best multiple of 10.

$$\begin{array}{r} 70 \\ 4\overline{)344} \\ \underline{280} \end{array} \qquad \begin{array}{r} \boxed{80} \\ 4\overline{)344} \\ 320 \end{array} \qquad \begin{array}{r} 90 \\ 4\overline{)344} \\ 360 \end{array}$$

too small   too large

Step 4: $24 \div 4 = \boxed{6}$.

$$\begin{array}{r} 686 \\ 6 \\ 80 \\ 600 \\ 4\overline{)2{,}744} \\ 2{,}400 \\ \hline 344 \\ 320 \\ \hline 24 \\ 24 \\ \hline 0 \end{array}$$

1. Look at $5\overline{)3{,}645}$.

   a. Is the quotient greater than 10? 100? 1,000?

$$\begin{array}{r} 10 \\ 5\overline{)3{,}645} \\ \underline{50} \end{array} \qquad \begin{array}{r} 100 \\ 5\overline{)3{,}645} \\ \underline{500} \end{array} \qquad \begin{array}{r} 1{,}000 \\ 5\overline{)3{,}645} \\ \underline{5{,}000} \end{array}$$

   b. Which multiple of 100 is the best?

$$\begin{array}{r} 600 \\ 5\overline{)3{,}645} \\ \underline{3{,}000} \end{array} \qquad \begin{array}{r} 700 \\ 5\overline{)3{,}645} \\ \underline{3{,}500} \end{array} \qquad \begin{array}{r} 800 \\ 5\overline{)3{,}645} \\ \underline{4{,}000} \end{array}$$

c. Which multiple of 10 should you choose?

$$\begin{array}{r} 700 \\ 5\overline{)3{,}645} \\ 3{,}500 \\ \hline 145 \end{array}$$

d. Copy and complete the division. Check.

2. Give your first estimate. Do not complete.

   a. $4\overline{)952}$ **b.** $5\overline{)2{,}375}$ **c.** $6\overline{)4{,}524}$

3. Divide and check.

   a. $3\overline{)852}$ **b.** $8\overline{)5{,}112}$ **c.** $7\overline{)2{,}842}$

EXERCISES

Divide.

1. $2\overline{)754}$ 2. $4\overline{)984}$ 3. $8\overline{)6{,}344}$ 4. $7\overline{)3{,}780}$

5. $6\overline{)2{,}256}$ 6. $5\overline{)1{,}355}$ 7. $3\overline{)693}$ 8. $5\overline{)2{,}380}$

9. $7\overline{)5{,}271}$ 10. $7\overline{)2{,}989}$ 11. $2\overline{)648}$ 12. $9\overline{)5{,}364}$

13. $8\overline{)4{,}384}$ 14. $2\overline{)748}$ 15. $4\overline{)2{,}472}$ 16. $3\overline{)699}$

17. $6\overline{)4{,}326}$ 18. $9\overline{)8{,}064}$ 19. $4\overline{)692}$ 20. $3\overline{)843}$

21. $2\overline{)942}$ 22. $3\overline{)783}$ ★ 23. $3\overline{)4{,}644}$ ★ 24. $4\overline{)9{,}980}$

Solve these mini-problems.

25. Pizza.
    488 slices.
    4 slices for each child.
    How many children?

26. 1,428 hamburgers.
    2 for each child.
    How many children?

TWO-STEP PROBLEMS

Sometimes it takes two steps to solve a problem.

Jerry had 8 marbles. He won 6 more. Then he lost 5. How many does he have now?

Think!　Step 1: $8 + 6 = 14$　Add number won.
Step 2: $14 - 5 = 9$　Subtract number lost to find how many now.

1. There were 11 people on the bus. At the next stop, 4 people got on and 2 people got off. How many are on the bus now?

   a. Step 1: $11 + 4 = \square$　　How many were there after 4 got on?

   b. Step 2: $\square - 2 = \triangle$　　How many were left after 2 got off?

2. Mr. Dubovik had $20. He spent $3.98 for a hat and $7.48 for groceries. How much did he have left?

   a. Step 1: $\$3.98 + \$7.48 = \square$　　How much was spent in all?

   b. Step 2: $\$20.00 - \square = \triangle$　　How much was left?

3. Sometimes a step is hidden.

   Mrs. Alston bought 3 dozen apples for $.07 an apple. How much did she pay in all?

   a. Step 1: $3 \times 12 = \square$　　How many apples did she buy?

   b. Step 2: $\$.07 \times \square = \triangle$　　How much did she pay?

Solve these problems.

1. An airplane was traveling from Los Angeles to New York City. It stopped in Chicago. There were 191 passengers when it left for Los Angeles. At Chicago 68 passengers got off and 79 got on. How many passengers were on the plane then?

2. Mr. Tucker is driving from Yorktown to Jamestown, a distance of 450 kilometers. He has driven through Smithsville and Two-Dot. How far does he have to go to Jamestown?

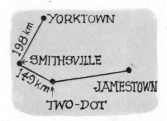

3. Mrs. Jones bought 3 dozen eggs. She has used 15. How many does she have left?

4. There were 10 yellow pencils and 2 red pencils in each pencil box. Mr. George bought 5 boxes. How many pencils did he buy?

5. Mr. Cruz saw this sign at a supermarket. How much would he pay for 3 kilograms of apples? 8 kilograms of apples?

6. Marge bought 3 pens at 49¢ each, 4 erasers at 15¢ each, and 2 boxes of crayons at 79¢ each. How much did she pay for the crayons and pens?

We often have a remainder when we divide.

38 boys.

9 on a team.

How many teams?

quotient
↓

$$\begin{array}{r} 4\,r\,2 \\ 9\overline{)38} \\ 36 \\ \hline 2 \end{array}$$

↑
remainder

Check

$$\begin{array}{r} 9 \\ \times\,4 \\ \hline 36 + 2 = 38 \end{array}$$

There are 4 teams. Two boys are not on a team.

1. Try 41 ÷ 7.

   a. What is the quotient?

   b. What is the remainder?

   c. Check the division.

$$\begin{array}{r} 5\,r\,6 \\ 7\overline{)41} \\ 35 \\ \hline 6 \end{array}$$

2. What is the remainder for 42 ÷ 7?

3. Divide each of these numbers by 3.

   9, 10, 11, 12, 13, 14, 15, 16

   a. List all remainders.

   b. Is each remainder less than 3?

4. Divide each of these numbers by 4.

   9, 10, 11, 12, 13, 14, 15, 16

   a. List all remainders.

   b. Is each remainder less than 4?

The remainder is always less than the number we divide by.

$$\begin{array}{r} 8\,r\,2 \\ 3\overline{)26} \\ 24 \\ \hline 2 \end{array}$$ 2 is less than 3.

5. Which have remainders that are too large?
   Correct the divisions.

   a. $\begin{array}{r} 7\,r\,9 \\ 7\overline{)58} \\ 49 \\ \hline 9 \end{array}$
   b. $\begin{array}{r} 9\,r\,5 \\ 9\overline{)86} \\ 81 \\ \hline 5 \end{array}$
   c. $\begin{array}{r} 7\,r\,7 \\ 4\overline{)35} \\ 28 \\ \hline 7 \end{array}$

6. Divide.

   a. $4\overline{)27}$　　b. $8\overline{)329}$　　c. $7\overline{)5,000}$

EXERCISES

Divide.

1. $6\overline{)40}$　　2. $8\overline{)40}$　　3. $7\overline{)65}$　　4. $9\overline{)56}$

5. $2\overline{)75}$　　6. $3\overline{)84}$　　7. $5\overline{)87}$　　8. $6\overline{)75}$

9. $8\overline{)438}$　　10. $7\overline{)524}$　　11. $9\overline{)734}$　　12. $4\overline{)92}$

13. $3\overline{)416}$　　14. $5\overline{)684}$　　15. $8\overline{)5,847}$　　16. $9\overline{)7,340}$

17. $4\overline{)3,946}$　　18. $7\overline{)3,124}$　　19. $2\overline{)847}$　　20. $6\overline{)5,456}$

★21. Draw a flow chart on how to check division.

205

Consider 326 ÷ 40.

Step 1: Is the quotient greater than 1? 10? 100?

$$\begin{array}{r} 1 \\ 40\overline{)326} \\ \underline{40} \end{array} \qquad \begin{array}{r} 10 \\ 40\overline{)326} \\ \underline{400} \end{array} \qquad \begin{array}{r} 100 \\ 40\overline{)326} \\ \underline{4000} \end{array}$$

The quotient is between 1 and 10.

Step 2: Find the best estimate.

$$\text{too} \quad \begin{array}{r} 7 \\ 40\overline{)326} \\ \end{array} \qquad \begin{array}{r} 8 \\ 40\overline{)326} \\ \end{array} \qquad \begin{array}{r} 9 \\ 40\overline{)326} \\ \end{array} \quad \text{too}$$
$$\text{small} \longrightarrow \underline{280} \qquad \underline{320} \qquad \underline{360} \longleftarrow \text{large}$$

8 is the best estimate.

Step 3: Complete. Check.

$$\begin{array}{r} 8\,\text{r}\,6 \\ 40\overline{)326} \\ \underline{320} \\ 6 \end{array} \qquad \begin{array}{c} \text{Check} \\ 40 \\ \underline{\times 8} \\ 320 + 6 = 326 \end{array}$$

1. Let's divide $50\overline{)326}$.

a. Is the quotient between 1 and 10?

$$\begin{array}{r} 1 \\ 50\overline{)326} \\ \underline{50} \end{array} \qquad \begin{array}{r} 10 \\ 50\overline{)326} \\ \underline{500} \end{array}$$

b. What is the best estimate? Complete and check.

$$\begin{array}{r} 5 \\ 50\overline{)326} \\ \underline{250} \end{array} \qquad \begin{array}{r} 6 \\ 50\overline{)326} \\ \underline{300} \end{array} \qquad \begin{array}{r} 7 \\ 50\overline{)326} \\ \underline{350} \end{array}$$

2. Divide.

    a. $20\overline{)186}$ **b.** $30\overline{)294}$ **c.** $60\overline{)473}$

3. Let's divide $20\overline{)564}$.

    a. Is the quotient greater than 10? 100?

$$\begin{array}{r} 1 \\ 20\overline{)564} \\ 20 \end{array} \qquad \begin{array}{r} 10 \\ 20\overline{)564} \\ 200 \end{array} \qquad \begin{array}{r} 100 \\ 20\overline{)564} \\ 2000 \end{array}$$

    b. Which multiple of 10 is the best?

$$\begin{array}{r} 20 \\ 20\overline{)564} \\ 400 \end{array} \qquad \begin{array}{r} 30 \\ 20\overline{)564} \\ 600 \end{array}$$

    c. What should you estimate next?

$$\begin{array}{r} 20 \\ 20\overline{)564} \\ 400 \\ \hline 164 \end{array}$$

    d. Complete the division. Check.

4. Tell your first estimate. Do not complete.

    a. $10\overline{)635}$ **b.** $20\overline{)635}$ **c.** $30\overline{)635}$

5. Divide and check.

    a. $10\overline{)276}$ **b.** $30\overline{)987}$ **c.** $40\overline{)3,874}$

EXERCISES

Tell your first estimate. Do not complete.

    1. $60\overline{)521}$ **2.** $70\overline{)483}$ **3.** $80\overline{)286}$

    4. $90\overline{)962}$ **5.** $50\overline{)748}$ **6.** $20\overline{)1,521}$

    7. $70\overline{)6,284}$ **8.** $80\overline{)5,474}$ **9.** $40\overline{)2,659}$

Divide.

10. $60\overline{)251}$ **11.** $30\overline{)200}$ **12.** $70\overline{)627}$

13. $90\overline{)627}$ **14.** $30\overline{)186}$ **15.** $80\overline{)742}$

16. $70\overline{)500}$ **17.** $30\overline{)108}$ **18.** $10\overline{)891}$

19. $20\overline{)486}$ **20.** $40\overline{)1,365}$ **21.** $70\overline{)2,493}$

22. $50\overline{)658}$ **23.** $40\overline{)591}$ **24.** $70\overline{)1,861}$

25. $80\overline{)3,642}$ ★ **26.** $20\overline{)3,472}$ ★ **27.** $30\overline{)8,971}$

Solve this problem.

28. A shoemaker made 1,350 shoes. He made 30 shoes a day, 5 days a week. How many weeks did it take?

Keeping Fit

Add.

1.   48
  + 24

2.   736
  + 249

3.   4,986
  + 3,785

4.   87,264
  + 29,847

Subtract.

5.   42
  − 29

6.   703
  − 278

7.   1,782
  −   894

8.   24,007
  − 13,642

Multiply.

9. 234
  × 4

10. 4,987
   × 4

11.   72
  × 86

12. 849
  × 96

ESTIMATING WITH DIVISION

We can use our first estimate to tell **about** how many.

46 children.
9 rows.
About how many in a row?

Our first estimate is 5.
We say there are **about**
5 children in a row.

1. 43 days.
7 days in a week.
About how many
weeks?

2. 121 bottles.
6 in a carton.
About how many
cartons?

3. 910 days.
30 days in a month.
About how many
months?

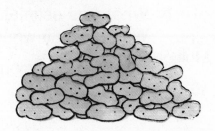

4. 412 potatoes.
8 in a kilogram.
About how many
kilograms?

A SHORT FORM FOR DIVISION

Compare the forms.

Step 1:

Long Form	Short Form
40	4
6)252	6)252
240	240
12	12
Estimate 40.	Estimate 40.
Write 40.	Write 4 in tens place.

Step 2:

Long Form

```
    42
    2
   40
6)252
  240
   12
   12
    0
```

Estimate 2.
Write 2.
Add.

Short Form

```
   42
6)252
  240
   12
   12
    0
```

Estimate 2.
Write 2 in ones place.
Division completed.

1. Try 348 ÷ 7 in the short form.

```
     4
7)348
  280
```

  a. What was estimated?
How was it written?

```
      49 r 5
7)348
  280
   68
   63
    5
```

  b. What was estimated?
Where was it written?

  c. Check the division.

2. Here is an example with a 3-digit quotient.

Long Form   *Short Form*

$$
\begin{array}{r}
497 \text{ r } 1 \\
7 \\
90 \\
400 \\
3\overline{)1{,}492} \\
1{,}200 \\
\hline
292 \\
270 \\
\hline
22 \\
21 \\
\hline
1
\end{array}
\qquad
\begin{array}{r}
4 \\
3\overline{)1{,}492} \\
1{,}200 \\
\hline
292
\end{array}
\qquad
\begin{array}{r}
49 \\
3\overline{)1{,}492} \\
1{,}200 \\
\hline
292 \\
270 \\
\hline
22
\end{array}
\qquad
\begin{array}{r}
497 \text{ r } 1 \\
3\overline{)1{,}492} \\
1{,}200 \\
\hline
292 \\
270 \\
\hline
22 \\
21 \\
\hline
1
\end{array}
$$

How was each estimate recorded in the short form?

3. Divide. Use the short form.

a. $9\overline{)873}$ **b.** $6\overline{)384}$ **c.** $2\overline{)961}$ **d.** $3\overline{)2{,}946}$

EXERCISES

Divide. Use the short form.

1. $2\overline{)77}$ **2.** $3\overline{)89}$ **3.** $4\overline{)395}$ **4.** $6\overline{)500}$

5. $7\overline{)333}$ **6.** $7\overline{)347}$ **7.** $6\overline{)928}$ **8.** $4\overline{)700}$

9. $3\overline{)2{,}425}$ **10.** $4\overline{)3{,}807}$ **11.** $6\overline{)524}$ **12.** $9\overline{)826}$

13. $8\overline{)5{,}000}$ **14.** $7\overline{)4{,}000}$ **15.** $6\overline{)949}$ **16.** $5\overline{)625}$

Solve this problem.

17. Marcia, Carlina, and Susan shared 198 marbles equally. How many did each girl have?

MULTIPLES OF 10—SHORT FORM

Look at $697 \div 20$.

$$\begin{array}{r} 3 \\ 20\overline{)697} \\ 600 \\ \hline 97 \end{array}$$

Write 3 in tens place.

$$\begin{array}{r} 34\,r\,17 \\ 20\overline{)697} \\ 600 \\ \hline 97 \\ 80 \\ \hline 17 \end{array}$$

Write 4 in ones place.
Division completed.

1. Look at $697 \div 30$.

   a. What was estimated?
      How was it written?

$$\begin{array}{r} 2 \\ 30\overline{)697} \\ 600 \\ \hline \end{array}$$

   b. What was estimated?
      Where was it written?

   c. Check the division.

$$\begin{array}{r} 23\,r\,7 \\ 30\overline{)697} \\ 600 \\ \hline 97 \\ 90 \\ \hline 7 \end{array}$$

2. Divide. Use the short form.

   a. $50\overline{)987}$ **b.** $60\overline{)3,740}$ **c.** $90\overline{)5,000}$

EXERCISES

Divide.

1. $20\overline{)750}$ **2.** $20\overline{)525}$ **3.** $30\overline{)487}$ **4.** $60\overline{)847}$

5. $50\overline{)600}$ **6.** $50\overline{)1,683}$ **7.** $60\overline{)5,243}$ **8.** $40\overline{)953}$

9. $30\overline{)847}$ **10.** $80\overline{)900}$ **11.** $90\overline{)8,111}$ **12.** $50\overline{)804}$

Divide.

1. $4\overline{)120}$ 2. $8\overline{)400}$ 3. $9\overline{)7,200}$

4. $5\overline{)85}$ 5. $7\overline{)392}$ 6. $3\overline{)192}$

7. $2\overline{)536}$ 8. $3\overline{)492}$ 9. $6\overline{)5,190}$

10. $7\overline{)30}$ 11. $5\overline{)49}$ 12. $6\overline{)185}$

13. $8\overline{)499}$ 14. $8\overline{)3,502}$ 15. $3\overline{)797}$ 16. $60\overline{)454}$

17. $70\overline{)362}$ 18. $20\overline{)425}$ 19. $30\overline{)987}$ 20. $50\overline{)705}$

ACTIVITY

Copy this drawing without lifting your pencil and without tracing over any lines. List the numbers to show the order in which you made the drawing.

Example   5, 10, 9, 1, 4, 3,
2, 8, 7, 6, 6, 11

Line 6 was retraced to get to 11.
This path is wrong.

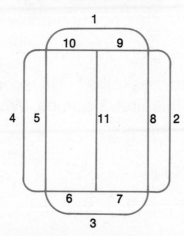

213

AVERAGES

Miguel took 4 arithmetic tests. His average score was 90.

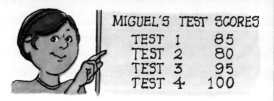

MIGUEL'S TEST SCORES

TEST 1	85
TEST 2	80
TEST 3	95
TEST 4	100

$$360 \div 4 = 90$$

↑   ↑   ↑

sum of   number   average
all tests   of tests   score

1. Sue received these scores.

Sue's Test Scores

Test 1: 85
Test 2: 95
Test 3: 75

a. What was her highest score? her lowest score?

b. Find the sum of all her scores.

c. How many tests did she take?

d. Divide the sum by the number of tests. What was Sue's average score?

We find the **average** by:
(1) Finding the sum of the numbers.
(2) Dividing the sum by the number of addends.

2. David played basketball. He scored 15, 19, and 20 points in his first 3 games. What was his average score?

3. Find the average.

     a. 5, 3, 4   **b.** 7, 8, 9, 4   **c.** 70, 80, 75

Find the average.

1. 3, 7, 2   **2.** 2, 6, 5, 3   **3.** 4, 8

4. 6, 2, 7   **5.** 4, 2   **6.** 14, 12, 16

7. 40, 50, 45   **8.** 10, 0, 8, 2   **9.** 35, 42, 58

10. 90, 90, 90, 90   ★ **11.** 20, 30, 40, 50, 60

Solve these problems.

HEALTH CHART	
Weight	*Height*
Bob 62 kg	114 cm
Paul 66 kg	135 cm
John 55 kg	129 cm

12. What is the average weight of the three boys?

13. What is the average height of the three boys?

Keeping Fit

Add.

	1.	**2.**	**3.**	**4.**
	36	821	395	4,268
	+95	426	27	2,454
		+928	+864	+ 878

Subtract.

	5.	**6.**	**7.**	**8.**
	42	876	1,498	4,000
	−29	−248	− 987	−2,948

DOLLARS AND CENTS

Mr. Ostrow bought 5 tickets for the football game. He paid $4.75. How much did each ticket cost?

STEP 1	STEP 2
$$\begin{array}{r} 95 \\ 5\overline{)475} \\ 450 \\ \hline 25 \\ 25 \\ \hline \end{array}$$	95¢ or $.95
Think of $4.75 as 475 cents. Divide.	Write the answer in money notation.

1. Consider $3\overline{)\$1.71}$.

   a. Think of $1.71 as 171¢. Divide $3\overline{)171}$.

   b. Write the answer using money notation.

2. Divide.

   a. $4\overline{)\$1.00}$ **b.** $5\overline{)\$3.75}$ **c.** $4\overline{)\$.36}$

Divide.

1. $2\overline{)\$.98}$ 2. $7\overline{)\$6.65}$ 3. $4\overline{)\$.32}$ 4. $8\overline{)\$1.52}$

5. $3\overline{)\$1.44}$ 6. $5\overline{)\$1.75}$ 7. $4\overline{)\$.24}$ 8. $6\overline{)\$3.42}$

Solve these mini-problems.

9. Apples.
   3 for $.39
   How much for 1?

10. Oranges.
    5 for $1.00
    How much for 3?

GEOLOGISTS

1. Mr. Gray Eagle is an oil geologist. He collected 6 core samples from a drilling site. It takes him 3 days to study one of the samples. How long will it take him to study the 6 samples?

2. In a recent year the average cost of drilling an oil well was $70 a meter. Estimate how much it would cost to drill a well 1,887 meters deep.

3. Some geologists must travel to do their work. Ms. Chin drove the following distances during a 4-week period: 268 kilometers, 583 kilometers, 483 kilometers, and 466 kilometers. What was the average distance she drove per week?

4. In one week Mr. Arnold spent 25 hours studying core samples. He spent 14 hours studying fossils. Planning his next field trip took 12 hours of his time. How many hours did he work that week?

5. A state highway department hired 4 geologists to plan a new road. Their ages were 41, 29, 62, and 28. What was their average age?

CHAPTER REVIEW

Divide. [190]

1. 6)480 **2.** 9)540 **3.** 8)3,200

4. 4)84 **5.** 3)16 **6.** 4)$3.52
[198] [204] [216]

7. 5)485 **8.** 3)780 **9.** 7)4,280
[198] [200] [204]

10. 9)7,110 **11.** 2)999 **12.** 30)100
[200] [204] [206]

13. 70)482 **14.** 20)542 **15.** 80)5,000
[206] [206] [206]

Find the average. [214]

16. 15, 17 **17.** 20, 40, 35, 5

Solve these problems.

18. Allen bought 3 kilograms of grapes for $4.44. How much did each kilogram cost?
[216]

19. This month Carol had scores of 80, 93 and 85 on her history tests. What was her average score?
[214]

20. Ed bought three shirts for $2.98 each. He gave the clerk $10. How much change did he receive?
[202]

Brainteaser

Paul has 80¢. He has twice as many nickels as dimes. How many nickels and how many dimes does he have?

CHAPTER TEST

Divide.

1. $7\overline{)560}$　　　　2. $2\overline{)1,200}$　　　　3. $8\overline{)6,400}$

4. $2\overline{)84}$　　　　5. $8\overline{)512}$　　　　6. $3\overline{)\$1.62}$

7. $8\overline{)912}$　　　　8. $7\overline{)4,952}$　　　　9. $8\overline{)5,144}$

10. $40\overline{)153}$　　　　11. $10\overline{)94}$　　　　12. $90\overline{)555}$

13. $50\overline{)824}$　　　　14. $20\overline{)986}$　　　　15. $70\overline{)6,000}$

Find the average.

16. 75, 85　　　　　　17. 63, 74, 85

Solve these problems.

18. Mrs. Almar bought 3 tickets for $2.85. How much did each ticket cost?

19. Mr. Twitchell bought 2 shirts for $6.98 each. He gave the clerk a $20 bill. How much change did he receive?

Brainteaser

1. A farmer planted an orchard of 16 trees. They were in 10 rows, with 4 trees in each row. Draw a picture showing how she did this.

'2. There were 13 cookies in 6 rows. In each row there were 3 cookies. Draw a picture to show this.

9 FRACTIONS

FRACTIONS

Fractions are numbers that tell about parts of things. They can answer the question, "What part?"

What part shaded?	Think	Write	Read
	1 out of 2 parts shaded	$\frac{1}{2}$	one half
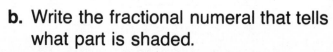	3 out of 5 parts shaded	$\frac{3}{5}$	three fifths

Fractional numerals like $\frac{1}{2}$ and $\frac{3}{5}$ are symbols used to name **fractions.**

1. Look at this pie.

   a. Complete.

   ___ out of ___ parts are shaded.

   b. Write the fractional numeral that tells what part is shaded.

   c. Read the fractional numeral.

2. a. What part of the apples are shaded?

   b. Write the fractional numeral.

   c. Read it.

3. Read these fractional numerals.

a. $\frac{0}{2}$, $\frac{1}{2}$, $\frac{2}{2}$, $\frac{3}{2}$, $\frac{4}{2}$, $\frac{5}{2}$ **b.** $\frac{0}{3}$, $\frac{1}{3}$, $\frac{2}{3}$, $\frac{3}{3}$, $\frac{4}{3}$, $\frac{5}{3}$

c. $\frac{0}{4}$, $\frac{1}{4}$, $\frac{2}{4}$, $\frac{3}{4}$, $\frac{4}{4}$, $\frac{5}{4}$ **d.** $\frac{0}{10}$, $\frac{1}{10}$, $\frac{2}{10}$, $\frac{3}{10}$, $\frac{4}{10}$, $\frac{5}{10}$

$\frac{3}{8}$ ← numerator
$\phantom{\frac{3}{8}}$ ← denominator

4. Name the numerators. Name the denominators.

a. $\frac{1}{8}$ **b.** $\frac{2}{7}$ **c.** $\frac{5}{6}$ **d.** $\frac{7}{2}$ **e.** $\frac{0}{3}$

EXERCISES

Write a fractional numeral to tell what part is shaded.

1. 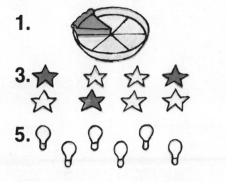 **2.**

3. 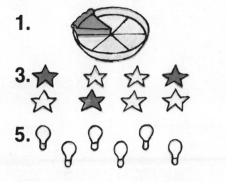 **4.**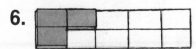

5. 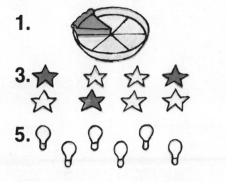 **6.**

Write fractional numerals.

7. 3 out of 4   **8.** 2 out of 9   **9.** 3 out of 14

10. 1 out of 3   **11.** 4 out of 5   **12.** 0 out of 6

Name the numerators. Name the denominators.

13. $\frac{7}{8}$ **14.** $\frac{10}{11}$ **15.** $\frac{5}{2}$ **16.** $\frac{6}{7}$ **17.** $\frac{9}{5}$

221

PARTS OF A WHOLE

When talking about parts of a whole, we think of parts of the same size.

$\dfrac{1}{2}$ ← number of parts shaded
← parts of the same size in all

$\dfrac{3}{4}$ ← number of parts shaded
← parts of the same size in all

1. Which shows $\frac{1}{2}$ of a whole shaded?

a.   **b.**   **c.**

2. Draw a picture to show each as part of a whole.

a. $\frac{3}{10}$ **b.** $\frac{1}{6}$ **c.** $\frac{3}{8}$ **d.** $\frac{7}{7}$

EXERCISES

Which show $\frac{1}{4}$ of a whole shaded?

1.   **2.**   **3.**   **4.**

Which show $\frac{2}{3}$ of a whole shaded?

5.   **6.**   **7.**   **8.**

Draw a picture to show each as a part of a whole.

9. $\frac{1}{3}$ **10.** $\frac{3}{4}$ **11.** $\frac{1}{5}$ **12.** $\frac{4}{9}$ **13.** $\frac{6}{6}$

222

PARTS OF A SET

 $\dfrac{1}{2}$ ←number of members shaded
←number of members in the whole set

 $\dfrac{3}{4}$ ←number of airplanes in the set
←number of members in the whole set

1. Which show $\frac{2}{3}$ of a set shaded?

a. **b.** **c.**

2. What part of each set is shaded?

a. **b.**

3. Look at this set.

  a. How many members are in the set?

  b. What part of the set are the airplanes?

  c. What part of the set is the car?

  d. What part of the set are the people?

Use this set.

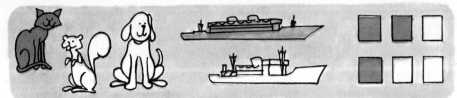

1. What part of the set are the animals? the ships? the squares?

2. What part of the set is shaded? not shaded?

Draw pictures of sets. Shade them to show these fractional numerals.

3. $\frac{5}{6}$ 4. $\frac{7}{8}$ 5. $\frac{2}{3}$ 6. $\frac{1}{3}$ 7. $\frac{3}{7}$ 8. $\frac{4}{4}$

Solve these problems.

9. 7 days in a week. What part of a week is 2 days?

10. 100 centimeters in a meter. What part of a meter is 33 centimeters?

11. 60 minutes in an hour. What part of an hour is 19 minutes?

12. 12 in a dozen. What part of a dozen is 7?

13. 52 weeks in a year. What part of a year is 23 weeks?

14. 100 years in a century. What part of a century is 11 years?

FINDING PARTS OF SETS

$\triangle \triangle \triangle$	$\frac{1}{2}$ of 6 = 3	$\triangle \triangle \triangle$	$\frac{1}{3}$ of 6 = 2
$\triangle \triangle \triangle$	6 ÷ 2 = 3	$\triangle \triangle \triangle$	6 ÷ 3 = 2
We can find $\frac{1}{2}$ by dividing by 2.		We can find $\frac{1}{3}$ by dividing by 3.	

1. Complete.

   a. $\frac{1}{2}$ of 8 = ___

   8 ÷ 2 = ___

   b. $\frac{1}{4}$ of 12 = ___

   12 ÷ 4 = ___

2. Complete.

   a. $\frac{1}{3}$ of 12 = ___

   b. $\frac{1}{4}$ of 20 = ___

EXERCISES

Complete.

1. $\frac{1}{4}$ of 12 = ___

   12 ÷ 4 = ___

2. $\frac{1}{6}$ of 12 = ___

   12 ÷ 6 = ___

Complete.

3. $\frac{1}{8}$ of 32 = ___

4. $\frac{1}{5}$ of 40 = ___

5. $\frac{1}{6}$ of 30 = ___

6. $\frac{1}{5}$ of 30 = ___

7. $\frac{1}{4}$ of 24 = ___

8. $\frac{1}{8}$ of 24 = ___

MINI-PROBLEMS

1. 4 sticks. $\frac{1}{4}$ red. How many red sticks?

2. 24 cm of ribbon. $\frac{1}{3}$ cut. How many centimeters cut?

3. 60 minutes in an hour. $\frac{1}{4}$ hour. How many minutes?

4. 100 cents in a dollar. $\frac{1}{4}$ of a dollar. How many cents?

5. Eggs: 12 in a dozen. $\frac{1}{4}$ dozen. How many eggs?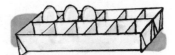

6. 50 apples. $\frac{1}{2}$ rotten. How many ripe?

7. Toy: Regular price, $1.98. On sale, $\frac{1}{2}$ price. How much?

8. Joe's dad: 81 kilograms. Joe $\frac{1}{9}$ as heavy. Joe's weight?

★9. Mary's dad: 36 years old. Mary: $\frac{1}{3}$ as old. Mary's sister: $\frac{1}{2}$ as old as Mary. How old is Mary's sister?

CHOOSING THE CORRECT OPERATION

Write +, −, ×, or ÷ to show which operation or operations you should use. Do not solve.

Example   Mr. Anders bought 3 radios. Each cost $39.95. He gave the clerk $150. How much change did he get back?

Answer: ×, then −.

1. The dogs at the Fernwood Kennel were fed 2,471 kilograms of food in May. The same amount of food was used each day. How many kilograms of food were used each day?

2. The tallest TV tower is in Fargo, North Dakota. It is 629 meters tall. The second highest is 461 meters tall. It is near Moscow in the U.S.S.R. How much taller is the tower in Fargo?

3. Mary saw a sign that read, "8 pencils for 72¢." She bought 3 pencils. How much did she pay?

4. Mrs. Esaku collected insects. She had 328 beetles, 194 bees, and 156 butterflies. How many insects did she have in all?

5. In one week Kathy cut 13 lawns and watered 25 lawns. She received $2.75 for cutting each lawn. For watering each lawn she received $.75. How much did she receive for cutting the lawns?

6. Mr. Hanson bought 2 dozen eggs for $.79 a dozen. He bought a liter of milk for $.44 and a loaf of bread for $.49. How much did he spend in all?

EQUIVALENT FRACTIONAL NUMERALS

$\frac{1}{2}$ OF THE CIRCLE IS SHADED.

$\frac{2}{4}$ OF THE CIRCLE IS SHADED.

Fractional numerals that name the same number are called **equivalent fractional numerals.** We show this with an equation. $\frac{1}{2} = \frac{2}{4}$

1. Look at these pictures.

   a. What part of A is shaded?   A

   b. What part of B is shaded?

   c. Is the same amount shaded in each?

   d. Complete: $\frac{1}{3} = \frac{\square}{6}$.

   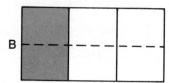

2. Look at this picture.

   a. Which two fractional numerals tell what part is shaded? $\frac{3}{6}, \frac{2}{3}, \frac{1}{2}$

   b. Write an equation to show they are equivalent fractional numerals.

3. Write two fractional numerals that tell what part is shaded.

Which two fractional numerals tell what part of each is shaded?

1.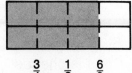

$\frac{3}{4}$, $\frac{1}{2}$, $\frac{6}{8}$

2.

$\frac{1}{3}$, $\frac{2}{6}$, $\frac{3}{2}$

3.

$\frac{1}{4}$, $\frac{2}{3}$, $\frac{3}{12}$

4.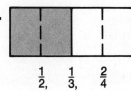

$\frac{1}{2}$, $\frac{1}{3}$, $\frac{2}{4}$

5.

$\frac{2}{3}$, $\frac{3}{4}$, $\frac{6}{8}$

6.

$\frac{1}{2}$, $\frac{2}{3}$, $\frac{6}{9}$

Write two equivalent fractional numerals that tell what part is shaded.

7.

8.

9.

10.

11.

12.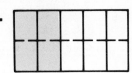

13.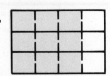

14.

15.

★ Write three equivalent fractional numerals that tell what part is shaded.

16.

17.

229

See:		
Think:	2 out of 4 circles are shaded	1 out of 2 smaller sets is shaded
Write:	$\frac{2}{4}$	$\frac{1}{2}$
So:		$\frac{2}{4} = \frac{1}{2}$

1. Look at this set.

   a. How many stars are there in all? How many stars are green?

   b. How many smaller sets are there? How many smaller sets are green?

   c. Complete: $\frac{5}{10} = \frac{\square}{2}$.

2. Here is another set.

   a. Which two fractional numerals tell what part is shaded?
   $$\frac{1}{2}, \quad \frac{2}{6}, \quad \frac{1}{3}$$

   b. Write an equation showing they are equivalent fractional numerals.

3. Write two fractional numerals that tell what part is shaded.

230

Which two fractional numerals tell what part is shaded?

1.

$\frac{1}{3}, \frac{1}{2}, \frac{2}{3}, \frac{3}{6}$

2.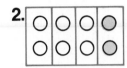

$\frac{2}{8}, \frac{1}{2}, \frac{1}{4}, \frac{6}{8}$

3.

$\frac{1}{3}, \frac{1}{2}, \frac{4}{8}$

4.

$\frac{3}{12}, \frac{9}{12}, \frac{1}{4}, \frac{3}{4}$

5.

$\frac{8}{12}, \frac{4}{6}, \frac{2}{3}, \frac{4}{12}$

6.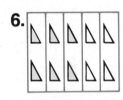

$\frac{3}{5}, \frac{4}{10}, \frac{6}{10}$

Write two fractional numerals that tell what part is shaded.

7.

8.

9.

10.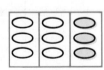

11.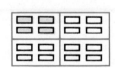

12.

★ Write three fractional numerals that tell what part is shaded.

13.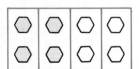

14.

THE NUMBER LINE AND FRACTIONS

This number line shows whole numbers.

We can cut each part in half.

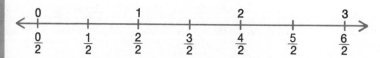

We can cut each part in thirds.

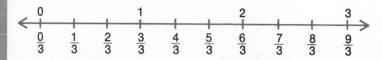

1. a. How are the parts cut in the number line below?

b. Read the fractional numerals.

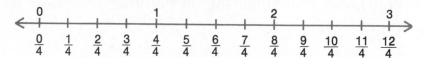

2. We can use the number line to compare fractions.

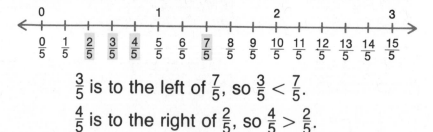

$\frac{3}{5}$ is to the left of $\frac{7}{5}$, so $\frac{3}{5} < \frac{7}{5}$.

$\frac{4}{5}$ is to the right of $\frac{2}{5}$, so $\frac{4}{5} > \frac{2}{5}$.

Complete.

a. $\frac{2}{5}$ is to the _____ of $\frac{0}{5}$, so $\frac{2}{5} \equiv \frac{0}{5}$.

b. $\frac{7}{5}$ is to the _____ of $\frac{13}{5}$, so $\frac{7}{5} \equiv \frac{13}{5}$.

3. Draw a number line like this. Show sixths on it.

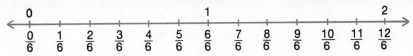

Use your number line. Compare. Use =, >, or <.

a. $\frac{1}{6} \equiv \frac{3}{6}$ **b.** $\frac{6}{6} \equiv \frac{5}{6}$ **c.** $\frac{11}{6} \equiv \frac{9}{6}$

d. $\frac{0}{6} \equiv \frac{12}{6}$ **e.** $\frac{5}{6} \equiv \frac{5}{6}$ **f.** $\frac{10}{6} \equiv \frac{12}{6}$

EXERCISES

1. Draw a number line like this. Show fourths on it.

Use your number line. Compare. Use =, >, or <.

2. $\frac{1}{4} \equiv \frac{3}{4}$ **3.** $\frac{4}{4} \equiv \frac{7}{4}$ **4.** $\frac{5}{4} \equiv \frac{3}{4}$

5. $\frac{5}{4} \equiv \frac{9}{4}$ **6.** $\frac{8}{4} \equiv \frac{0}{4}$ **7.** $\frac{10}{4} \equiv \frac{10}{4}$

8. $\frac{2}{4} \equiv \frac{3}{4}$ **9.** $\frac{11}{4} \equiv \frac{11}{4}$ **10.** $\frac{7}{4} \equiv \frac{6}{4}$

Keeping Fit

Add.

1.	**2.**	**3.**	**4.**
2,948	5,873	$35.95	34,963
+7,382	+7,429	+87.44	+78,478

Subtract.

5.	**6.**	**7.**	**8.**
8,003	3,493	$19.00	48,247
−2,916	− 847	−12.94	−39,683

NAMES FOR WHOLE NUMBERS

$\frac{0}{3}$ names the same number as 0.

$\frac{3}{3}$ names the same number as 1.

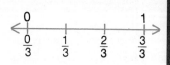

1. Look at these number lines.

   a. List four fractional numerals for 0.

   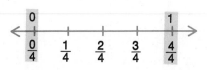

   b. Look at the fractional numerals for 0. what is the numerator in each?

   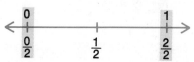

   c. List four fractional numerals for 1.

   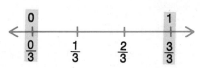

   d. Look at the fractional numerals for 1. How do the numerators and denominators compare?

   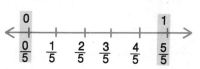

2. Use this number line.

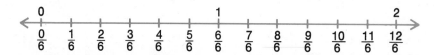

   a. What fractional numeral names 1?

   b. Name the fractions less than 1.

   c. Compare the numerators to the denominators for the fractions less than 1. What do you find?

   d. Name the fractions greater than 1.

   e. Compare the numerators to the denominators for the fractions greater than 1. What do you find?

3. Compare. Use =, <, or >.

a. $\frac{3}{4} \equiv 1$ **b.** $\frac{7}{6} \equiv 1$ **c.** $\frac{3}{3} \equiv 1$

1. List five fractional numerals for 0; for 1.

2. List five fractional numerals for numbers greater than 1; for numbers less than 1.

Compare. Use =, > or <.

3. $\frac{2}{3} \equiv 1$ **4.** $\frac{4}{3} \equiv 1$ **5.** $\frac{3}{9} \equiv 1$

6. $\frac{4}{7} \equiv 1$ **7.** $1 \equiv \frac{9}{5}$ **8.** $\frac{5}{5} \equiv 1$

9. $1 \equiv \frac{7}{8}$ **10.** $1 \equiv \frac{8}{7}$ **11.** $1 \equiv \frac{8}{8}$

Keeping Fit

Multiply.

1. $\begin{array}{r} 72 \\ \times 5 \\ \hline \end{array}$ **2.** $\begin{array}{r} 68 \\ \times 9 \\ \hline \end{array}$ **3.** $\begin{array}{r} 649 \\ \times 8 \\ \hline \end{array}$ **4.** $\begin{array}{r} 407 \\ \times 4 \\ \hline \end{array}$

5. $\begin{array}{r} 3{,}467 \\ \times 6 \\ \hline \end{array}$ **6.** $\begin{array}{r} \$71.49 \\ \times 9 \\ \hline \end{array}$ **7.** $\begin{array}{r} 87 \\ \times 36 \\ \hline \end{array}$ **8.** $\begin{array}{r} 52 \\ \times 48 \\ \hline \end{array}$

Divide.

9. $4\overline{)58}$ **10.** $7\overline{)95}$ **11.** $8\overline{)4{,}982}$ **12.** $80\overline{)4{,}982}$

13. Find the average: 46, 50, 61, 47.

USING THE NUMBER LINE

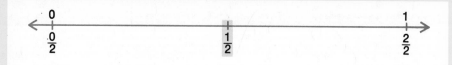

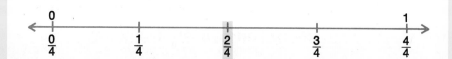

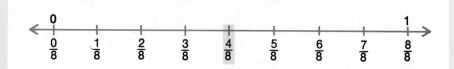

$$\frac{1}{2} = \frac{2}{4} = \frac{4}{8}$$

These are equivalent fractional numerals. They all go with the same point on the number line.

1. Look at the number lines.

   a. Give a fractional numeral equivalent to $\frac{1}{4}$.

   b. Give a fractional numeral equivalent to $\frac{6}{8}$.

2. Make true sentences. Use the number lines.

   a. $\frac{2}{8} = \frac{\square}{4}$ **b.** $\frac{0}{8} = \frac{\square}{4}$ **c.** $\frac{4}{4} = \frac{\triangle}{2}$

   d. $\frac{0}{2} = \frac{\triangle}{8}$ **e.** $\frac{1}{4} = \frac{\triangle}{8}$ **f.** $\frac{8}{8} = \frac{\square}{4}$

3. True or false?

   a. $\frac{6}{8} = \frac{3}{4}$ **b.** $\frac{0}{4} = \frac{1}{2}$ **c.** $\frac{8}{8} = \frac{4}{4}$

Make true sentences. Use the number lines.

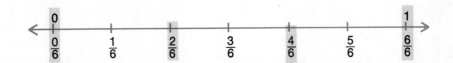

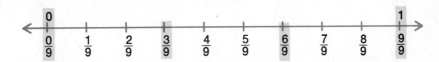

1. $\dfrac{1}{3} = \dfrac{\square}{6}$

2. $\dfrac{4}{6} = \dfrac{\triangle}{9}$

3. $\dfrac{0}{9} = \dfrac{\square}{6}$

4. $\dfrac{2}{6} = \dfrac{\square}{3}$

5. $\dfrac{3}{3} = \dfrac{\triangle}{9}$

6. $\dfrac{6}{9} = \dfrac{\triangle}{3}$

7. $\dfrac{0}{6} = \dfrac{\square}{3}$

8. $\dfrac{2}{3} = \dfrac{\triangle}{6}$

9. $\dfrac{6}{6} = \dfrac{\triangle}{3}$

True or false?

10. $\dfrac{3}{9} = \dfrac{1}{3}$

11. $\dfrac{6}{9} = \dfrac{3}{3}$

12. $\dfrac{0}{3} = \dfrac{0}{9}$

13. $\dfrac{2}{6} = \dfrac{3}{9}$

14. $\dfrac{9}{9} = \dfrac{3}{6}$

15. $\dfrac{6}{9} = \dfrac{4}{6}$

Brainteaser

Complete.

1. $\dfrac{1}{3}$ of 12 = 4, so $\dfrac{2}{3}$ of 12 = ___

2. $\dfrac{3}{4}$ of 12 = ___

3. $\dfrac{2}{3}$ of 9 = ___

4. $\dfrac{2}{5}$ of 10 = ___

5. $\dfrac{4}{7}$ of 28 = ___

237

WRITING LISTS

Study these number lines.

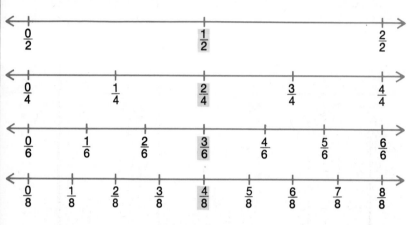

These are some names for $\frac{1}{2}$: $\frac{1}{2}$, $\frac{2}{4}$, $\frac{3}{6}$, $\frac{4}{8}$.

1. Look at the names for $\frac{1}{2}$.

    a. What pattern do you see for the numerators? the denominators?

    b. What fractional numeral for $\frac{1}{2}$ would come after $\frac{4}{8}$?

    c. List the next five names for $\frac{1}{2}$ in order.

2. This shows names for $\frac{1}{2}$.

$$\frac{1}{2}, \frac{2}{4}, \frac{3}{6}, \frac{4}{8}, \frac{5}{10}, \frac{6}{12}, \frac{7}{14}, \cdots$$

    a. What do the three dots tell us?

    b. How many names could we have for $\frac{1}{2}$?

238

3. These are some names for $\frac{2}{3}$: $\frac{2}{3}, \frac{4}{6}, \frac{6}{9}, \frac{8}{12}, \frac{10}{15}$.

a. What patterns do you see?

b. Write the next three numerals for $\frac{2}{3}$.

c. List the equivalent fractional numerals for $\frac{2}{3}$.

4. Write the next four equivalent fractional numerals for each.

a. $\frac{1}{4}, \frac{2}{8}, \frac{3}{12}, \cdots$

b. $\frac{2}{5}, \frac{4}{10}, \frac{6}{15}, \cdots$

EXERCISES

Write the next four equivalent fractional numerals for each.

1. $\frac{1}{3}, \frac{2}{6}, \frac{3}{9}, \cdots$

2. $\frac{3}{4}, \frac{6}{8}, \frac{9}{12}, \cdots$

3. $\frac{1}{5}, \frac{2}{10}, \frac{3}{15}, \cdots$

4. $\frac{4}{5}, \frac{8}{10}, \frac{12}{15}, \cdots$

5. $\frac{1}{6}, \frac{2}{12}, \frac{3}{18}, \cdots$

6. $\frac{1}{7}, \frac{2}{14}, \frac{3}{21}, \cdots$

7. $\frac{1}{8}, \frac{2}{16}, \frac{3}{24}, \cdots$

8. $\frac{3}{8}, \frac{6}{16}, \frac{9}{24}, \cdots$

Brainteaser

1. Use the digit 1 six times to make a sum of 12.

2. Use the digit 3 three times to make a product of 3.

BUILDING LISTS

This is the list of equivalent fractional numerals for $\frac{1}{4}$:

$$\frac{1}{4}, \frac{2}{8}, \frac{3}{12}, \frac{4}{16}, \frac{5}{20}, \frac{6}{24}, \cdots$$

Let's see how they were built.

$$\frac{1 \times 1}{4 \times 1} = \frac{1}{4} \qquad \frac{1 \times 2}{4 \times 2} = \frac{2}{8} \qquad \frac{1 \times 3}{4 \times 3} = \frac{3}{12}$$

$$\frac{1 \times 4}{4 \times 4} = \frac{4}{16} \qquad \frac{1 \times 5}{4 \times 5} = \frac{5}{20} \qquad \frac{1 \times 6}{4 \times 6} = \frac{6}{24}$$

1. Look at the fractional numerals above.

   a. How did we get $\frac{1}{4} = \frac{5}{20}$?

   b. How did we get $\frac{1}{4} = \frac{6}{24}$?

2. **a.** Multiply the numerator and denominator of $\frac{1}{4}$ by 7. What fractional numeral do you get?

   b. What comes next after $\frac{6}{24}$?

3. Consider $\frac{3}{4}$.

   a. Complete.

   $$\frac{3 \times 1}{4 \times 1} = \frac{\square}{4}, \qquad \frac{3 \times 2}{4 \times 2} = \frac{\square}{8}, \qquad \frac{3 \times 3}{4 \times 3} = \frac{9}{\triangle}$$

   $$\frac{3 \times 4}{4 \times 4} = \frac{12}{\triangle}, \qquad \frac{3 \times 5}{4 \times 5} = \frac{\square}{\triangle} \qquad \frac{3 \times 6}{4 \times 6} = \frac{\square}{\triangle}$$

   b. List the equivalent fractional numerals you have written for $\frac{3}{4}$.

4. Write four fractional numerals equivalent to each.

a. $\frac{1}{5}$ **b.** $\frac{2}{3}$ **c.** $\frac{1}{12}$

Write four fractional numerals equivalent to each.

1. $\frac{1}{3}$ **2.** $\frac{1}{8}$ **3.** $\frac{1}{6}$ **4.** $\frac{5}{6}$

5. $\frac{1}{10}$ **6.** $\frac{7}{10}$ **7.** $\frac{3}{5}$ **8.** $\frac{3}{8}$

9. $\frac{4}{5}$ **10.** $\frac{9}{10}$ **11.** $\frac{7}{8}$ **12.** $\frac{5}{12}$

★ Complete.

13. $\frac{1 \times \square}{4 \times \square} = \frac{2}{8}; \frac{1}{4} = \frac{\square}{8}$ **14.** $\frac{4 \times \square}{5 \times \square} = \frac{\triangle}{10}; \frac{4}{5} = \frac{\triangle}{10}$

15. $\frac{3}{4} = \frac{\square}{8}$ **16.** $\frac{3}{5} = \frac{\triangle}{10}$ **17.** $\frac{1}{6} = \frac{2}{\square}$

Draw these.

1. $\overleftrightarrow{AB}$ **2.** $\overrightarrow{CD}$ **3.** $\angle EFG$

4. A simple closed curve

5. A right angle ABC

6. $\angle DEF$ smaller than a right angle

7. $\angle LMH$ larger than a right angle

8. $\overline{AB}$ and $\overline{CD}$ as parallel line segments

241

A TEST FOR EQUIVALENCE

Let's see if $\frac{2}{3} = \frac{4}{6}$ and if $\frac{2}{3} = \frac{3}{4}$.

$2 \times 6 = 12$
$3 \times 4 = 12$
so $\frac{2}{3} = \frac{4}{6}$

$2 \times 4 = 8$
$3 \times 3 = 9$
so $\frac{2}{3}$ is not equivalent to $\frac{3}{4}$

If the cross products are the same, the fractional numerals are equivalent.

1. Let's check $\frac{3}{4}$ and $\frac{6}{8}$.

   a. Multiply: $3 \times 8 =$ ___ , $4 \times 6 =$ ___ .

   b. Are the cross products the same?

   c. Are the fractional numerals equivalent?

2. Which pairs are equivalent?

   a. $\frac{1}{2}, \frac{3}{6}$ b. $\frac{1}{3}, \frac{2}{5}$ c. $\frac{2}{5}, \frac{3}{4}$

EXERCISES

Which pairs are equivalent?

1. $\frac{1}{2}, \frac{4}{6}$ 2. $\frac{1}{2}, \frac{5}{10}$ 3. $\frac{2}{4}, \frac{4}{8}$ 4. $\frac{1}{2}, \frac{1}{3}$

5. $\frac{2}{3}, \frac{2}{4}$ 6. $\frac{4}{8}, \frac{3}{7}$ 7. $\frac{3}{4}, \frac{6}{8}$ 8. $\frac{4}{8}, \frac{1}{2}$

ANNOUNCERS

In a recent year there were 13,600 radio announcers. There were 2,400 television announcers.

1. How many more announcers were on radio than television?

2. How many radio and television announcers were there in all?

3. A television station broadcasts programs for 18 hours each day. It has 13 minutes of commercials each hour. How many minutes of commercials did it have each day?

This table shows how a radio station used one hour.

4. What part of the hour is sports?

5. What part of the hour is music?

6. How many minutes were news and commercials?

Time	Content
9 min	News
4 min	Weather
5 min	Sports
30 min	Music
12 min	Commercials

Keeping Fit

Divide.

1. $3\overline{)900}$ **2.** $4\overline{)64}$ **3.** $5\overline{)317}$

4. $6\overline{)942}$ **5.** $20\overline{)60}$ **6.** $20\overline{)97}$

Estimate each sum.

7. 49	**8.** 91	**9.** 476	**10.** $6.78
75	89	289	9.23
+23	+90	+723	+8.99

Estimate each difference.

11. 49	**12.** 476	**13.** $8.72	**14.** $8.50
−25	−199	−5.59	−2.63

Estimate each product.

15. 48	**16.** 95	**17.** 37	**18.** 276
×6	×8	×9	×3

Compare. Use =, >, or <.

19. 693 ⬚ 639   **20.** 976 ⬚ 899

21. 4,986 ⬚ 5,000   **22.** 6,489 ⬚ 6,489

Solve these mini-problems.

23. 87 boys.
96 girls.
How many students
and teachers?

24. Had $10.00.
Bought 3 toy cars.
$.59 each.
How much left?

25. 87 boys.
96 girls.
133 marbles.
How many children?

26. 276 cars in the lot.
198 left the lot.
99 came into the lot.
How many now in the lot?

CHAPTER REVIEW

Name the numerators. Name the denominators. [220]

1. $\frac{7}{16}$ 2. $\frac{3}{4}$ 3. $\frac{5}{9}$ 4. $\frac{10}{9}$

Draw a picture to show each as a part of a whole. [222]

5. $\frac{2}{3}$ 6. $\frac{1}{4}$ 7. $\frac{7}{8}$ 8. $\frac{2}{5}$

Draw a picture to show each as a part of a set. [223]

9. $\frac{1}{5}$ 10. $\frac{5}{6}$ 11. $\frac{1}{2}$ 12. $\frac{3}{7}$

Write a fractional numeral to tell what part is shaded.

13. [220]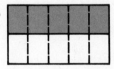

14. [220]

15. [220]

Complete. [225]

16. $\frac{1}{4}$ of 8 = ___   17. $\frac{1}{3}$ of 15 = ___

18. $\frac{1}{4}$ of 20 = ___   19. $\frac{1}{2}$ of 32 = ___

Write two fractional numerals that tell what part is shaded. [228, 230]

20. 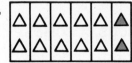   21.    22.

23.   24.   25.

Compare. Use =, >, or <. [232, 234]

26. $\frac{3}{4} \equiv 1$ **27.** $1 \equiv \frac{1}{7}$ **28.** $\frac{9}{6} \equiv 1$ **29.** $1 \equiv \frac{8}{8}$

Look at the number lines. Complete. [236]

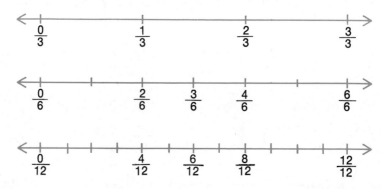

30. $\frac{0}{3} = \frac{\square}{6}$ **31.** $\frac{2}{6} = \frac{\square}{12}$ **32.** $\frac{12}{12} = \frac{\square}{3}$

33. $\frac{6}{12} = \frac{\square}{6}$ **34.** $\frac{1}{3} = \frac{\square}{6}$ **35.** $\frac{2}{3} = \frac{\square}{12}$

Write the next four equivalent fractional numerals for each. [238]

36. $\frac{2}{3}, \frac{4}{6}, \frac{6}{9}, \ldots$ **37.** $\frac{1}{4}, \frac{2}{8}, \frac{3}{12}, \ldots$

38. $\frac{3}{8}, \frac{6}{16}, \frac{9}{24}, \ldots$ **39.** $\frac{1}{5}, \frac{2}{10}, \frac{3}{15}, \ldots$

Write four fractional numerals equivalent to each. [240]

40. $\frac{1}{6}$ **41.** $\frac{2}{3}$ **42.** $\frac{1}{4}$ **43.** $\frac{2}{5}$

Solve these mini-problems. [226]

44. 8 cats. $\frac{1}{2}$ with collars. How many with collars?

45. 12 dogs. $\frac{1}{2}$ collies. How many collies?

CHAPTER TEST

1. Name the denominator in $\frac{3}{8}$.

2. Draw a picture to show $\frac{1}{3}$ of a whole shaded.

3. Draw a picture to show $\frac{1}{3}$ of a set shaded.

Write a fractional numeral to tell what part is shaded.

4.   **5.**

Complete.

6. $\frac{1}{3}$ of 12 = ___   **7.** $\frac{1}{2}$ of 20 = ___

Write two fractional numerals that tell what part is shaded.

8.   **9.**

Compare. Use =, <, or >.

10. $\frac{2}{3} \equiv 1$ **11.** $\frac{5}{4} \equiv 1$ **12.** $1 \equiv \frac{6}{6}$ **13.** $1 \equiv \frac{10}{7}$

Write four fractional numerals equivalent to each.

14. $\frac{1}{3}$ **15.** $\frac{3}{4}$ **16.** $\frac{3}{5}$ **17.** $\frac{1}{2}$

Solve these mini-problems.

18. 6 apples. $\frac{1}{2}$ rotten.
How many rotten?

19. 9 candles. $\frac{1}{3}$ red.
How many red?

10 ADDING AND SUBTRACTING

ADDING FRACTIONS

Mike ate $\frac{1}{3}$ of a candy bar.

Susie also ate $\frac{1}{3}$ of the candy bar.

How much did they eat in all?

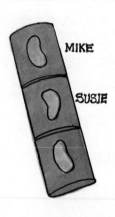

MIKE

SUSIE

1 third	$\frac{1}{3}$	
+ 1 third	$+\frac{1}{3}$	$\frac{1}{3} + \frac{1}{3} = \frac{2}{3}$
2 thirds	$\frac{2}{3}$	

1. Al ate $\frac{2}{8}$ of the cake.

   George ate $\frac{1}{8}$ of the same cake.
   How much did they eat in all?

   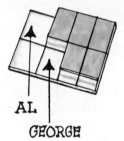

   AL

   GEORGE

   a. What numbers should you add?

   b. Complete: $\frac{2}{8} + \frac{1}{8} = \frac{\square}{8}$.

2. Jan ran $\frac{1}{5}$ kilometer.

   Then she walked $\frac{2}{5}$
   kilometer. How far did she go?

   ran   walked

   $\frac{0}{5}$ $\frac{1}{5}$ $\frac{2}{5}$ $\frac{3}{5}$ $\frac{4}{5}$ $\frac{5}{5}$

   a. What numbers should you add?

   b. Complete: $\frac{1}{5} + \frac{2}{5} = \frac{\square}{5}$.

248

3. Observe. What pattern do you see?

$$\frac{1}{3} + \frac{1}{3} = \frac{2}{3} \qquad \frac{2}{8} + \frac{1}{8} = \frac{3}{8} \qquad \frac{1}{5} + \frac{2}{5} = \frac{3}{5}$$

To add fractions with the same denominator: (1) add the numerators, (2) use the denominator.

$$\frac{3}{7} + \frac{2}{7} = \frac{3+2}{7} \qquad\qquad \frac{3}{7}$$
$$= \frac{5}{7} \qquad\qquad +\frac{2}{7}$$
$$\overline{\frac{5}{7}}$$

4. Copy and complete.

a. $\frac{1}{6} + \frac{1}{6} = \frac{1+1}{6}$

$\quad = \frac{\square}{6}$

b. $\frac{4}{9} + \frac{2}{9} = \frac{4+\square}{9}$

$\quad = \frac{\triangle}{9}$

5. Add.

a. $\frac{1}{4} + \frac{2}{4}$

b. $\frac{2}{5} + \frac{2}{5}$

c. $\frac{1}{6} + \frac{3}{6}$

EXERCISES

Add.

1. $\frac{1}{10} + \frac{3}{10}$

2. $\frac{1}{5} + \frac{1}{5}$

3. $\frac{2}{7} + \frac{3}{7}$

4. $\frac{7}{12} + \frac{2}{12}$

5. $\frac{1}{5} + \frac{3}{5}$

6. $\frac{4}{8} + \frac{3}{8}$

7. $\frac{3}{8} + \frac{3}{8}$

★**8.** $\frac{1}{7} + \frac{2}{7} + \frac{3}{7}$

9. $\frac{2}{9}$
$+\frac{5}{9}$

10. $\frac{0}{4}$
$+\frac{3}{4}$

11. $\frac{6}{13}$
$+\frac{5}{13}$

12. $\frac{5}{11}$
$+\frac{4}{11}$

SUBTRACTING FRACTIONS

Mama hippopotamus takes her bath in a pool $\frac{4}{5}$ full of water. The pool is $\frac{1}{5}$ full when Baby hippo bathes. How much fuller is the pool for Mama hippo?

$\frac{4}{5} - \frac{1}{5} = \frac{3}{5}$

$$\begin{array}{r} \frac{4}{5} \\ -\frac{1}{5} \\ \hline \frac{3}{5} \end{array}$$

1. Mr. Skunk's tail is $\frac{3}{4}$ foot long. Mrs. Skunk's tail is $\frac{2}{4}$ foot long. How much longer is Mr. Skunk's tail?

Complete: $\frac{3}{4} - \frac{2}{4} = \frac{\square}{4}$.

2. Fluffy Rabbit ran $\frac{7}{10}$ mile. Squeaky Mouse ran $\frac{3}{10}$ mile. How much farther did Fluffy Rabbit run?

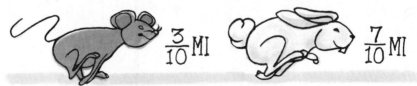

$\frac{3}{10}$MI $\frac{7}{10}$MI

Complete: $\frac{7}{10} - \frac{3}{10} = \frac{\square}{10}$.

3. Observe. What pattern do you see?

$$\frac{4}{5} - \frac{1}{5} = \frac{3}{5} \qquad \frac{3}{4} - \frac{2}{4} = \frac{1}{4} \qquad \frac{7}{10} - \frac{3}{10} = \frac{4}{10}$$

To subtract fractions with the same denominator: (1) subtract the numerators, (2) use the denominator.

$$\frac{8}{9} - \frac{3}{9} = \frac{8-3}{9} \qquad\qquad \begin{array}{r} \frac{8}{9} \\ -\frac{3}{9} \\ \hline \frac{5}{9} \end{array}$$
$$= \frac{5}{9}$$

4. Copy and complete.

a. $\dfrac{9}{10} - \dfrac{4}{10} = \dfrac{\square - 4}{10}$

$\qquad = \dfrac{\triangle}{10}$

b. $\dfrac{7}{11} - \dfrac{1}{11} = \dfrac{7-1}{\square}$

$\qquad = \dfrac{\triangle}{\square}$

5. Subtract.

a. $\dfrac{7}{8} - \dfrac{2}{8}$

b. $\dfrac{11}{12} - \dfrac{4}{12}$

c. $\dfrac{1}{5} - \dfrac{1}{5}$

EXERCISES

Subtract.

1. $\dfrac{11}{12} - \dfrac{7}{12}$

2. $\dfrac{6}{7} - \dfrac{5}{7}$

3. $\dfrac{6}{13} - \dfrac{2}{13}$

4. $\dfrac{6}{8} - \dfrac{1}{8}$

5. $\dfrac{4}{5} - \dfrac{3}{5}$

6. $\dfrac{7}{8} - \dfrac{0}{8}$

7. $\dfrac{4}{6} - \dfrac{4}{6}$

8. $\dfrac{7}{10} - \dfrac{3}{10}$

9. $\begin{array}{r} \frac{4}{5} \\ -\frac{1}{5} \\ \hline \end{array}$

10. $\begin{array}{r} \frac{7}{4} \\ -\frac{6}{4} \\ \hline \end{array}$

11. $\begin{array}{r} \frac{13}{16} \\ -\frac{9}{16} \\ \hline \end{array}$

12. $\begin{array}{r} \frac{7}{12} \\ -\frac{6}{12} \\ \hline \end{array}$

Keeping Fit

Write four fractional numerals equivalent to each.

1. $\frac{1}{2}$ 2. $\frac{1}{3}$ 3. $\frac{2}{3}$ 4. $\frac{1}{4}$

5. $\frac{3}{4}$ 6. $\frac{1}{5}$ 7. $\frac{5}{6}$ 8. $\frac{3}{8}$

Add.

9.	10.	11.	12.
906	4,287	7,685	$47.68
+ 899	+ 3,948	+ 3,009	+ 26.45

Subtract.

13.	14.	15.	16.
426	506	$97.65	8,000
− 116	− 219	− 18.49	− 4,903

Multiply.

17.	18.	19.	20.
87	381	$70.98	72
× 6	× 3	× 6	× 47

Divide.

21. $6\overline{)487}$ **22.** $3\overline{)2,424}$ **23.** $4\overline{)3,941}$ **24.** $30\overline{)498}$

What geometric figures are pictured?

25.   A

26.

27.

28.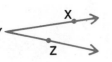

29.

30.

31.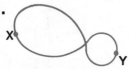

32.

33.

COMPARING FRACTIONS

Compare	Think	Write
$\frac{1}{3}$	$\frac{1}{3}$ is less than $\frac{2}{3}$	$\frac{1}{3} < \frac{2}{3}$
$\frac{2}{3}$	$\frac{2}{3}$ is greater than $\frac{1}{3}$	$\frac{2}{3} > \frac{1}{3}$

When the denominators are the same, we can compare the numerators.

1. Compare $\frac{2}{5}$ and $\frac{3}{5}$.

   a. Are the denominators the same?

   b. Compare the numerators using $<$ or $>$: 2 ≡ 3.

   c. Make true using $<$ or $>$: $\frac{2}{5}$ ≡ $\frac{3}{5}$.

2. Compare. Use $<$ or $>$.

   a. $\frac{1}{4}$ ≡ $\frac{3}{4}$ b. $\frac{4}{7}$ ≡ $\frac{2}{7}$ c. $\frac{1}{12}$ ≡ $\frac{3}{12}$

EXERCISES

Compare. Use $<$ or $>$.

1. $\frac{5}{6}$ ≡ $\frac{2}{6}$ 2. $\frac{2}{6}$ ≡ $\frac{5}{6}$ 3. $\frac{3}{4}$ ≡ $\frac{1}{4}$

4. $\frac{2}{5}$ ≡ $\frac{4}{5}$ 5. $\frac{5}{10}$ ≡ $\frac{6}{10}$ 6. $\frac{3}{8}$ ≡ $\frac{5}{8}$

7. $\frac{2}{4}$ ≡ $\frac{3}{4}$ 8. $\frac{1}{6}$ ≡ $\frac{4}{6}$ 9. $\frac{7}{8}$ ≡ $\frac{5}{8}$

10. $\frac{5}{11}$ ≡ $\frac{2}{11}$ 11. $\frac{7}{11}$ ≡ $\frac{5}{11}$ 12. $\frac{3}{7}$ ≡ $\frac{5}{7}$

We can compare $\frac{1}{2}$ and $\frac{1}{4}$ by looking at this picture. We see $\frac{1}{2} > \frac{1}{4}$.

$\frac{1}{2}$

$\frac{1}{4}$

We can also compare $\frac{1}{2}$ and $\frac{1}{4}$ this way.

Step 1 Names for $\frac{1}{2}$: $\frac{1}{2}, \frac{2}{4}, \frac{3}{6}, \ldots$

Names for $\frac{1}{4}$: $\frac{1}{4}, \frac{2}{8}, \frac{3}{12}, \ldots$

Step 2 Find names with the same denominator.

$$\frac{1}{2} = \frac{2}{4} \qquad \frac{1}{4} = \frac{1}{4}$$

Step 3 $\frac{2}{4} > \frac{1}{4}$ so $\frac{1}{2} > \frac{1}{4}$

1. Look at this picture to compare $\frac{1}{2}$ and $\frac{2}{3}$. Make true using $<$ or $>$: $\frac{1}{2} \equiv \frac{2}{3}$.

$\frac{1}{2}$

$\frac{2}{3}$

2. Let's use the other method to compare $\frac{1}{2}$ and $\frac{2}{3}$.

   a. Complete. List the first four names for $\frac{1}{2}$.

   $$\frac{1}{2}, \quad \frac{1 \times 2}{2 \times 2} = \frac{\square}{4}, \quad \frac{1 \times 3}{2 \times 3} = \frac{\triangle}{6}, \quad \frac{1 \times 4}{2 \times 4} = \frac{\triangledown}{8}$$

   b. List the first four names for $\frac{2}{3}$.

   c. Find names with the same denominator.

   d. Complete: $\frac{1}{2} = \frac{\square}{6}$, $\frac{2}{3} = \frac{\triangle}{6}$.

   e. Make true. Use $>$ or $<$.

   $$\frac{3}{6} \equiv \frac{4}{6} \text{ so } \frac{1}{2} \equiv \frac{2}{3}$$

3. Compare $\frac{1}{3}$ and $\frac{1}{4}$.

    a. List four names for $\frac{1}{3}$; for $\frac{1}{4}$.

    b. Find names with the same denominator.

    c. Make true using < or >: $\frac{1}{3} \equiv \frac{1}{4}$.

4. Compare using < or >: $\frac{1}{2} \equiv \frac{2}{5}$.

Compare. Use < or >.

  1. $\frac{1}{4} \equiv \frac{2}{3}$
    2. $\frac{1}{3} \equiv \frac{1}{2}$
    3. $\frac{1}{2} \equiv \frac{3}{5}$
    4. $\frac{3}{4} \equiv \frac{1}{5}$

  5. $\frac{3}{8} \equiv \frac{1}{4}$
    6. $\frac{1}{4} \equiv \frac{3}{5}$
    7. $\frac{2}{3} \equiv \frac{1}{2}$
    8. $\frac{3}{8} \equiv \frac{1}{3}$

  9. $\frac{1}{3} \equiv \frac{3}{4}$
  10. $\frac{1}{3} \equiv \frac{1}{5}$
  11. $\frac{1}{4} \equiv \frac{2}{5}$
  12. $\frac{2}{3} \equiv \frac{3}{4}$

Solve these mini-problems.

13. Tank of gas.
    Used $\frac{1}{8}$ on Monday.
    Used $\frac{3}{4}$ on Tuesday.
    Used more on which day?

14. Rope.
    A: $\frac{1}{4}$ inch thick.
    B: $\frac{5}{8}$ inch thick.
    Which rope is thicker?

15. Garden.
    $\frac{2}{3}$ roses.
    $\frac{1}{6}$ tulips.
    More roses or tulips?

To add fractions the denominators must be the same. We can add $\frac{1}{2}$ and $\frac{1}{4}$ this way.

Step 1	$\frac{1}{2} + \frac{1}{4}$	Compare denominators.
Step 2	Names for $\frac{1}{2}$: $\frac{1}{2}, \frac{2}{4}, \frac{3}{6}, \ldots$ Names for $\frac{1}{4}$: $\frac{1}{4}, \frac{2}{8}, \frac{3}{12}, \ldots$	Find names with the same denominator.
Step 3	$\frac{1}{2} + \frac{1}{4} = \frac{2}{4} + \frac{1}{4}$ $\qquad$ $\frac{1}{2} = \frac{2}{4}$ $\qquad = \frac{3}{4}$ $\qquad\qquad$ $+\frac{1}{4} = \frac{1}{4}$ $\qquad\qquad\qquad\qquad\qquad\qquad \frac{3}{4}$	Rename and add.

1. Consider $\frac{1}{3} + \frac{1}{6}$.

a. List some names for $\frac{1}{3}$; $\frac{1}{6}$.

b. Find names with the same denominator.

c. Complete.

$$\frac{1}{3} + \frac{1}{6} = \frac{\square}{6} + \frac{\triangle}{6}$$
$$= \frac{\square + \triangle}{6}$$
$$= \frac{\triangledown}{6}$$

$\frac{1}{3}$ $\qquad$ $\frac{2}{6}$

2. Copy and complete.

a. $\quad \frac{1}{3} = \frac{\square}{12}$
$\quad +\frac{1}{4} = \frac{\triangledown}{12}$
$\qquad\qquad \frac{\triangle}{12}$

b. $\quad \frac{1}{2} = \frac{\square}{10}$
$\quad +\frac{2}{5} = \frac{\triangledown}{10}$
$\qquad\qquad \frac{\triangle}{10}$

3. Add.

a. $\frac{1}{8} + \frac{1}{2}$ **b.** $\frac{1}{2} + \frac{1}{3}$ **c.** $\frac{2}{3} + \frac{1}{4}$

Add.

1. $\frac{1}{4} + \frac{3}{8}$ **2.** $\frac{1}{3} + \frac{1}{9}$ **3.** $\frac{3}{4} + \frac{1}{8}$ **4.** $\frac{1}{2} + \frac{3}{8}$

5. $\frac{2}{3} + \frac{3}{4}$ **6.** $\frac{1}{2} + \frac{2}{3}$ **7.** $\frac{1}{2} + \frac{5}{8}$ **8.** $\frac{1}{5} + \frac{2}{3}$

9. $\frac{3}{6} + \frac{1}{2}$ **10.** $\frac{3}{8} + \frac{3}{4}$ **11.** $\frac{1}{2} + \frac{1}{6}$ **12.** $\frac{1}{3} + \frac{3}{5}$

13. $\begin{array}{r} \frac{3}{5} \\ + \frac{1}{2} \\ \hline \end{array}$ **14.** $\begin{array}{r} \frac{1}{3} \\ + \frac{1}{6} \\ \hline \end{array}$ **15.** $\begin{array}{r} \frac{3}{4} \\ + \frac{1}{6} \\ \hline \end{array}$ **16.** $\begin{array}{r} \frac{2}{5} \\ + \frac{1}{3} \\ \hline \end{array}$

17. $\begin{array}{r} \frac{1}{3} \\ + \frac{3}{4} \\ \hline \end{array}$ **18.** $\begin{array}{r} \frac{3}{5} \\ + \frac{1}{10} \\ \hline \end{array}$ **19.** $\begin{array}{r} \frac{5}{8} \\ + \frac{1}{4} \\ \hline \end{array}$ **20.** $\begin{array}{r} \frac{1}{2} \\ + \frac{5}{6} \\ \hline \end{array}$

Solve these problems.

21. Jim sleeps $\frac{1}{3}$ of his day and plays $\frac{1}{6}$ of his day. What part of a day does he sleep and play?

22. Cathy grew $\frac{1}{10}$ meter last year and $\frac{1}{5}$ meter this year. How much did she grow during these 2 years?

★ **23.** Three girls shared a pizza. Stephanie ate $\frac{2}{8}$, Toni ate $\frac{1}{4}$, and Bobbi ate $\frac{1}{2}$. How much pizza was left?

We can subtract $\frac{3}{4} - \frac{1}{2}$ this way.

Step 1	$\frac{3}{4} - \frac{1}{2}$	Compare denominators.
Step 2	Names for $\frac{3}{4}$: $\frac{3}{4}, \frac{6}{8}, \frac{9}{12}, \ldots$ Names for $\frac{1}{2}$: $\frac{1}{2}, \frac{2}{4}, \frac{3}{6}, \ldots$	Find names with the same denominator.
Step 3	$\frac{3}{4} - \frac{1}{2} = \frac{3}{4} - \frac{2}{4}$ $\quad$ $\begin{aligned} \frac{3}{4} &= \frac{3}{4} \\ -\frac{1}{2} &= \frac{2}{4} \\ \hline &\frac{1}{4} \end{aligned}$ $\phantom{\frac{3}{4} - \frac{1}{2}} = \frac{3-2}{4}$ $\phantom{\frac{3}{4} - \frac{1}{2}} = \frac{1}{4}$	Rename and subtract.

1. Consider $\frac{1}{3} - \frac{1}{6}$.

$\quad$ **a.** List some names for $\frac{1}{3}$; for $\frac{1}{6}$.

$\quad$ **b.** Find names with the same denominator.

$\quad$ **c.** Complete.

$$\frac{1}{3} - \frac{1}{6} = \frac{\square}{6} - \frac{\triangle}{6}$$
$$= \frac{\square - \triangle}{6}$$
$$= \frac{\triangledown}{6}$$

2. Copy and complete.

$\quad$ **a.** $\begin{aligned} \frac{2}{3} &= \frac{\square}{12} \\ -\frac{1}{4} &= \frac{\triangledown}{12} \\ \hline &\frac{\triangle}{12} \end{aligned}$
$\qquad\qquad$ **b.** $\begin{aligned} \frac{4}{5} &= \frac{\square}{10} \\ -\frac{1}{2} &= \frac{\triangledown}{10} \\ \hline &\frac{\triangle}{10} \end{aligned}$

3. Subtract.

    a. $\frac{5}{6} - \frac{1}{2}$ **b.** $\frac{2}{3} - \frac{1}{2}$ **c.** $\frac{4}{5} - \frac{1}{3}$

Subtract.

1. $\frac{5}{6} - \frac{1}{3}$ **2.** $\frac{1}{2} - \frac{1}{6}$ **3.** $\frac{7}{8} - \frac{1}{4}$ **4.** $\frac{7}{8} - \frac{1}{2}$

5. $\frac{5}{8} - \frac{1}{4}$ **6.** $\frac{1}{3} - \frac{1}{4}$ **7.** $\frac{4}{5} - \frac{2}{3}$ **8.** $\frac{3}{4} - \frac{2}{3}$

9. $\begin{array}{r} \frac{1}{2} \\ -\frac{1}{4} \\ \hline \end{array}$ **10.** $\begin{array}{r} \frac{1}{2} \\ -\frac{1}{8} \\ \hline \end{array}$ **11.** $\begin{array}{r} \frac{3}{4} \\ -\frac{1}{6} \\ \hline \end{array}$ **12.** $\begin{array}{r} \frac{7}{8} \\ -\frac{3}{4} \\ \hline \end{array}$

13. $\begin{array}{r} \frac{2}{3} \\ -\frac{1}{4} \\ \hline \end{array}$ **14.** $\begin{array}{r} \frac{3}{8} \\ -\frac{1}{4} \\ \hline \end{array}$ **15.** $\begin{array}{r} \frac{1}{2} \\ -\frac{1}{5} \\ \hline \end{array}$ **16.** $\begin{array}{r} \frac{5}{8} \\ -\frac{1}{2} \\ \hline \end{array}$

★ **17.** Draw a flow chart on how to subtract fractions.

Solve these problems.

18. Ms. Davis had $\frac{2}{3}$ of a dozen eggs. She used $\frac{1}{4}$ of a dozen for a cake. What part of a dozen does she have left?

19. The cake used $\frac{1}{3}$ cup of sugar. The frosting used $\frac{3}{5}$ cup of sugar. How much more sugar was used in the frosting?

Estimate the sum by rounding each addend to the nearest ten.

1.	34	2.	63	3.	92
	58		21		47
	67		89		34
	+23		+54		+19

Estimate the sum by rounding each addend to the nearest dollar.

4.	$4.86	5.	$8.73	6.	$1.25	7.	$7.98
	+2.94		+3.47		+6.98		+8.19

Look at this angle.

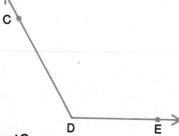

8. Name its sides.

9. Name its vertex.

10. Name the angle in two ways.

Which are parallel? Which intersect?

11. **12.** **13.** **14.**

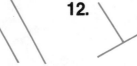

Look at this circle.

15. Name the center.

16. Name three radii.

17. Name a diameter.

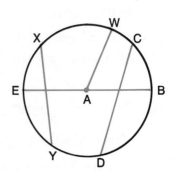

MINI-PROBLEMS WITH FRACTIONS

1. Time.
Ran: $\frac{1}{4}$ hour.
Walked: $\frac{1}{2}$ hour.
How long in all?

2. Distance.
School: $\frac{3}{4}$ kilometer.
Store: $\frac{1}{2}$ kilometer.
Difference?

3. Belt length.
Tom's: $\frac{1}{2}$ meter.
Joe's: $\frac{3}{5}$ meter.
Difference?

4. Snow.
$\frac{1}{10}$ meter on Sunday.
$\frac{1}{5}$ meter on Monday.
How much in all?

5. Test.
Joan: $\frac{2}{3}$ problems correct.
Jan: $\frac{8}{12}$ problems correct.
Who did better?

6. Pie.
Bob: ate $\frac{3}{8}$.
Al: ate $\frac{1}{8}$.
How much eaten?

7. Eggs.
$\frac{1}{6}$ dozen for a cake.
$\frac{1}{3}$ dozen for a pie.
How much in all?

8. Buttons.
Red: $\frac{1}{4}$ inch.
Blue: $\frac{1}{2}$ inch.
Difference?

9. Fish.
Sue's: $\frac{2}{10}$ kilogram.
Ann's: $\frac{3}{5}$ kilogram.
How much together?

★**10.** John's work.
$\frac{1}{2}$ in the morning.
$\frac{1}{3}$ in the afternoon.
How much left?

MIXED NUMERALS

Fractional Numeral		Mixed Numeral

$\frac{4}{3}$ 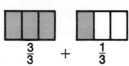 $1\frac{1}{3}$

$\frac{3}{3}$ + $\frac{1}{3}$

$\frac{7}{4}$  $1\frac{3}{4}$

$\frac{4}{4}$ + $\frac{3}{4}$

Numerals like $1\frac{1}{3}$ and $1\frac{3}{4}$ are called **mixed numerals.**

1. Look at these pictures.

   a. How many halves are shaded?

   b. Write the fractional numeral for the shaded part.

   c. How many wholes are shaded?

   d. What part of the second figure is shaded?

   e. Write a mixed numeral for all the shaded part.

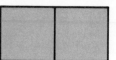

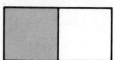

$$\frac{3}{2} = \frac{2}{2} + \frac{1}{2}$$
$$= 1 + \frac{1}{2}$$
$$= 1\frac{1}{2}$$

We read $1\frac{1}{2}$ as "one and one half."

2. Write a fractional numeral and a mixed numeral for the shaded part of each.

   a.   b.

3. Copy and complete to find a mixed numeral.

a. $\frac{6}{5} = \frac{5}{5} + \frac{1}{5}$

$= 1 + \underline{}$

$= \underline{}$

b. $\frac{9}{6} = \frac{6}{6} + \underline{}$

$= \underline{} + \underline{}$

$= \underline{}$

4. Write mixed numerals.

a. $\frac{7}{5}$ **b.** $\frac{11}{8}$ **c.** $\frac{9}{7}$

EXERCISES

Write a fractional numeral and a mixed numeral for the shaded part of each.

1.  **2.**

Write mixed numerals.

3. $\frac{5}{3}$ **4.** $\frac{5}{4}$ **5.** $\frac{8}{5}$ **6.** $\frac{5}{4}$ **7.** $\frac{7}{6}$

8. $\frac{11}{7}$ **9.** $\frac{9}{6}$ **10.** $\frac{13}{8}$ **11.** $\frac{15}{10}$ **12.** $\frac{12}{9}$

13. $\frac{6}{4}$ **14.** $\frac{9}{5}$ ★ **15.** $\frac{5}{2}$ ★ **16.** $\frac{7}{3}$ ★ **17.** $\frac{15}{4}$

Brainteaser

 Michael is $\frac{1}{4}$ as old as his father. When his father's age is divided by 2, 3, 4, 6, or 8, there is never a remainder. How old is Michael?

SUMS 1 AND GREATER

Sometimes when we add fractions the sum is 1.

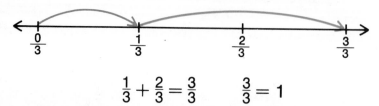

$$\frac{1}{3} + \frac{2}{3} = \frac{3}{3} \qquad \frac{3}{3} = 1$$

Sometimes when we add fractions the sum is greater than 1.

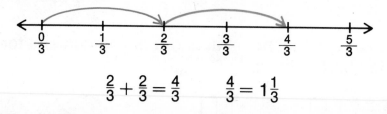

$$\frac{2}{3} + \frac{2}{3} = \frac{4}{3} \qquad \frac{4}{3} = 1\frac{1}{3}$$

1. Ken filled $\frac{5}{8}$ of a cup with water. Jack added $\frac{3}{8}$ of a cup more. How much water was in the cup?

 a. Complete: $\frac{5}{8} + \frac{3}{8} = \frac{\square}{8}$.

 b. Complete: $\frac{8}{8} = \square$.

 c. Is the cup full?

$$\begin{array}{r} \frac{5}{8} \\ +\frac{3}{8} \\ \hline \frac{8}{8} = 1 \end{array}$$

2. Copy and complete.

 a.
$$\begin{array}{r} \frac{3}{4} \\ +\frac{1}{4} \\ \hline \frac{4}{4} = \underline{} \end{array}$$

 b.
$$\begin{array}{r} \frac{4}{5} \\ +\frac{3}{5} \\ \hline \frac{7}{5} = \frac{5}{5} + \underline{} \\ = \underline{} \end{array}$$

264

3. Add. Give the sum as 1 or a mixed numeral.

a. $\frac{3}{5} + \frac{2}{5}$ **b.** $\frac{6}{10} + \frac{7}{10}$ **c.** $\frac{3}{6} + \frac{5}{6}$

Add. Give the sum as 1 or a mixed numeral.

1. $\frac{4}{5} + \frac{1}{5}$ **2.** $\frac{3}{7} + \frac{4}{7}$ **3.** $\frac{4}{7} + \frac{4}{7}$ **4.** $\frac{5}{9} + \frac{5}{9}$

5. $\frac{4}{6} + \frac{2}{6}$ **6.** $\frac{3}{4} + \frac{3}{4}$ **7.** $\frac{3}{10} + \frac{8}{10}$ **8.** $\frac{4}{5} + \frac{2}{5}$

9. $\frac{7}{9} + \frac{5}{9}$ **10.** $\frac{1}{9} + \frac{8}{9}$ **11.** $\frac{7}{12} + \frac{11}{12}$ **12.** $\frac{5}{8} + \frac{6}{8}$

13. $\begin{array}{r} \frac{3}{8} \\ + \frac{6}{8} \\ \hline \end{array}$ **14.** $\begin{array}{r} \frac{4}{5} \\ + \frac{4}{5} \\ \hline \end{array}$ **15.** $\begin{array}{r} \frac{5}{6} \\ + \frac{5}{6} \\ \hline \end{array}$ **16.** $\begin{array}{r} \frac{7}{11} \\ + \frac{10}{11} \\ \hline \end{array}$

17. $\begin{array}{r} \frac{4}{9} \\ + \frac{5}{9} \\ \hline \end{array}$ **18.** $\begin{array}{r} \frac{5}{7} \\ + \frac{6}{7} \\ \hline \end{array}$ **19.** $\begin{array}{r} \frac{7}{10} \\ + \frac{8}{10} \\ \hline \end{array}$ **20.** $\begin{array}{r} \frac{4}{11} \\ + \frac{8}{11} \\ \hline \end{array}$

21. $\begin{array}{r} \frac{7}{8} \\ + \frac{7}{8} \\ \hline \end{array}$ **22.** $\begin{array}{r} \frac{3}{7} \\ + \frac{4}{7} \\ \hline \end{array}$ **23.** $\begin{array}{r} \frac{5}{6} \\ + \frac{4}{6} \\ \hline \end{array}$ **24.** $\begin{array}{r} \frac{9}{10} \\ + \frac{3}{10} \\ \hline \end{array}$

Solve these mini-problems.

25. Dog food.

$\frac{3}{4}$ can for breakfast.

$\frac{1}{2}$ can for dinner.

How much in all?

26. Snake growth.

$\frac{3}{5}$ meter first year.

$\frac{7}{10}$ meter second year.

How much in all?

There were $2\frac{3}{8}$ chocolate cakes and $1\frac{1}{8}$ white cakes left after the party. How much cake was left in all?

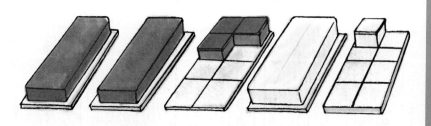

Add fractions	Add whole numbers
$2\frac{3}{8}$	$2\frac{3}{8}$
$+1\frac{1}{8}$	$+1\frac{1}{8}$
$\frac{4}{8}$	$3\frac{4}{8}$

1. Look at $3\frac{1}{6} + 2\frac{3}{6}$.

   a. What is the sum of the fractions? $\frac{1}{6} + \frac{3}{6} =$ ___

   $\begin{array}{r} 3\frac{1}{6} \\ +2\frac{3}{6} \\ \hline 5\frac{4}{6} \end{array}$

   b. What is the sum of the whole numbers? $3 + 2 =$ ___

   c. Read the sum.

2. Add.

   a. $\begin{array}{r} 3\frac{1}{3} \\ +4\frac{1}{3} \\ \hline \end{array}$
   b. $\begin{array}{r} 7\frac{1}{5} \\ +9\frac{2}{5} \\ \hline \end{array}$
   c. $\begin{array}{r} 78\frac{2}{7} \\ +68\frac{2}{7} \\ \hline \end{array}$
   d. $\begin{array}{r} 42\frac{1}{8} \\ +9 \\ \hline \end{array}$

Add.

1. $6\frac{1}{7}$
$+2\frac{5}{7}$

2. $3\frac{1}{8}$
$+4\frac{2}{8}$

3. $5\frac{3}{6}$
$+6\frac{1}{6}$

4. $4\frac{3}{8}$
$+4\frac{3}{8}$

5. $7\frac{3}{9}$
$+2\frac{1}{9}$

6. $7\frac{2}{10}$
$+6\frac{3}{10}$

7. $4\frac{1}{12}$
$+7\frac{10}{12}$

8. $9\frac{4}{11}$
$+6\frac{5}{11}$

9. $12\frac{5}{8}$
$+\ 6\frac{1}{8}$

10. $23\frac{4}{7}$
$+65\frac{1}{7}$

11. $38\frac{3}{8}$
$+29\frac{4}{8}$

12. $44\frac{1}{9}$
$+88\frac{3}{9}$

13. $7\frac{1}{2}$
$+9$

14. $38\frac{3}{4}$
$+29$

15. $126\frac{1}{4}$
$+328$

16. $18\frac{1}{9}$
$+18\frac{1}{9}$

17. $6\frac{1}{3}$
$+4\frac{1}{3}$

18. $19\frac{3}{8}$
$+27\frac{4}{8}$

★ **19.** $5\frac{1}{6}$
$+4\frac{1}{3}$

★ **20.** $15\frac{1}{3}$
$+28\frac{3}{5}$

Solve these problems.

21. John measured on his map. It was $2\frac{3}{10}$ centimeters from Lampo to Alpin. It was $4\frac{1}{10}$ centimeters from Alpin to Zado. How far would it measure from Lampo to Zado through Alpin?

22. Mrs. Brown had a board $2\frac{1}{10}$ meters long and a board $1\frac{2}{10}$ meters long. How much did she have in all?

SUBTRACTION: MIXED NUMERALS

Paul was making a bookcase. He had a board $4\frac{5}{10}$ meters long.

He cut off a piece $2\frac{3}{10}$ meters long. How much did he have left?

He worked the problem this way.

Subtract Fractions	Subtract Whole Numbers
$4\frac{5}{10}$	$4\frac{5}{10}$
$-2\frac{3}{10}$	$-2\frac{3}{10}$
$\frac{2}{10}$	$2\frac{2}{10}$

1. Let's subtract $6\frac{4}{6} - 2\frac{1}{6}$. Complete.

$$6\frac{4}{6}$$
$$-2\frac{1}{6}$$
$$4\frac{3}{6}$$

a. Subtract the fractions.

$$\frac{4}{6} - \frac{1}{6} = \underline{\quad}$$

b. Subtract the whole numbers.

$$6 - 2 = \underline{\quad}$$

c. Read the difference.

2. Subtract.

a. $3\frac{2}{3}$
$-1\frac{1}{3}$

b. $4\frac{3}{4}$
$-2\frac{1}{4}$

c. $67\frac{7}{8}$
$-49\frac{7}{8}$

d. $47\frac{3}{5}$
-9

268

Subtract.

1. $4\frac{7}{8}$
    $-1\frac{3}{8}$

2. $7\frac{5}{6}$
    $-2\frac{2}{6}$

3. $4\frac{9}{10}$
    $-2\frac{5}{10}$

4. $8\frac{7}{9}$
    $-2\frac{6}{9}$

5. $12\frac{7}{8}$
    $-6\frac{5}{8}$

6. $15\frac{5}{16}$
    $-9\frac{4}{16}$

7. $17\frac{5}{12}$
    $-8\frac{3}{12}$

8. $16\frac{7}{10}$
    $-9\frac{4}{10}$

9. $23\frac{3}{4}$
    $-14\frac{1}{4}$

10. $43\frac{5}{10}$
    $-19\frac{3}{10}$

11. $136\frac{4}{9}$
    $-98\frac{3}{9}$

12. $28\frac{5}{12}$
    $-19\frac{3}{12}$

13. $9\frac{1}{2}$
    $-8\frac{1}{2}$

14. $17\frac{3}{4}$
    $-8\frac{3}{4}$

15. $47\frac{2}{3}$
    $-19\frac{1}{3}$

16. $86\frac{5}{6}$
    $-28\frac{3}{6}$

17. $35\frac{3}{5}$
    $-17\frac{3}{5}$

18. $74\frac{5}{8}$
    -37

19. $58\frac{7}{9}$
    -2

20. $46\frac{2}{3}$
    -17

Solve these problems.

21. It takes $3\frac{3}{4}$ hours by train to Pintor. John has been traveling on the train for $1\frac{1}{4}$ hours. How much longer will it take John to get to Pintor?

★ 22. Solve this magic square. Each row, column, and diagonal must have the same sum.

3		
$2\frac{1}{2}$		$4\frac{1}{2}$
5	$1\frac{1}{2}$	

PROBLEM SOLVING

Sometimes replacing fractions with whole numbers can help us decide which operation to use.

Example   Britt needs $\frac{3}{4}$ liter of water. She has $\frac{1}{2}$ liter. How much more does she need?

Think: Replace $\frac{3}{4}$ with 4 and $\frac{1}{2}$ with 2.

How much more? We subtract.

Then: $\frac{3}{4} - \frac{1}{2} = \frac{3}{4} - \frac{2}{4}$

$= \frac{1}{4}$ liter

1. Maria practiced her swimming for $2\frac{1}{4}$ hours. She practiced diving for $1\frac{1}{4}$ hours. How long did she practice in all?

   a. Replace $2\frac{1}{4}$ with 2 and $1\frac{1}{4}$ with 1. Would you add or subtract?

   b. Solve the problem.

2. Liz ran $\frac{7}{10}$ kilometer. Then she walked $\frac{3}{5}$ kilometer. How much farther did she run than walk?

3. Joe bought $3\frac{3}{10}$ meters of red tape and $2\frac{1}{10}$ meters of blue tape. How much tape did he buy in all?

4. David got $\frac{2}{3}$ of his problems done in one minute. Kathy got $\frac{3}{4}$ of hers done in one minute. Who got more done? How much more?

PATTERNMAKERS

1. A large factory had 27 patternmakers working the day shift. It had 36 patternmakers working the night shift. How many patternmakers were there in all?

2. In a recent year there were about 19,000 patternmakers. They worked for many kinds of manufacturers. How many worked for automobile manufacturers?

3. There were 78 patterns made by 3 patternmakers. Each made the same number. How many patterns did each make?

Mrs. Alvarez, a patternmaker, was working from this blueprint.

4. What is the total length of sides A and C?

5. How much longer is side D than side B?

★ 6. What is the total length of all 6 sides?

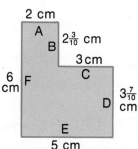

CHAPTER REVIEW

Add.

1. [248]
$$\frac{3}{10} + \frac{3}{10}$$

2. [248]
$$\frac{7}{16} + \frac{3}{16}$$

3. [256]
$$\frac{1}{2} + \frac{3}{8}$$

4. [256]
$$\frac{2}{5} + \frac{3}{10}$$

5. [256]
$$\frac{1}{2} + \frac{1}{3}$$

6. [256]
$$\frac{2}{3} + \frac{1}{4}$$

7. [266]
$$3\frac{5}{12} + 6\frac{3}{12}$$

8. [266]
$$4\frac{3}{5} + 2\frac{1}{5}$$

Add. Give the sum as 1 or a mixed numeral. [264]

9.
$$\frac{4}{7} + \frac{5}{7}$$

10.
$$\frac{6}{8} + \frac{7}{8}$$

11.
$$\frac{1}{9} + \frac{8}{9}$$

12.
$$\frac{2}{3} + \frac{2}{3}$$

Subtract.

13. [250]
$$\frac{7}{8} - \frac{3}{8}$$

14. [258]
$$\frac{1}{2} - \frac{1}{8}$$

15. [258]
$$\frac{5}{6} - \frac{1}{4}$$

16. [268]
$$12\frac{8}{10} - 9\frac{4}{10}$$

Compare. Use < or >. [253, 254]

17. $\frac{3}{4} \equiv \frac{2}{4}$ **18.** $\frac{3}{8} \equiv \frac{5}{16}$ **19.** $\frac{4}{5} \equiv \frac{7}{10}$ **20.** $\frac{1}{4} \equiv \frac{1}{3}$

Solve these problems.

21. Mr. Hopson had $\frac{1}{5}$ meter of red cloth and $\frac{1}{2}$ meter of blue cloth. How much cloth did he have in all?

22. Christina worked $8\frac{3}{4}$ hours on Monday and $7\frac{1}{4}$ hours on Tuesday. How much longer did she work on Monday?

CHAPTER TEST

Add.

1. $\frac{1}{5}$
$+\frac{2}{5}$

2. $\frac{7}{11}$
$+\frac{3}{11}$

3. $\frac{1}{3}$
$+\frac{1}{6}$

4. $\frac{3}{5}$
$+\frac{3}{10}$

5. $\frac{1}{2}$
$+\frac{2}{5}$

6. $\frac{1}{4}$
$+\frac{1}{3}$

7. $3\frac{3}{8}$
$+2\frac{2}{8}$

8. $7\frac{3}{9}$
$+4\frac{4}{9}$

Add. Give the sum as 1 or a mixed numeral.

9. $\frac{4}{9}$
$+\frac{5}{9}$

10. $\frac{1}{5}$
$+\frac{4}{5}$

11. $\frac{5}{6}$
$+\frac{5}{6}$

12. $\frac{7}{11}$
$+\frac{8}{11}$

Subtract.

13. $\frac{5}{6}$
$-\frac{1}{6}$

14. $\frac{1}{2}$
$-\frac{1}{3}$

15. $\frac{7}{8}$
$-\frac{3}{4}$

16. $3\frac{3}{8}$
$-2\frac{2}{8}$

Compare. Use < or >.

17. $\frac{2}{5}$ ⬚ $\frac{3}{5}$ **18.** $\frac{3}{6}$ ⬚ $\frac{2}{3}$ **19.** $\frac{3}{4}$ ⬚ $\frac{1}{3}$ **20.** $\frac{3}{5}$ ⬚ $\frac{7}{10}$

Solve these problems.

21. Joe spent $\frac{1}{4}$ hour on a bus and $\frac{1}{2}$ hour on a train. How long was he on the bus and train in all?

22. Frances bought $3\frac{7}{10}$ meters of rope and $1\frac{1}{10}$ meters of wire. How much more rope did she buy?

POLYGONS

1. a. Mark three points on your paper. Name them using letters *A*, *B*, and *C*.

A• •B

•C

b. Connect the points with line segments.

c. Is your figure a simple closed curve?

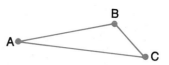

A simple closed curve which is made of line segments is called a **polygon.**

2. Draw a polygon with four line segments.

Which are polygons?

1.

2.

3.

4.

5. ◯

6.

7.

8.

9.

List the first four equivalent fractional numerals for each.

1. $\frac{3}{8}$ 2. $\frac{1}{4}$ 3. $\frac{2}{3}$ 4. $\frac{1}{3}$

5. $\frac{1}{5}$ 6. $\frac{1}{2}$ 7. $\frac{3}{4}$ 8. $\frac{2}{5}$

Add.

9.	275	10.	6,984	11.	5,476	12.	$ .25
	312		5,426		3,948		4.98
	+498		+3,219		+ 764		+7.82

13. $\frac{3}{8}$ 14. $\frac{3}{8}$ 15. $\frac{1}{4}$ 16. $3\frac{5}{8}$

   $+\frac{2}{8}$ $+\frac{1}{4}$ $+\frac{1}{3}$ $+4\frac{2}{8}$

Subtract.

17.	475	18.	6,742	19.	8,007	20.	$9.65
	−288		−3,465		−3,988		−4.89

21. $\frac{4}{7}$ 22. $\frac{5}{8}$ 23. $\frac{1}{2}$ 24. $6\frac{3}{4}$

   $-\frac{2}{7}$ $-\frac{1}{4}$ $-\frac{1}{5}$ $-2\frac{1}{4}$

Multiply.

25.	78	26.	145	27.	4,982	28.	$.75
	×7		×3		×8		×24

Divide.

29. $6\overline{)540}$ 30. $8\overline{)6,276}$ 31. $7\overline{)5,342}$ 32. $40\overline{)862}$

Find the average.

33. 19, 13, 25, 23   34. 8, 0, 4

275

TRIANGLES

1. Look at the triangles above.

   a. How many sides does a triangle have?

   b. $\overline{AC}$ is one side of triangle *ABC*.
   Name the other two sides of triangle *ABC*.

2. Look at triangle *LMN*.
   One angle is ∠*LMN*.

   a. How many more an-
   gles are there?

   b. Name them.

3. Look at triangle *ABC*.
   Point *A* is a vertex
   (plural — vertices).

   a. How many more ver-
   tices are there?

   b. Name them.

   A **triangle** has three
   sides, three angles,
   and three vertices.

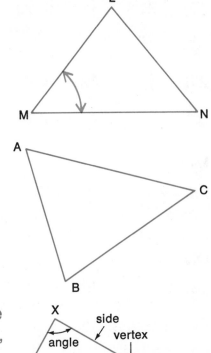

4. Look at these triangles.

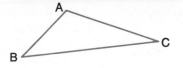 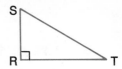

Which triangle has a right angle?

A triangle with a right angle is called a **right triangle.** Triangle *HIJ* is a right triangle.

Look at triangle *DEF*.

1. Name its sides.

2. Name its angles.

3. Name its vertices.

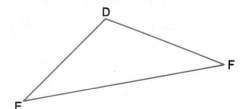

Look at these triangles.

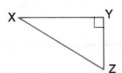 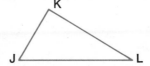

4. Which triangle has a right angle? Name the right angle.

5. Which triangle has two sides the same length?

6. Use the corner of your book to draw a right angle. Make a right triangle from your angle. Label the right angle *M* and the other two angles *L* and *O*.

277

Here are pictures of another special kind of polygon.
They are called **rectangles.**

1. Look at the rectangles above.

a. How many sides does each have?

b. Name the sides of rectangle *ABCD.*

c. How many right angles can you find in rectangle
ABCD? rectangle *LMNO*? rectangle *WXYZ*?

A rectangle has four sides and four right angles.

2. Find $\overline{AD}$ and $\overline{BC}$ in this rectangle. We say they are **opposite**
sides.

a. Name 2 more opposite sides.

b. Measure $\overline{AD}$ and $\overline{BC}$. How
do their lengths compare?

c. Measure $\overline{AB}$ and $\overline{DC}$. How
do their lengths compare?

The opposite sides of a rectangle have the same
length.

3. We call this figure a **square.**

    a. Is it a rectangle? Tell why.

    b. Measure all four sides. How do the lengths compare?

A square is a special kind of rectangle. All four of its sides have the same length.

4. Which are rectangles? Which are squares?

    a.   **b.**   **c.**   **d.**

Which are rectangles? Which are squares?

1.   **2.**   **3.**

4.   **5.**   **6.**

7.   **8.**   **9.**

Look at this rectangle.

10. Name two pairs of opposite sides.

11. Which side has the same length as $\overline{RS}$? as $\overline{ST}$?

R   S

U   T

279

DIAGONALS

1. $\overline{AC}$ is called a **diagonal**.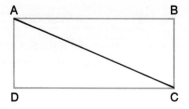

   a. A diagonal separates a rectangle into two triangles. Name them.

   b. The rectangle has another diagonal. Name it.

2. Measure the diagonals in each rectangle. What do you find?

   a.  b.   c.

The two diagonals in any rectangle or any square have the same length.

EXERCISES

Name the diagonals of each.

1.  2.   3.

4. In Exercise 1, $\overline{AC}$ is 3 centimeters long. How long is $\overline{BD}$?

Copy each figure. Then draw its diagonals.

5.   6.   7.

CERAMIC ENGINEERS

1. Some ceramic engineers help plan new factories. Mrs. Johnson designed a new glassware factory. It could produce 785 glasses an hour. Estimate how many glasses it could produce in 8 hours.

2. Mr. Ortega found that he had to fire one clay to 1,085 degrees. Another clay had to be fired to 1,471 degrees. How much hotter was the firing temperature of the second clay?

3. Glasses were packed in cartons. Each carton held 30 glasses. How many cartons would be needed to pack 5,700 glasses?

4. Before the final firing of some pottery, a glaze is applied. This glaze is applied by hand. One worker can glaze 40 plates in an hour. How many workers will be needed to glaze 360 plates in one hour?

5. It takes 18 hours to fire a glaze. Ms. Malone developed a new glaze that could be fired in 14 hours. What is the difference in the time needed to fire these glazes?

SLIDES AND TURNS

1. a. Make a figure like this one and cut it out.

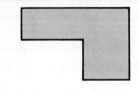

b. Put it on your desk.

c. Slide it to the right.   Slide it to the left.

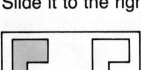   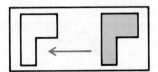

d. Did the figure change shape or size?

In a **slide,** a figure does not change shape or size.

2. a. Turn your figure clockwise.

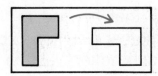

b. Turn your figure counterclockwise.

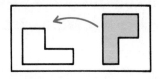

c. Turn your figure like this.

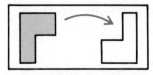

d. Did the figure change shape or size?

In a **turn,** a figure does not change shape or size.

3. Which show slides? Which show turns?

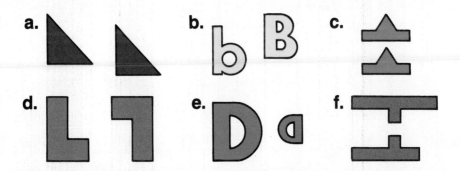

a. b. c.

d. e. f.

Which show slides? Which show turns?

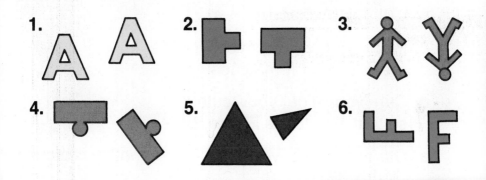

1. 2. 3.

4. 5. 6.

7. Make a figure like this one.
Cut it out.

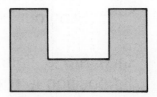

Trace around the figure on
a piece of paper.

Slide the figure to a different position and trace
it again.

8. Trace two more slides.

These show **flips.**

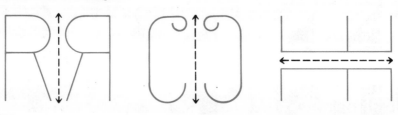

1. Take a piece of paper. Turn it over. We call that a **flip.**

2. Let's see if these figures are flips of each other.

   a. Trace Figure A.

   b. Cut out the tracing.

   c. Place your cutout over Figure A so that it matches.

   d. Can you slide your cutout so that it matches Figure B?

   e. Can you turn your cutout so that it matches Figure B?

   f. Flip your cutout. Does it match Figure B?

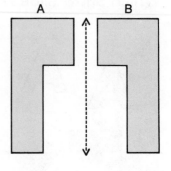

In a **flip** a figure does not change size or shape. Its position is **reversed.**

Figure

Flip line

Its flip

284

3. Which pairs look like flips?

a.   **b.**   **c.**

Which pairs look like flips?

1.   **2.**    **3.**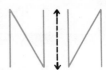

4.   **5.** 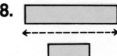   **6.**

7. 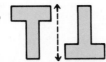   **8.** 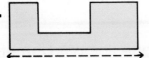   **9.**

★ Trace each figure and its flip line. Draw a flip of the figure.

10.    **11.**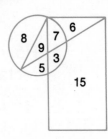

Brainteaser

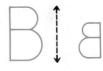

1. Find the sum of the numbers in the circle.

2. Find the sum of the numbers in the rectangle, but not in the triangle.

285

SYMMETRY

If we fold each figure on the dotted line, each half is a flip of the other.

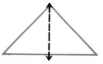

We call these figures **symmetric**.
The dotted lines are the **lines of symmetry**.

1. Which are symmetric?

a.    b.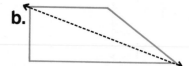

c. 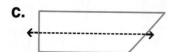   d.

2. Trace these. Draw a line of symmetry.

a.   b.   c.

3. Some figures have more than one line of symmetry.

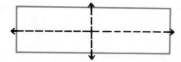

a. How many lines of symmetry are shown in the rectangle?

b. How many more lines of symmetry could you find for the circle?

286

4. Trace each figure. Draw as many lines of symmetry as you can.

a.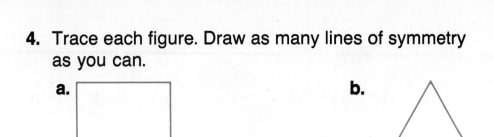

b.

5. Look around your room. What things are symmetric?

Which are symmetric?

1.

2.

3.

4.

5.

6.

7.

8.

9.

Trace each figure. Draw as many lines of symmetry as you can.

10.

11.

12.

13.

14.

15.

AT THE GROCERY STORE

Mrs. Chin taught her children, Bob and Mary, how to shop at a grocery store.

1. They needed 1 bag of carrots. How much did it cost?

Bob wanted an orange. His mother showed him how to find the cost by dividing. She told him that the store usually rounds the remainder up to the next cent. One orange cost 10¢.

$$\begin{array}{r} 9 \text{ r } 4 \\ 5\overline{)49} \\ 45 \\ \hline 4 \end{array}$$

2. How much would 2 oranges cost?

3. Mrs. Chin needed 5 apples for an apple pie. How much did 5 apples cost?

4. The family had salad for dinner. What was the total cost of 1 bag of carrots, 1 bag of celery, and 1 head of lettuce?

5. What was the cost of a half kilogram of grapes?

288

Mrs. Chin, Mary, and Bob saw a sign for sales on certain items. Mrs. Chin said that sometimes sale prices were not good buys.

Item	Regular price	Sale price
tomatoes	35¢ per can	3 cans for $1.00
eggs	79¢ per dozen	2 dozen for $1.49
tuna fish	59¢ per can	2 cans for $1.29

Here is how they checked the tomatoes.

3 cans at 35¢ each would be $1.05.
Sale price is $1.00.

6. Is the sale price a good buy?

7. Check the tuna fish. Complete.

2 cans at 59¢ each would be ____ .
Sale price is ____ .
Is the sale price a good buy?

Check to find out which is the better buy.

8. Frozen peas: 35¢ a package or 6 for $2.00.

9. Orange juice: 39¢ a bottle or 3 for $1.00.

10. Bread: 40¢ a loaf or 2 for 85¢.

11. Steak: $3.49 a kilogram or 2 kilograms for $7.

12. Cookies: 67¢ a box or 3 for $1.91.

13. Candy: 49¢ a bag or 2 bags $1.00.

1. **Trace this pattern. Include the tabs.**

2. **Cut out your pattern.**

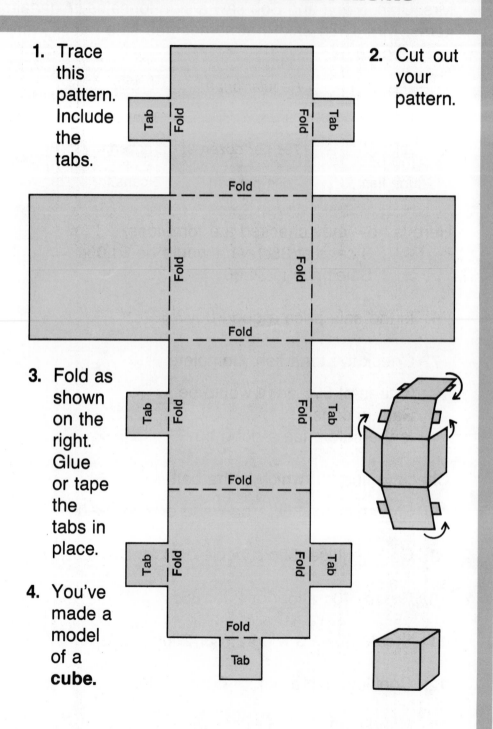

3. **Fold as shown on the right. Glue or tape the tabs in place.**

4. **You've made a model of a cube.**

5. Use your cube and this picture.

edge

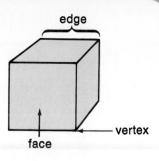

   a. How many faces are there?

   b. What figure is each face?

   c. Count the number of edges; of vertices.

vertex

face

6. This is a picture of a **rectangular prism.** It looks like a box.

   a. Is each face a square?

   b. Count the number of faces; of edges; of vertices.

A rectangular prism has 6 faces, 12 edges, and 8 vertices. A cube is a special rectangular prism. Each face is a square.

EXERCISES

Which look like rectangular prisms? Which look like cubes?

1.

2.

3.

4.

5.

6.

7.

8.

9.

These are pictures of other geometric figures.

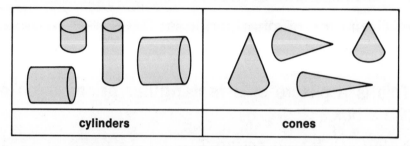

| cylinders | cones |

1. You can make a paper model of a cylinder. Hold the ends of a piece of paper together as shown.

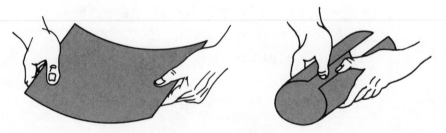

a. Think of tracing the top of your cylinder. What kind of figure would you get?

b. What figure would you get if you traced the bottom of your cylinder?

c. Open your paper model of a cylinder and spread it out flat. What kind of a figure is it?

2. Which look like cylinders?

a. 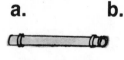   **b.**   **c.**

3. Let's make a model of a cone.

a. Trace this drawing.   **b.** Cut it out.

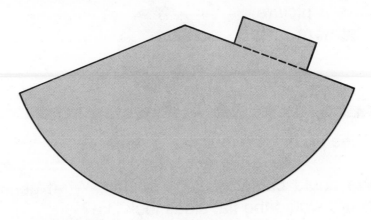

c. Attach the tab with tape or glue.

 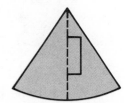

d. Trace the bottom of the cone. What figure is it?

EXERCISES

Which look like cylinders? Which look like cones?

1.    **2.**    **3.**

4.   **5.**   **6.**

7.    **8.**    **9.**

This is a picture of a **sphere.**

1. Does an orange look like a sphere?

2. We could cut an orange in half. What geometric figure would the flat sides look like?

3. We could cut an orange anywhere. What figure would the flat sides look like?

Which look like spheres?

1.   2.    3.

4.   5.   6.

7.   8.   9.

Compare. Use =, >, or <.

1. $\frac{1}{3}$ ⬚ $\frac{2}{3}$

2. $\frac{3}{4}$ ⬚ $\frac{1}{4}$

3. $\frac{1}{2}$ ⬚ $\frac{1}{3}$

4. $\frac{1}{4}$ ⬚ $\frac{3}{8}$

Add.

5.
$$\begin{array}{r} 35 \\ 47 \\ 83 \\ + \ 9 \\ \hline \end{array}$$

6.
$$\begin{array}{r} 498 \\ 276 \\ 95 \\ + 348 \\ \hline \end{array}$$

7.
$$\begin{array}{r} \$8.76 \\ 9.24 \\ 6.34 \\ + 9.98 \\ \hline \end{array}$$

8.
$$\begin{array}{r} 927 \\ 259 \\ 46 \\ + \ \ 1 \\ \hline \end{array}$$

9.
$$\begin{array}{r} \frac{1}{4} \\ + \frac{3}{4} \\ \hline \end{array}$$

10.
$$\begin{array}{r} \frac{3}{8} \\ + \frac{1}{4} \\ \hline \end{array}$$

11.
$$\begin{array}{r} \frac{2}{4} \\ + \frac{3}{4} \\ \hline \end{array}$$

12.
$$\begin{array}{r} 3\frac{4}{11} \\ + 6\frac{5}{11} \\ \hline \end{array}$$

Subtract.

13.
$$\begin{array}{r} 86 \\ - \ 9 \\ \hline \end{array}$$

14.
$$\begin{array}{r} 498 \\ - 399 \\ \hline \end{array}$$

15.
$$\begin{array}{r} \$8.75 \\ - 3.86 \\ \hline \end{array}$$

16.
$$\begin{array}{r} 8,004 \\ - 3,297 \\ \hline \end{array}$$

17.
$$\begin{array}{r} \frac{6}{8} \\ - \frac{3}{8} \\ \hline \end{array}$$

18.
$$\begin{array}{r} \frac{3}{4} \\ - \frac{3}{8} \\ \hline \end{array}$$

19.
$$\begin{array}{r} \frac{3}{4} \\ - \frac{2}{3} \\ \hline \end{array}$$

20.
$$\begin{array}{r} 6\frac{7}{8} \\ - 1\frac{1}{8} \\ \hline \end{array}$$

Multiply.

21.
$$\begin{array}{r} 37 \\ \times 9 \\ \hline \end{array}$$

22.
$$\begin{array}{r} 476 \\ \times 8 \\ \hline \end{array}$$

23.
$$\begin{array}{r} 6,249 \\ \times 5 \\ \hline \end{array}$$

24.
$$\begin{array}{r} 876 \\ \times 25 \\ \hline \end{array}$$

Divide.

25. $8\overline{)64}$

26. $9\overline{)72}$

27. $3\overline{)120}$

28. $7\overline{)6,300}$

29. $3\overline{)48}$

30. $4\overline{)948}$

31. $7\overline{)480}$

32. $30\overline{)492}$

CHAPTER REVIEW

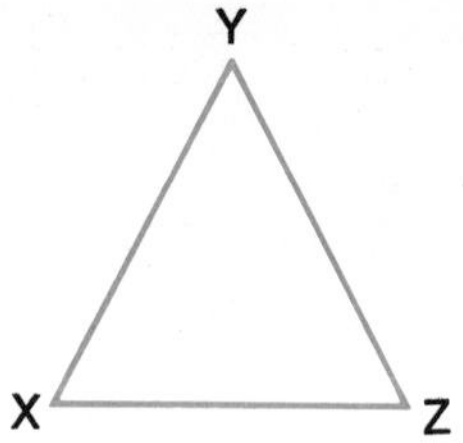

1. Name the sides of triangle *XYZ*.
[276]

2. Name the angles of triangle *XYZ*.
[276]

3. Name the vertices of triangle *XYZ*.
[276]

Which show slides? Which show turns? [282]

4.

5.

6.

Which pairs look like flips? [284]

7.

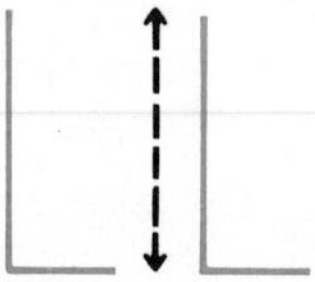

8.

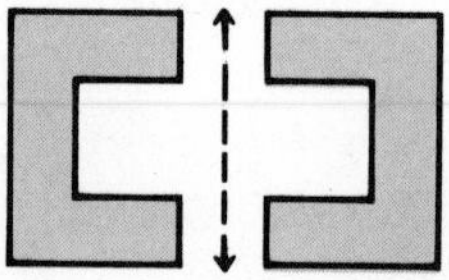

9.

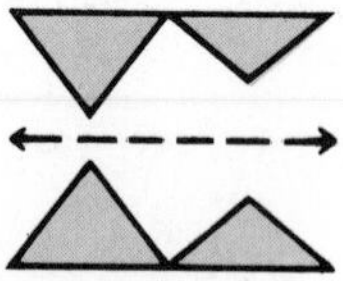

Trace each figure. Draw as many lines of symmetry as you can. [286]

10.

11.

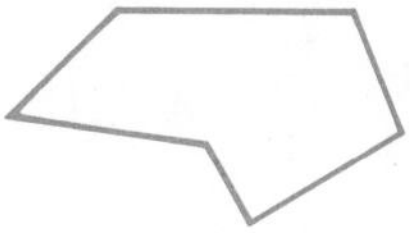

12.

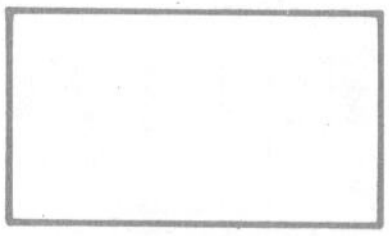

13. Look at figures 10–12. Which are squares? Which are rectangles? [278]

Match each figure with a name. Use each name once.

14.
[290]

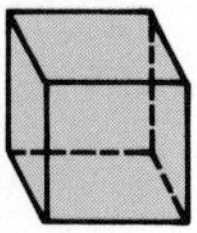

15.
[292]

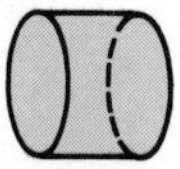

16.
[294]

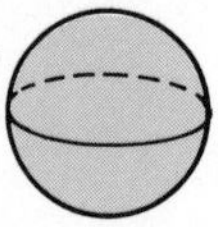

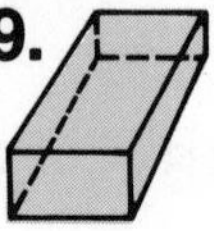

cone
rectangular prism
cube
sphere
cylinder
right triangle

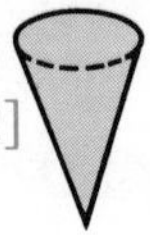

17.
[276]

18.
[292]

19.
[290]

CHAPTER TEST

Match each figure with a name. Use each name once.

1.   2.   3.

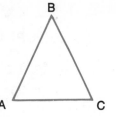

| rectangular prism |
| square |
| sphere |
| cube |
| rectangle |
| right triangle |
| polygon |
| cone |
| cylinder |

4.   5.   6.

7.   8.  9.

10. Name the sides of triangle *ABC*.

11. Name the angles of triangle *ABC*.

12. Name the vertices of triangle *ABC*.

Which show slides? Which show turns?

13.   14.   15.

Which pairs look like flips?

16. 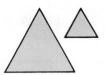   17. 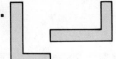   18.

Trace each figure. Draw as many lines of symmetry as you can.

19.   20.   21.

12 MEASUREMENT

LENGTH: METRIC SYSTEM

A **centimeter (cm)** is a metric unit of length.
It is used to measure short things.

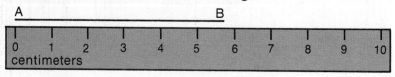

The measure of $\overline{AB}$ is 6 centimeters.

1. Look at $\overline{CD}$.

    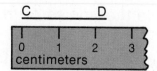

    a. Is it closer to 2 cm
    or to 3 cm?

    b. What is its length to the nearest centimeter?

2. Draw a line segment 3 cm long.

EXERCISES

Measure each to the nearest centimeter.

1. _____   2. _____

3. _____

Draw line segments of these lengths.

4. 1 cm   **5.** 7 cm   **6.** 5 cm   **7.** 10 cm

CENTIMETERS, METERS, KILOMETERS

The **meter (m)** is another metric unit of length.

1 centimeter   ——
1 meter = 100 centimeters

1. We can change meters to centimeters. Complete.

a. 3 m = 3 × 1 m
     = 3 × 100 cm
     = ____ cm

b. 6 m = 6 × 1 m
     = 6 × ____ cm
     = ____ cm

2. We can change centimeters to meters. Complete.

a. 400 cm = 4 × 100 cm
     = 4 × 1 m
     = ____ m

b. 200 cm = 2 × 100 cm
     = ____ × 1 m
     = ____ m

3. Copy and complete.

a. 8 m = ____ cm

b. 5 m = ____ cm

c. 700 cm = ____ m

d. 900 cm = ____ m

4. Let's change 325 cm. Complete.

Example   325 cm = 300 cm + 25 cm
                   = 3 m + 25 cm or 3 m 25 cm

a. 825 cm = ____ m ____ cm

b. 505 cm = ____ m ____ cm

c. 6 m 42 cm = ____ cm

d. 3 m 9 cm = ____ cm

132 cm

THAT'S 1m 32cm

5. Kilometers are used for longer distances. How far is it from Apple Valley to Peachville?

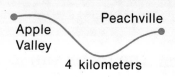

Peachville

Apple Valley

4 kilometers

1 kilometer (km) = 1,000 meters

6. Complete.

a. 2 km = ____ m   **b.** 5,000 m = ____ km

c. 2,793 m = 2 km ____ m   **d.** 9 km 500 m = ____ m

7. What would you use to measure these, cm, m, or km?

a. A pin   **b.** A scout hike   **c.** A person's jump

EXERCISES

Complete.

1. 5 m = ____ cm   **2.** 600 cm = ____ m

3. 345 cm = ____ m ____ cm   **4.** 2 m 47 cm = ____ cm

5. 5 km = ____ m   **6.** 6,000 m = ____ km

7. 8,637 m = ____ km ____ m   **8.** 9 km 237 m = ____ m

9. 3,500 m = ____ km ____ m   **10.** 2 km 807 m = ____ m

What would you use to measure these, cm, m, or km?

11. A mouse   **12.** A house   **13.** A long road

14. A spoon   **15.** A tree   **16.** A bee

LITERS

The **liter (L)** is a metric unit used to measure liquids.

1 LITER   ½ LITER   ¼ LITER

1. How many $\frac{1}{4}$ L does it take to make $\frac{1}{2}$ L?

2. Complete.

a. two L = ____ $\frac{1}{2}$ L

b. one L = ____ $\frac{1}{4}$ L

c. two $\frac{1}{2}$ L = ____ L

d. four $\frac{1}{4}$ L = ____ $\frac{1}{2}$ L

EXERCISES

Complete.

1. two L = ____ $\frac{1}{4}$ L

2. three $\frac{1}{2}$ L = ____ $\frac{1}{4}$ L

3. four $\frac{1}{2}$ L = ____ L

4. two $\frac{1}{4}$ L = ____ $\frac{1}{2}$ L

Solve this problem.

5. Arnold wants to buy 1 liter of ice cream. He could buy 1 liter for $1.05 or two $\frac{1}{2}$ liters for 55¢ each. Which is the better buy?

GRAM, KILOGRAM, METRIC TON

The **gram** is a unit of weight in the metric system. A small paper clip weighs about 1 gram.

1,000 grams(g) = 1 kilogram(kg)
1,000 kilograms = 1 metric ton(t)

1. The gram is used to weigh light things.
   Complete.

   a. 2,000 g = ___ kg

   b. 1,500 g = ___ kg ___ g

   c. 3,325 g = ___ kg ___ g

2. The kilogram is used to weigh heavier things.
   Complete.

   a. 3 kg = ___ g

   b. 9 kg = ___ g

   c. 5 kg 625 g = ___ g

3. The metric ton is used to weigh very heavy things.
   Complete.

   a. 5 t = ___ kg

   b. 9 t 986 kg = ___ kg

   c. 3,486 kg = ___ t ___ kg

302

4. Which one would you use to weigh each, g, kg, or t?

    a. a feather   **b.** a person

    c. an elephant   **d.** a pen

    e. a truck load of cement   **f.** a sack of potatoes

EXERCISES

Complete.

1. $3,000 \text{ g} = \_\_\_\_ \text{ kg}$ **2.** $6,000 \text{ g} = \_\_\_\_ \text{ kg}$

3. $4,650 \text{ g} = \_\_\_ \text{ kg} \_\_\_ \text{ g}$ **4.** $5,804 \text{ g} = \_\_\_ \text{ kg} \_\_\_ \text{ g}$

5. $7 \text{ kg} = \_\_\_ \text{ g}$ **6.** $6 \text{ kg } 300 \text{ g} = \_\_\_ \text{ g}$

7. $9 \text{ kg } 705 \text{ g} = \_\_\_ \text{ g}$ **8.** $6 \text{ t} = \_\_\_ \text{ kg}$

9. $4,000 \text{ kg} = \_\_\_ \text{ t}$ **10.** $7,489 \text{ kg} = \_\_\_ \text{ t} \_\_\_ \text{ kg}$

11. $8 \text{ t } 942 \text{ kg} = \_\_\_ \text{ kg}$ **12.** $4 \text{ t } 400 \text{ kg} = \_\_\_ \text{ kg}$

★**13.** $\frac{1}{2} \text{ kg} = \_\_\_ \text{ g}$ ★**14.** $\frac{1}{4} \text{ kg} = \_\_\_ \text{ g}$

Which one would you use to weigh each, g, kg, or t?

15. a football   **16.** a football player

17. a sack of apples   **18.** a truck load of apples

19. an apple   **20.** a pencil

21. a package of butter   **22.** a ship's cargo

ADDING AND SUBTRACTING MEASURES

Alonso made 2 jumps:
3 m 25 cm and 4 m 50 cm.
What was the total length?

$$\begin{array}{r} 3 \text{ m } 25 \text{ cm} \\ +4 \text{ m } 50 \text{ cm} \\ \hline 7 \text{ m } 75 \text{ cm} \end{array}$$

To add these lengths: add centimeters to centimeters, add meters to meters.

1. We can add kilometers and meters.

    a. Add meters.

    b. Add kilometers.
$$\begin{array}{r} 3 \text{ km } 250 \text{ m} \\ +7 \text{ km } 482 \text{ m} \\ \hline \end{array}$$

    c. What is the sum?

2. Add.

    a.
$$\begin{array}{r} 46 \text{ m } 29 \text{ cm} \\ +89 \text{ m } 38 \text{ cm} \\ \hline \end{array}$$
    b.
$$\begin{array}{r} 48 \text{ km } 362 \text{ m} \\ +79 \text{ km } 467 \text{ m} \\ \hline \end{array}$$

3. We can add weights the same way.

    Examples
$$\begin{array}{r} 112 \text{ kg } 400 \text{ g} \\ +314 \text{ kg } 362 \text{ g} \\ \hline 426 \text{ kg } 762 \text{ g} \end{array} \qquad \begin{array}{r} 17 \text{ t } 176 \text{ kg} \\ +9 \text{ t } 376 \text{ kg} \\ \hline 26 \text{ t } 552 \text{ kg} \end{array}$$

    Add.

    a.
$$\begin{array}{r} 861 \text{ kg } 421 \text{ g} \\ +198 \text{ kg } 98 \text{ g} \\ \hline \end{array}$$
    b.
$$\begin{array}{r} 47 \text{ t } 764 \text{ kg} \\ +98 \text{ t } 219 \text{ kg} \\ \hline \end{array}$$

4. We can subtract measures.

Examples

82 m 36 cm	4 kg 362 g
− 14 m 18 cm	− 2 kg 135 g
68 m 18 cm	2 kg 227 g

Subtract.

a. 42 m 88 cm
− 29 m 37 cm

b. 876 kg 450 g
− 198 kg 184 g

Add.

1. 37 m 25 cm
+ 37 m 25 cm

2. 428 km 312 m
+ 146 km 398 m

3. 21 kg 147 g
+ 68 kg 223 g

4. 500 t 376 kg
+ 297 t 186 kg

5. 92 kg 490 g
+ 32 kg 364 g

★ **6.** 52 m 86 cm
+ 29 m 14 cm

Subtract.

7. 7 m 40 cm
− 4 m 19 cm

8. 42 km 288 m
− 29 km 137 m

9. 46 km 426 m
− 19 km 316 m

10. 94 t 149 kg
− 28 t 127 kg

11. 86 kg 450 g
− 19 kg 184 g

12. 500 t 376 kg
− 297 t 186 kg

★ **13.** 28 m 25 cm
− 14 m 50 cm

★ **14.** 416 kg 392 g
− 296 kg 411 g

305

MEASURING TEMPERATURE

We use a thermometer to measure temperature. The unit of measure is called a **degree** (°).

These thermometers are marked with the **Celsius (C)** scale.

IN BOILING WATER   IN BLOCK OF ICE

1. Water boils at 100°C on the Celsius scale.

    a. At what temperature does water freeze?

    b. What is the difference between the boiling and freezing temperatures on the Celsius scale?

2. Thermometer A shows 32°C.

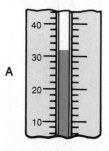 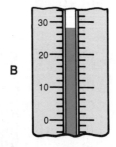 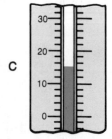

    a. What temperature is shown on thermometer B?

    b. What temperature is shown on thermometer C?

    c. Which shows the warmest temperature?

3. This thermometer shows 15 degrees below zero. We write −15°C.

a. If the temperature rises to 0°C, how many degrees would it rise?

b. If the temperature rises 10°, what would the thermometer read?

EXERCISES

What is the temperature?

1.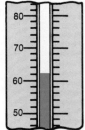

2.

3.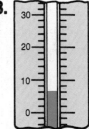

4.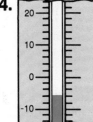

5.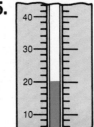

6.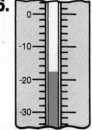

Complete.

7. Temperature: Was 9°C. Rose 8°. Temperature now?

8. Temperature: Was 9°C. Fell 8°. Temperature now?

9. Temperature: Was −3°C. Fell 6°. Temperature now?

10. Temperature: Was 12°C. Fell 6°. Temperature now?

Study these clocks.

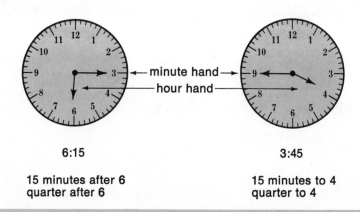

6:15

15 minutes after 6
quarter after 6

3:45

15 minutes to 4
quarter to 4

1. Complete to tell the time.

a.

___ : ___

___ minutes after ___

b.

___ : ___

___ minutes to ___

2. There are 24 hours in a day. Most clocks show only 12 hours. We use **am** or **pm**.

> 12 noon: The sun is usually overhead.
> 12 noon to 12 midnight: Time is labeled pm.
> 12 midnight: It is usually dark.
> 12 midnight to 12 noon: Time is labeled am.

We sleep at 5:35 am and eat dinner at 5:35 pm.
Label each as am or pm.

a. Breakfast — 7:15   **b.** School — 2:25

3. There are 60 minutes in an hour.
How many minutes are in 3 hours? 8 hours?

4. There are 60 seconds in a minute.
How many seconds are in 2 minutes? 10 minutes?

Give the time in two different ways.

1.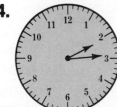

2.

3.

4.

5.

6.

Label each as am or pm.

7. Lunch — 12:15

8. Homework — 4:30

9. Shopping — 10:45

10. Baseball — 3:45

How many minutes are in each?

11. 2 hours

12. 5 hours

13. 12 hours

How many seconds are in each?

14. 3 minutes

15. 8 minutes

16. 20 minutes

★ **17.** How many seconds are in an hour? in a day?

309

ADDING AND SUBTRACTING TIME

It is 11:00 am.
In 1 hour it will be 12 noon.
In 2 hours it will be 1:00 pm.
1 hour ago it was 10:00 am.
4 hours ago it was 7:00 am.

1. What time will it be 4 hours after each?

    a. 3:00 pm   **b.** 6:21 am   **c.** 9:00 pm

2. What time was it 3 hours before each?

    a. 10:15 am   **b.** 2:00 am   **c.** 11:25 pm

3. We can add 1 hour and 13 minutes to 3:45.

ADD MINUTES

```
  3 hours  45 minutes
+ 1 hour   13 minutes
           58 minutes
```

ADD HOURS

```
  3 hours  45 minutes
+ 1 hour   13 minutes
  4 hours  58 minutes
           or 4:58
```

What time will it be 4 hours and 30 minutes after 5:24?

4. We can subtract 6 hours and 15 minutes from 9:31.

SUBTRACT MINUTES

```
  9 hours  31 minutes
- 6 hours  15 minutes
           16 minutes
```

SUBTRACT HOURS

```
  9 hours  31 minutes
- 6 hours  15 minutes
  3 hours  16 minutes
           or 3:16
```

What time was it 3 hours and 35 minutes before 7:50?

310

What time will it be 2 hours later?

1. 5:25 pm   **2.** 10:00 pm   **3.** 11:15 am

What time was it 4 hours earlier?

4. 9:15 am   **5.** 3:00 pm   **6.** 1:09 pm

What time will it be 1 hour and 27 minutes later?

7. 2:23 pm   **8.** 7:30 am   **9.** 10:14 am

What time was it 1 hour and 12 minutes earlier?

10. 2:23 pm   **11.** 7:30 am   **12.** 10:14 am

ADVERTISING WORKERS

1. Ms. Jefferson and Mr. Salcedo began a job at 9:10 am. It took them 1 hour and 33 minutes. What time did they finish?

2. Mrs. Sanchez takes a train home from work. The train ride takes 35 minutes. The train leaves at 5:20. At what time will she get home?

3. Ms. Jacobs wrote the copy for 268 grocery ads. She also wrote 450 car ads. How many ads did she write in all?

CUSTOMARY SYSTEM

Rulers in the customary system are maked in inches.
Each inch is marked into parts. Study these rulers.

Marked in halves

Marked in fourths

1. This line segment
   measures $\frac{3}{4}$ inch.
   Measure these.

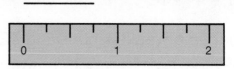

   a. ─────────────── b. ──────────

2. Draw line segments of these lengths.

   a. $\frac{1}{2}$ inch   **b.** $\frac{3}{4}$ inch   **c.** $3\frac{1}{4}$ inches

3. This ruler is divided into eighths.

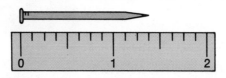

   a. How many eighth inches are in each inch?

   b. What is the length of the nail?

4. Measure these.

   a. ─────────   b. ──────

5. Draw a line segment $\frac{7}{8}$ inch long.

312

6. Let's measure this segment to the nearest $\frac{1}{8}$ inch.

A———————————————————B

Is the length of $\overline{AB}$ closer to $1\frac{5}{8}$ or $1\frac{6}{8}$?

$\overline{AB}$ is $1\frac{5}{8}$ inches long to the nearest $\frac{1}{8}$ inch. It is closer to $1\frac{5}{8}$ inches than to $1\frac{4}{8}$ inches or $1\frac{6}{8}$ inches.

7. Measure to the nearest $\frac{1}{8}$ inch.

    a. _____   **b.** _____   **c.** _____

EXERCISES

Draw line segments of these lengths.

1. $1\frac{1}{2}$ inches   **2.** $\frac{1}{4}$ inch   **3.** $2\frac{3}{4}$ inches

4. $1\frac{1}{4}$ inches   **5.** $\frac{1}{8}$ inch   **6.** $\frac{5}{8}$ inch

7. $1\frac{7}{8}$ inches   **8.** $2\frac{3}{8}$ inches   **9.** $4\frac{1}{8}$ inches

Measure to the nearest $\frac{1}{8}$ inch.

10. _____   **11.** _____

12. _____   **13.** _____

14. _____   **15.** _____

LENGTH: CUSTOMARY SYSTEM

Some units of length in the customary system are the **inch (in.)**, the **foot (ft)**, the **yard (yd)**, and the **mile (mi)**.

_____ 1 inch _____

1 foot = 12 inches
1 yard = 3 feet or 36 inches
1 mile = 5,280 feet

1. We can change feet to inches. Complete.

a. 2 ft = 2 × 1 ft
= 2 × 12 in.
= ____ in.

b. 5 ft = 5 × 1 ft
= 5 × ____ in.
= ____ in.

c. 3 ft = ____ in.

d. 9 ft = ____ in.

2. We can change yards to inches and to feet.

Examples   2 yd = 2 × 1 yd
= 2 × 36 in.
= 72 in.

2 yd = 2 × 1 yd
= 2 × 3 ft
= 6 ft

Complete.

a. 4 yd = ____ ft

b. 6 yd = ____ in.

3. To change feet to yards divide by 3. Complete.

a. 12 ft = 4 yd because
12 ÷ 3 = ____ .

b. 21 ft = ____ yd

314

4. To change miles to feet, multiply by 5,280.

    a. 2 mi = ____ ft   **b.** 9 mi = ____ ft

5. Which one would you use to measure these, in., ft, yd, or mi?

    a. A pen   **b.** The length of a highway

EXERCISES

Complete.

1. 4 ft = ____ in.   **2.** 8 ft = ____ in.

3. 15 ft = ____ in.   **4.** 3 yd = ____ in.

5. 4 yd = ____ in.   **6.** 5 yd = ____ in.

7. 5 yd = ____ ft   **8.** 9 yd = ____ ft

9. 7 yd = ____ ft   **10.** 15 ft = ____ yd

11. 24 ft = ____ yd   **12.** 18 ft = ____ yd

13. 4 mi = ____ ft   **14.** 5 mi = ____ ft

15. 8 mi = ____ ft   ★ **16.** 2 mi = ____ in.

Which one would you use to measure these, in., ft, yd, or mi?

17. The distance to the moon   **18.** A nail

19. The height of the ceiling   **20.** Your height

21. The length of a river   **22.** A pen

MEASURING LIQUIDS

We use these units to measure liquids.

2 cups = 1 pint (pt)
2 pints = 1 quart (qt)
4 quarts = 1 gallon (gal)

1. Complete.

a. 1 qt = ____ cups   **b.** 2 gal = ____ pt

2. Which is more?

a. 7 pt or 3 qt   **b.** 9 pt or 2 gal

Complete.

1. 2 gal = ____ qt   **2.** 2 pt = ____ cups

3. 1 gal = ____ pt   **4.** 2 qt = ____ pt

5. $\frac{1}{2}$ gal = ____ qt   **6.** $\frac{1}{2}$ gal = ____ pt

Which is more?

7. 6 cups or 4 pt   **8.** 8 cups or 2 qt

9. 9 pt or 1 gal   **10.** 14 pt or 2 gal

OUNCES, POUNDS, TONS

The **ounce (oz)**, **pound (lb)**, and **ton** are units of weight in the customary system.

1 oz   1 lb

1 ton

1 pound = 16 ounces
1 ton   = 2,000 pounds

1. We multiply by 16 to change pounds to ounces. Complete.

   a. 2 lb = ____ oz   **b.** 10 lb = ____ oz

2. Look at this balance scale.

   How many ounces are needed to make it balance?

   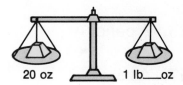

   20 oz   1 lb ___ oz

3. Complete.

   a. 22 oz = 1 lb ____ oz   **b.** 30 oz = ____ lb 14 oz

   c. 25 oz = ____ lb ____ oz   **d.** 19 oz = ____ lb ____ oz

4. We multiply by 2,000 to change tons to pounds. Complete.

   a. 2 tons = ____ lb   **b.** 5 tons = ____ lb

5. Which one would you use to weigh these, ton, lb, or oz?

   a. A robin   **b.** A person   **c.** A truck

Complete.

1. 4 lb = ____ oz   **2.** 6 lb = ____ oz

3. 9 lb = ____ oz   **4.** 12 lb = ____ oz

5. 21 oz = ___ lb ___ oz   **6.** 27 oz = ___ lb ___ oz

7. 18 oz = ___ lb ___ oz   **8.** 31 oz = ___ lb ___ oz

9. 6 tons = ____ lb   **10.** 9 tons = ____ lb

11. 8 tons = ____ lb   ★ **12.** 1 ton = ____ oz

Which one would you use to weigh these, ton, lb, or oz?

13. A dog   **14.** A jet plane

15. A pencil   **16.** A whale

17. A baseball   **18.** A baseball player

Keeping Fit

Add.

1.	48	**2.**	975	**3.**	2,894	**4.**	15,486
	26		648		3,987		29,692
	+ 32		+ 78		+ 4,912		+ 51,296

Multiply.

5.	59	**6.**	509	**7.**	63	**8.**	176
	× 4		× 8		× 34		× 49

FAHRENHEIT SCALE

This thermometer is marked with the **Fahrenheit (F)** scale.

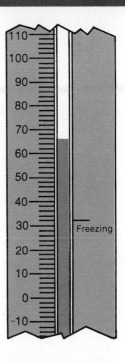

1. Water boils at 212°F. At what temperature does water freeze?

2. What is the temperature on the thermometer on the right?

3. On a warm day in Chicago, the temperature was 72°F. At night the temperature fell 24°. What was the temperature then?

EXERCISES

What is the temperature?

1.

2.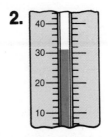

3.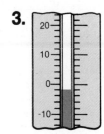

4. Temperature: Was 14°F. Rose 12°. What is it now?

5. Temperature: Was 48°F. Fell 20°. What is it now?

6. Temperature: Was 48°F. Rose 20°. What is it now?

1. Consider this triangle.

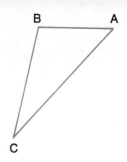

a. Use your centimeter ruler. Measure AB; BC; CA.

b. Add the lengths of the three sides. What is the distance around the triangle?

The distance around a figure is called the **perimeter.** We find the perimeter of a polygon by adding the lengths of its sides.

2. Find the perimeters.

a.

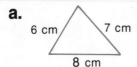

6 cm   7 cm
8 cm

b.

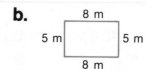

8 m
5 m   5 m
8 m

c.

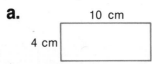

6 m
6 m   6 m
6 m

d.

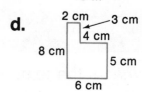

2 cm   3 cm
4 cm
8 cm
5 cm
6 cm

3. Find the perimeters.

a.

10 cm
4 cm

b.

3 m

4. Mr. Tago wants a fence around his property. His property is in the shape of a rectangle. It is 118 m long and 93 m wide. How many meters of fencing does he need?

Use your centimeter ruler to find the perimeters.

1.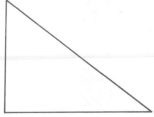

2.

Find the perimeters.

3.
4 cm
2 cm
3 cm

4.
29 m
13 m   13 m
29 m

5.
5 mi
5 mi   5 mi
5 mi

6.
1 cm
2 cm

7.
16 km   16 km
20 km

8.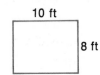
10 ft
8 ft

9.
7 yd

10.
14 in.
4 in.
7 in. 6 in.
10 in.
7 in.

11.
4 in.
5 in.
7 in.
5 in.
9 in.   2 in.

Solve these problems.

12. Noriko has a fenced in area for her dog. It is a rectangle, 15 meters by 20 meters. How many meters of fence does she have?

★ **13.** Lot A is a square, 60 feet on each side. Lot B is a rectangle, 50 feet by 75 feet. Which lot has the larger perimeter?

AREA

We use units like this to find length.

1 cm

We use units like this to find area. This is 1 **square centimeter.** We write 1 cm².

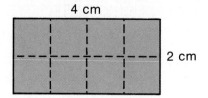

1 cm

1 cm

---

1. How many square centimeters cover the inside of this rectangle?

4 cm

2 cm

We say the area of this rectangle is 8 square centimeters (8 cm²). Area is a measure that tells how many square units fit into the inside of a figure.

2. This is 1 **square inch (in.²).** We can use it to find area.

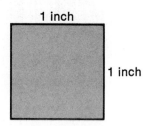

1 inch

1 inch

a. How many square inches cover the inside of this rectangle?

b. Find the area of this rectangle.

3 inches

1 inch

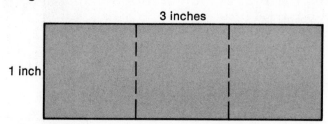

3. Find the areas.

a.  3 in.

4 in.

b. 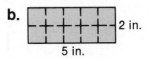 2 in.

5 in.

c. 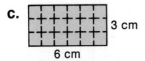 3 cm

6 cm

d. 3 cm

3 cm

Find the areas.

1. 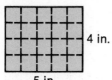 4 in.

5 in.

2. 10 cm
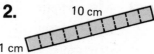
1 cm

3. 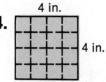 2 cm

6 cm

4. 4 in.
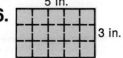 4 in.

5. 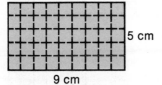 5 cm

9 cm

6. 5 in.
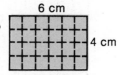 3 in.

7. 7 in.
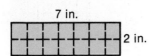 2 in.

8. 6 cm
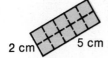 4 cm

9.

2 cm 5 cm

10. 4 in.
2 in.

FINDING AREAS BY MULTIPLYING

Ms. Hotinski is covering a small area with mirror tiles. Each tile is 1 square centimeter.

5 cm

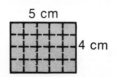

4 cm

1. a. How many tiles will Ms. Hotinski need?

b. What is the area of the rectangle?

2. Ms. Hotinski thought, "I have 4 rows with 5 in each row. 4 × 5 = 20. The area is 20 cm²." Is she correct?

We can find the area of a rectangle by multiplying length by width.

3 m

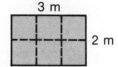

2 m

3 × 2 = 6
The area is 6 **square meters (m²).**

3. Look at this rectangle.

a. Count to find the area.

b. Think 4 rows of 7. Multiply to find the area.

7 m

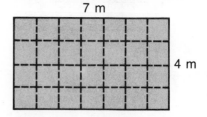

4 m

4. Find the areas by multiplying.

a.

5 m

2 m

b.

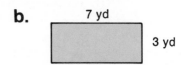

7 yd

3 yd

Find the areas by multiplying.

1. 9 cm / 4 cm

2. 8 cm / 2 cm

3. 8 m / 5 m

4. 23 m / 3 m

5. 12 m / 9 m

6. 10 km / 10 km

7. 16 km / 13 km

8. 34 cm / 15 cm

9. 5 ft

10. 7 cm / 4 cm

Solve these problems.

11. Mrs. Diaz's living room is a rectangle, 7 meters by 6 meters. How many square meters of carpet will she need to carpet the room?

12. Debbie wants to tile her workroom. It is a square, 4 meters on each side. How many square meters of tile does she need?

VOLUME

We use different units of measure to measure length, area, and volume.

To measure length, we use length measure.

———

To measure area, we use square measure.

To measure **volume,** we use **cubic** measure.

To measure volume, we find the number of cubes that will fit inside a figure.

1. How many cubes are in this figure?

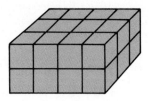

The volume of this box is 24 cubic units.

2. Find the volumes.

a.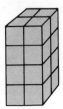

b.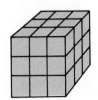

Find the volumes.

1.

2.

3.

4.

5.

6.

7.

8.

9.

10.

11.

12.

13.

14.

15.

16.

17.

18.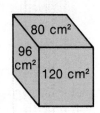

Brainteaser

The areas of the top, end, and side of a rectangular prism are shown. What is the total area of the surface?

80 cm²
96 cm²
120 cm²

PROBLEM SOLVING USING PICTURES

Sometimes drawing pictures helps to solve a problem.

Ellen put a fence around a garden. It was 3 meters long and $1\frac{1}{4}$ meters wide. How much fence did she use?

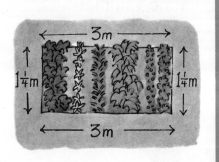

Add: $3 + 3 + 1\frac{1}{4} + 1\frac{1}{4} = 8\frac{2}{4}$ meters.

Solve these problems. Use the pictures to help you.

1. Mr. Dill put grass in his yard, which is shaped like a square. Each side is 25 meters long. How many square meters did he cover?

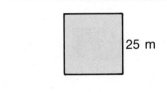

25 m

2. Sue biked $\frac{2}{3}$ mile and walked $\frac{1}{4}$ mile. How far did she travel?

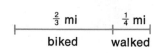

Solve these problems. Draw pictures to help you.

3. Ms. Woods fenced in a yard for her dog. The yard was shaped like a square. Each side was 50 meters long. How many meters of fence did she use?

4. Bob painted the floor of a garage. The floor was shaped like a rectangle. It was 8 meters long and 5 meters wide. How much area did he paint?

Add.

1. 947
    + 268

2. 1,379
    + 896

3. 476
    938
    + 287

4. 3,594
    8,689
    + 4,407

5. $\frac{2}{4}$
    $+\frac{1}{4}$

6. $\frac{1}{2}$
    $+\frac{1}{4}$

7. $\frac{1}{2}$
    $+\frac{1}{3}$

8. $1\frac{3}{8}$
    $+9\frac{1}{8}$

Subtract.

9. 43
    − 19

10. 876
    − 498

11. 500
    − 276

12. 4,915
    − 1,876

13. $\frac{4}{5}$
    $-\frac{1}{5}$

14. $\frac{2}{3}$
    $-\frac{1}{2}$

15. $\frac{1}{4}$
    $-\frac{1}{8}$

16. $3\frac{7}{10}$
    $-1\frac{4}{10}$

Multiply.

17. 49
    × 7

18. 87
    × 90

19. 46
    × 64

20. 728
    × 34

Divide.

21. $3\overline{)25}$

22. $3\overline{)250}$

23. $5\overline{)2,514}$

24. $50\overline{)248}$

What is each figure?

25.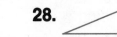

26. $\longrightarrow$

27. $\diagdown$

28.

29. ▭

30. ▢

31. △

32. ◯

329

CHAPTER REVIEW

1. Measure this segment to the nearest centimeter.
[298]
_____

Find the perimeters. [320]

2.

6 cm
14 cm
12 cm

3.
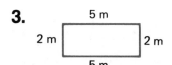
5 m
2 m
2 m
5 m

4.
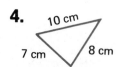
10 cm
7 cm
8 cm

Find the areas. [324]

5.

8 cm
3 cm

6.
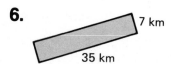
7 km
35 km

7.
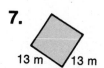
13 m
13 m

Find the volumes. [326]

8.

9.

10.

Complete.

11. 4 m = ___ cm
[299]

12. 600 cm = ___ m
[299]

13. 3 km = ___ m
[299]

14. 3,000 m = ___ km
[299]

15. 493 cm = ___ m ___ cm
[299]

16. 3 m 42 cm = ___ cm
[299]

17. 5 km 694 m = ___ m
[299]

18. 1,476 m = ___ km ___ m
[299]

19. 5 kg = ___ g
[302]

20. 7,000 g = ___ kg
[302]

21. 3 t = ___ kg
[302]

22. 4,000 kg = ___ t
[302]

23. 4 t 295 kg = ___ kg
[302]

24. 2,348 kg = ___ t ___ kg
[302]

25. four $\frac{1}{2}$ L = ___ L

[301]

26. two L = ___ $\frac{1}{4}$ L

[301]

27. 4 hours = ___ minutes

[308]

28. 5 minutes = ___ seconds

[308]

Add or subtract. [304]

29.	27 cm	**30.**	17 kg 10 g	**31.**	5 m 14 cm
	+ 56 cm		− 9 kg 3 g		+9 m 29 cm

What is the temperature? [306]

32.

33.

34.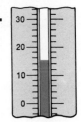

35. Temperature: Was 15°C. Fell 6°. Temperature now?

[306]

Give the time. [308]

36.

37.

38.

Label each as am or pm. [308]

39. Breakfast − 7:15

40. Dinner − 6:00

Solve these problems. [310, 324]

41. What time will it be 3 hours and 28 minutes after 9:10?

42. Bea wants to cover the top of her desk. It is 2 meters long and 1 meter wide. What is the area?

331

CHAPTER TEST

1. Measure this segment to the nearest centimeter.

2. Find the perimeter.

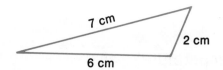

3. Find the area.

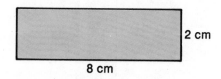

4. Find the volume.

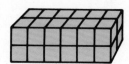

Complete.

5. 3 m = ____ cm

6. 4,000 m = ____ km

7. 726 cm = ____ m ____ cm

8. 4 km 897 m = ____ m

9. 3 kg = ____ g

10. 2,000 kg = ____ t

11. 5,468 g = ____ kg ____ g

12. 4 t 368 kg = ____ kg

13. two L = ____ $\frac{1}{2}$ L

14. four $\frac{1}{4}$ L ____ L

15. 3 minutes = ____ seconds

16. 2 hours = ____ minutes

Add or subtract.

17. 7 m
     +8 m

18. 17 m 68 cm
     − 9 m 19 cm

19. 12 kg 6 g
     +18 kg 9 g

What is the temperature?

20.

21.

22. Temperature: Was 8°C. Rose 6°. Temperature now?

Give the time.

23.

24.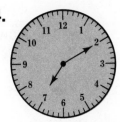

Label each as am or pm.

25. School is out—3:30

26. School begins—9:00

Solve these problems.

27. What time was it 3 hours and 18 minutes before 7:35?

28. Mrs. Case wants to cover a floor with a rug. The floor is 5 meters long and 3 meters wide. What is the area of the floor?

13 GRAPHS AND PROBABILITY

This is a seating chart for Mr. Anderson's class.

Seat 6	George	Eiko	Ray	Yvonne	Will
Seat 5	Gil	Kali	Richard	Marita	Terry
Seat 4	Julie	Denise	Laura	Oscar	Ruth
Seat 3	Vic	Kathy	Soichi	Kayleen	Jack
Seat 2	Susan	Amy	Irene	Gene	Camila
Seat 1	Al	Joe	Paul	Miguel	Sara
	Row 1	Row 2	Row 3	Row 4	Row 5

1. Each student has a special code. Try to crack it.

   a. Al's code is (1, 1). Give his row; his seat.

   b. Susan's code is (1, 2). Give her row; her seat.

   c. What row is Amy in? What seat? Give her code.

2. Give the special codes for these students.

   a. Paul　　　**b.** Gene　　　**c.** Vic　　　**d.** Kali

3. Name the students with these codes.

   a. (4, 1)　　**b.** (1, 4)　　**c.** (4, 3)　　**d.** (3, 4)

Sometimes we use a **pair of numbers.** When the order of the pair is important, we call them **ordered pairs.**

4. Which students have 3 as a first number? 3 as a second number?

5. Which students have pairs that add to 7?

This is the seating chart for the school orchestra. Each student has a code like in Mr. Anderson's class.

	Row 1	Row 2	Row 3	Row 4	Row 5	Row 6
Seat 4	Janice	Jason	Nancy	Tom	Nat	Abni
Seat 3	Sue	Marge	Alex	Steve	Linda	Neil
Seat 2	Peg	Anita	Mike	Nick	Rose	Lula
Seat 1	Chris	Bob	Carol	Marie	Ted	Deena

Give the codes for these students.

1. Chris   2. Steve   3. Rose   4. Bob

5. Neil   6. Nancy   7. Sue   8. Alex

Name the students with these codes.

9. $(1,3)$ 10. $(3,1)$ 11. $(2,4)$ 12. $(3,2)$

13. $(6,2)$ 14. $(5,4)$ 15. $(4,4)$ 16. $(5,3)$

17. Which students have 4 as a first number? 4 as a second number?

18. Which students have pairs that add to 8? multiply to 10?

19. Which students have pairs with both numbers the same?

335

READING PICTOGRAPHS

Graphs are used to show facts. Here is one kind of graph. It is called a **pictograph.**

FISH CAUGHT ON MONDAY

Name	Number of Fish Caught
Robert	⤬ ⤬
John	⤬ ⤬ ⤬ ⤬
Alice	⤬ ⤬ ⤬ ⤬ ⤬ ⤬ ⤬
Betty	⤬ ⤬ ⤬ ⤬ ⤬ ⤬

Each symbol ⤬ represents 1 fish

1. Look at the graph.

   a. How many fish did John catch?

   b. Who caught the most fish? How many?

   c. How would 10 fish be shown?

2. In this pictograph each complete symbol represents 2 fish. Each half of a symbol represents 1 fish.

FISH CAUGHT ON TUESDAY

Name	Number of Fish Caught
Robert	⤬ ⤬ ⤬ ⤬
John	⤬ ⤬ ⤜
Alice	⤬ ⤬ ⤬ ⤜
Betty	⤬ ⤜

Each symbol ⤬ represents 2 fish

   a. How many fish did each child catch?

   b. How would 11 fish be shown?

STUDENTS IN FOURTH GRADE

Teacher	Number of Students
Ms. Liu	웃 웃 웃 웃 웃 웃 웃
Mr. Blake	웃 웃 웃 웃 웃 웃 웃 ⸃
Miss Carney	웃 웃 웃 웃 웃 웃
Mrs. Thomas	웃 웃 웃 웃 웃 웃 ⸃

Each symbol 웃 represents 4 children

1. Which teacher has the most children? The least?

2. How many children are in each fourth grade class?

3. How would 34 children be shown on the pictograph?

BERRIES PICKED BY BETTY

Day	Number of Boxes Picked
Monday	🪣 🪣
Tuesday	🪣 🪣
Wednesday	🪣 🪣 🪣
Thursday	🪣 🪣 🪣 🪣

Each symbol 🪣 represents 6 boxes

4. How many boxes did Betty pick on each day?

5. How many boxes did Betty pick in all?

6. Find the average number of boxes Betty picked a day.

7. Betty picked 15 boxes on Friday. How would it be shown?

DRAWING A PICTOGRAPH

1. Let's make a pictograph to show these facts.

MEMBERS IN THE SCHOOL CLUBS	
Club	Number of Members
Sports	25
Outing	5
Cooking	10
Chess	15

a. Label the graph. The title goes on top.

MEMBERS IN THE SCHOOL CLUBS

Club	Number of Members
Sports	
Outing	
Cooking	
Chess	

b. Choose a picture symbol.

c. Decide how many each symbol represents. Which would be better: 1 symbol for 1 member,
1 symbol for 3 members, or
1 symbol for 5 members?
Tell why.

d. Decide how many symbols to draw for each club. Check this graph. Is it correct?

MEMBERS IN THE SCHOOL CLUBS

Club	Number of Members
Sports	⚇ ⚇ ⚇ ⚇ ⚇
Outing	⚇
Cooking	⚇ ⚇
Chess	⚇ ⚇ ⚇

Each symbol ⚇ represents 5 members

2. Make a pictograph to show these facts.

a. Label the graph.

b. Choose a picture symbol.

c. Decide how many each symbol should represent.

d. Draw the symbols in the graph.

PAPERS SOLD BY CHUCK	
Day	Number of papers
Monday	32
Tuesday	20
Wednesday	36
Thursday	16
Friday	40

EXERCISES

Draw a pictograph for each set of facts.

1.

SCHOOL ELECTION	
Candidate	Number of Votes
Theresa	7
George	4
Harold	14
Maria	12

2.

CLUB ELECTION	
Candidate	Number of Votes
Mr. Black	200
Ms. Brown	150
Mrs. Jones	250

3.

NEWSPAPERS SOLD BY MR. SATO	
Day	Number of Newspapers
Monday	75
Tuesday	150
Wednesday	100
Thursday	125
Friday	175

4.

BOOKS SOLD IN MAY	
Week	Number of books
First	25
Second	40
Third	35
Fourth	45

BAR GRAPHS

Bar graphs show facts quickly. This bar graph shows the number of papers David sold one week. Use it to solve the problems below.

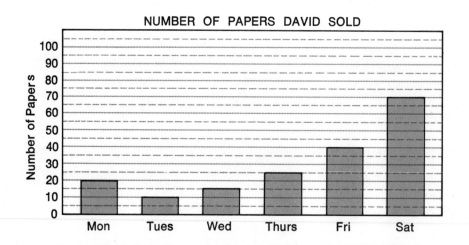

NUMBER OF PAPERS DAVID SOLD

1. Which day did David sell the most papers?

2. Which day did he sell the least papers?

3. The side shows the scale. How is it labeled?

4. How many did he sell on Monday? on Tuesday?

5. Look at Wednesday. Did he sell more than 10? less than 20? Estimate how many he sold.

6. About how many did he sell on Thursday?

7. How many more did he sell on Saturday than on Friday?

8. If he sold 35 on Sunday, how would it be shown?

Solve. Use the bar graph below.

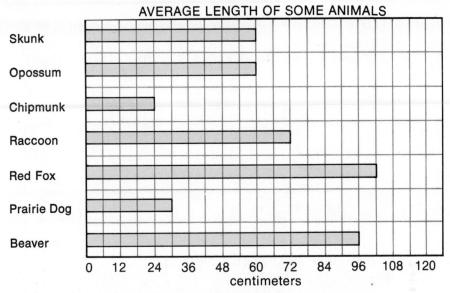

AVERAGE LENGTH OF SOME ANIMALS

Skunk
Opossum
Chipmunk
Raccoon
Red Fox
Prairie Dog
Beaver

0   12   24   36   48   60   72   84   96   108   120
centimeters

9. Which animal is the longest? the shortest?

10. The bottom shows the scale. How is it labeled?

11. How long is the skunk?

12. How long is the raccoon?

13. How long is the opossum?

14. How much longer is the beaver than the chipmunk?

15. About how long is the prairie dog? the red fox?

Brainteaser

A man has two jars. One holds 5 liters and the other holds 3 liters. How can he get exactly 7 liters of water using only the two jars?

1. Let's make a bar graph to show this information.

Children	Number of meters ball is thrown
Mary	25
Sam	35
Joan	30
Frank	20

a. Draw two segments like this.

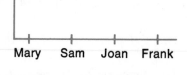

b. Label the bottom.

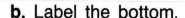
Mary   Sam   Joan   Frank

c. Choose a scale for the side. Would units of 1, 2, 5, or 10 be best? Let's try units of 5.

d. Mark off the scale and label it.

e. Copy this graph and put in the bars.

f. Finish your graph by giving it a title.

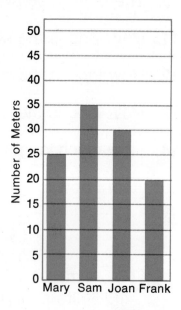

2. Make another graph with the same information. Use units of 10 on your scale.

3. Make a bar graph to show this information.

Student	Hours of TV a week
John	10
Roy	12
Abbie	6
Donna	8

a. Label the side as shown.

b. Choose a scale for the bottom and label it.

c. Put in the bars.

d. Give the graph a title.

John

Roy

Abbie

Donna

Make a bar graph to show each set of facts.

1.

RUNNING CONTEST	
Child	Time in seconds
June	8
John	6
Paul	10
Donna	14
Mary	9

2.

STAMPS IN COLLECTION	
Child	Number of Stamps
Nancy	40
Sandra	30
Howard	25
Robert	50

FINISH

★ **3.** Draw a flow chart on how to make a bar graph.

343

Keeping Fit

What is the value of each underlined digit?

1. 4<u>9</u>8

2. 7<u>4</u>6,297

3. 6,<u>2</u>91

4. 3,2<u>1</u>6,407

5. 78<u>4</u>

6. <u>9</u>,876,291

Add.

7.
```
   9
   8
   7
 + 6
```

8.
```
   86
   85
   89
 + 98
```

9.
```
   4,982
   6,784
      99
 +   497
```

10.
```
  $7.68
   9.47
   1.36
 + 8.05
```

11. $\frac{3}{9}$ $+\frac{4}{9}$

12. $\frac{1}{3}$ $+\frac{1}{6}$

13. $\frac{3}{8}$ $+\frac{7}{8}$

14. $24\frac{3}{7}$ $+96\frac{2}{7}$

Subtract.

15.
```
   71
 - 38
```

16.
```
   497
 - 398
```

17.
```
   98,765
 - 56,789
```

18.
```
  $9.46
 - 8.19
```

19. $\frac{7}{11}$ $-\frac{2}{11}$

20. $\frac{1}{2}$ $-\frac{2}{10}$

21. $\frac{3}{4}$ $-\frac{1}{3}$

22. $61\frac{2}{3}$ $-19\frac{1}{3}$

Multiply.

23.
```
   78
  × 4
```

24.
```
  976
  × 5
```

25.
```
  4,287
  ×   6
```

26.
```
  $18.94
  ×    7
```

Divide.

27. $3\overline{)27}$

28. $9\overline{)270}$

29. $6\overline{)40}$

30. $4\overline{)1,325}$

THE BASEBALL

Each major league baseball is made the same way. It has a cork and rubber center. The center is covered with 337 meters of thread. This is wrapped with horsehide and is held together with 108 stitches.

1. How many meters of thread are used inside 5 baseballs?

2. Can 3 baseballs be made with a kilometer of thread?

3. How many stitches are in 8 balls? 1 dozen balls?

4. A baseball club bought 47 dozen balls. How many balls did they get?

5. Mr. Rit bought 4 baseballs. Each ball cost $4.98. How much change did he receive from a $20 bill?

6. A baseball club bought 96 baseballs for its 8 teams. Each team received the same number of balls. How many balls did each team receive?

PROBABILITY

1. Flip a penny. What two sides can come up? There are two **possible outcomes** when we flip a penny.

2. **a.** Flip a penny 50 times. List your results like this.

heads	tails
~~////~~ / / /	~~////~~ / /

b. Is the number of heads about the same as the number of tails?

> We say the chance or probability of getting a head is 1 out of 2.
>
> 1 chance
> 2 possible outcomes

c. What is the probability of getting a tail?

d. Is the probability of getting a tail the same as getting a head?

3. **a.** How many equal parts are on this spinner?

b. How many of the parts are red?

c. The probability of the pointer stopping on red is 1 out of 3. What is the probability of the pointer stopping on blue? on green?

There are four different colored marbles in a box. Close your eyes and pick a marble.

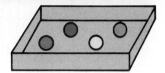

1. How many marbles or possible outcomes are there?

2. How many of the marbles are green?

3. What is the probability of picking a green marble?

4. What is the probability of picking a red marble? a blue marble? a yellow marble?

What is the probability of the pointer stopping on red?

5. 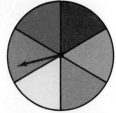   **6.** 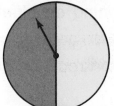   **7.**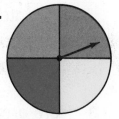

What is the probability of picking a yellow ball?

★**8.** 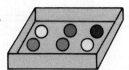   **9.** 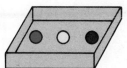   **10.**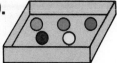

Brainteaser

Move the sticks so that the numbers in each part have the same sum.

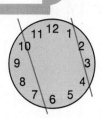

347

1. a. How many marbles are in the box?

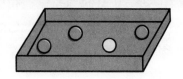

b. How many are red?

The probability of picking a red marble with your eyes closed is 3 out of 4.

        3 chances (red marbles)
        4 possible outcomes (marbles in all)

2. a. How many equal parts are there on the spinner?

b. How many are blue?

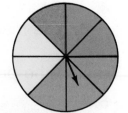

c. What is the probability of the pointer stopping on blue?

d. What is the probability of the pointer stopping on yellow? on red? on green?

3. Here are two spinners.

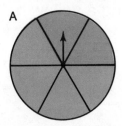
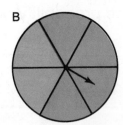

a. How many equal parts are there in all in spinner A? in spinner B?

b. How many equal parts are red in spinner A? spinner B?

c. Which spinner should stop on red more often?

Look at this box.

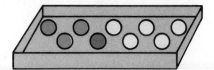

1. How many marbles are there in all?

2. How many are yellow?

3. What is the probability of picking a yellow marble?

4. What is the probability of picking a red marble? a blue marble?

What is the probability of picking a blue marble?

5.

6.

7.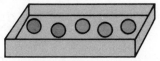

8.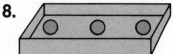

Which spinner, A or B, from each set should stop on blue more often?

9.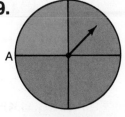

10.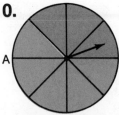

11.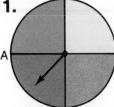

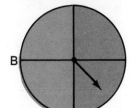

349

Keeping Fit

Divide.

1. $5\overline{)45}$ **2.** $7\overline{)287}$

3. $4\overline{)346}$ **4.** $90\overline{)630}$

5. $30\overline{)390}$ **6.** $80\overline{)976}$

Multiply.

7. $\begin{array}{r} 86 \\ \times 20 \end{array}$ **8.** $\begin{array}{r} 359 \\ \times 14 \end{array}$ **9.** $\begin{array}{r} 702 \\ \times 36 \end{array}$ **10.** $\begin{array}{r} \$4.19 \\ \times 58 \end{array}$

Compare. Use $<$, $>$, or $=$.

11. $75 \equiv 83$ **12.** $4{,}792 \equiv 4{,}972$ **13.** $646 \equiv 646$

14. $68 \equiv 63$ **15.** $1{,}085 \equiv 1{,}174$ **16.** $329 \equiv 287$

Subtract.

17. $\begin{array}{r} 65 \\ -47 \end{array}$ **18.** $\begin{array}{r} 328 \\ -109 \end{array}$ **19.** $\begin{array}{r} 50{,}003 \\ -21{,}698 \end{array}$ **20.** $\begin{array}{r} \$7.24 \\ -5.09 \end{array}$

21. $\begin{array}{r} \frac{8}{13} \\ -\frac{5}{13} \end{array}$ **22.** $\begin{array}{r} \frac{1}{3} \\ -\frac{2}{9} \end{array}$ **23.** $\begin{array}{r} \frac{1}{2} \\ -\frac{2}{5} \end{array}$ **24.** $\begin{array}{r} 84\frac{3}{4} \\ -16\frac{1}{4} \end{array}$

Add.

25. $\begin{array}{r} 8 \\ 6 \\ +9 \end{array}$ **26.** $\begin{array}{r} 74 \\ 58 \\ +32 \end{array}$ **27.** $\begin{array}{r} 4{,}654 \\ 7{,}921 \\ +8{,}096 \end{array}$ **28.** $\begin{array}{r} \$3.72 \\ 6.48 \\ +15.30 \end{array}$

29. $\begin{array}{r} \frac{8}{17} \\ +\frac{7}{17} \end{array}$ **30.** $\begin{array}{r} \frac{3}{8} \\ +\frac{1}{4} \end{array}$ **31.** $\begin{array}{r} \frac{5}{6} \\ +\frac{4}{6} \end{array}$ **32.** $\begin{array}{r} 31\frac{2}{5} \\ +87\frac{1}{5} \end{array}$

BOTANISTS

1. A botanist studies plants. There are over three hundred thousand kinds of plants in the world. Write the standard numeral for this number.

2. George Washington Carver was a famous botanist. He developed ways to use plants to improve the soil in fields. He was born in 1864. How many years ago was that?

3. A person eats about 750 kilograms of food a year. How many kilograms would 4 people eat in one year?

Mrs. Gray Eagle is experimenting with corn plants. She is searching for ways to increase the amount of grain one plant will produce.

4. For one experiment she examined 20 plant-cell samples each week. The experiment lasted 28 weeks. How many samples did she examine?

5. She worked 12 hours on her experiments one day. She spent $\frac{1}{4}$ of the time measuring and recording plant growth. How many hours was this?

CHAPTER REVIEW

Give the codes for these students. [334]

	Row 1	Row 2
Seat 5	Ali	Eric
Seat 4	Lewis	Jo
Seat 3	Peg	Maria
Seat 2	Isao	Bob
Seat 1	Bev	Cesar

1. Lewis

2. Maria

3. Isao

4. Ali

5. Jo

6. Bev

7. Bob

8. Eric

FIRST PLACE SWIMMING AWARDS

Name	Number of Awards Won
Tina	🎖🎖🎖🎖🎖🎖 ⌇
Britt	🎖🎖🎖🎖
Fran	🎖🎖🎖🎖🎖 ⌇

Each symbol 🎖 represents 2 medals

How many awards did each girl win? [336]

9. Tina

10. Britt

11. Fran

What score did Bob get on each? [340]

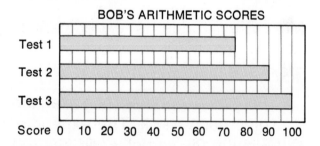

BOB'S ARITHMETIC SCORES

Test 1

Test 2

Test 3

Score 0 10 20 30 40 50 60 70 80 90 100

12. Test 1

13. Test 3

What is the probability of the pointer stopping on red?

14. [346]

15. [346]

16. [348]

352

CHAPTER TEST

Give the codes for these students.

	Row 1	Row 2
Seat 2	Ines	Ron
Seat 1	Jane	Sele

1. Ines

2. Jane

3. Ron

4. Sele

HOME RUNS MADE IN ONE YEAR

Name	Number of Home runs
Stan	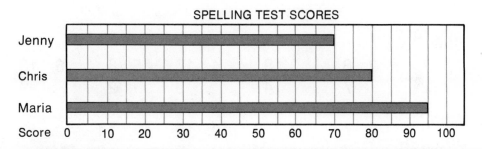
Lori	
Carl	

Each symbol ⊖ represents 2 home runs

How many home runs did each make?

5. Stan

6. Lori

7. Carl

SPELLING TEST SCORES

Jenny — 70
Chris — 80
Maria — 95

Score 0 10 20 30 40 50 60 70 80 90 100

What spelling test score did each receive?

8. Jenny

9. Chris

10. Maria

What is the probability of picking a red ball if your eyes are closed?

11.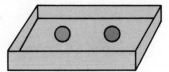

12.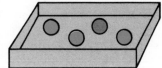

PRACTICE EXERCISES

Add.

1. 3 <u>7</u>	**2.** 2 <u>6</u>	**3.** 0 <u>8</u>	**4.** 5 <u>8</u>	**5.** 1 <u>2</u>	**6.** 7 <u>0</u>
7. 1 <u>6</u>	**8.** 2 <u>7</u>	**9.** 4 <u>1</u>	**10.** 2 <u>2</u>	**11.** 6 <u>4</u>	**12.** 5 <u>7</u>
13. 3 <u>8</u>	**14.** 6 <u>7</u>	**15.** 8 <u>8</u>	**16.** 2 <u>9</u>	**17.** 0 <u>9</u>	**18.** 3 <u>6</u>
19. 3 <u>2</u>	**20.** 9 <u>5</u>	**21.** 7 <u>6</u>	**22.** 8 <u>9</u>	**23.** 9 <u>3</u>	**24.** 2 <u>8</u>
25. 5 <u>5</u>	**26.** 7 <u>9</u>	**27.** 9 <u>6</u>	**28.** 9 <u>9</u>	**29.** 6 <u>8</u>	**30.** 8 <u>4</u>

Subtract.

1. 7 <u>2</u>	**2.** 8 <u>7</u>	**3.** 9 <u>4</u>	**4.** 17 <u>9</u>	**5.** 8 <u>2</u>	**6.** 13 <u>9</u>
7. 9 <u>7</u>	**8.** 7 <u>7</u>	**9.** 12 <u>5</u>	**10.** 10 <u>9</u>	**11.** 14 <u>6</u>	**12.** 13 <u>6</u>
13. 9 <u>3</u>	**14.** 10 <u>3</u>	**15.** 12 <u>9</u>	**16.** 7 <u>3</u>	**17.** 14 <u>7</u>	**18.** 8 <u>4</u>
19. 8 <u>3</u>	**20.** 6 <u>2</u>	**21.** 12 <u>4</u>	**22.** 15 <u>7</u>	**23.** 6 <u>3</u>	**24.** 10 <u>6</u>
25. 16 <u>8</u>	**26.** 15 <u>9</u>	**27.** 12 <u>6</u>	**28.** 16 <u>7</u>	**29.** 5 <u>3</u>	**30.** 11 <u>2</u>

Multiply.

1. 1 2	**2.** 3 2	**3.** 5 6	**4.** 9 6	**5.** 6 3	**6.** 5 7
7. 9 9	**8.** 6 2	**9.** 0 3	**10.** 3 8	**11.** 2 7	**12.** 4 0
13. 5 5	**14.** 4 9	**15.** 4 4	**16.** 7 6	**17.** 8 2	**18.** 7 7
19. 9 1	**20.** 8 5	**21.** 9 8	**22.** 4 3	**23.** 0 6	**24.** 3 3
25. 9 3	**26.** 4 6	**27.** 6 8	**28.** 2 4	**29.** 7 4	**30.** 9 7
31. 8 0	**32.** 6 6	**33.** 2 2	**34.** 7 3	**35.** 1 5	**36.** 0 2
37. 8 1	**38.** 1 1	**39.** 7 8	**40.** 0 5	**41.** 6 1	**42.** 8 8
43. 5 2	**44.** 5 4	**45.** 0 0	**46.** 2 9	**47.** 4 1	**48.** 0 7
49. 3 1	**50.** 0 9	**51.** 3 5	**52.** 1 0	**53.** 1 7	**54.** 5 9
55. 0 7	**56.** 3 9	**57.** 4 2	**58.** 9 4	**59.** 5 8	**60.** 4 7
61. 8 7	**62.** 6 7	**63.** 7 2	**64.** 6 4	**65.** 3 6	**66.** 7 9

Divide.

1. $9\overline{)81}$ 2. $1\overline{)0}$ 3. $6\overline{)24}$ 4. $7\overline{)56}$

5. $2\overline{)6}$ 6. $3\overline{)12}$ 7. $1\overline{)2}$ 8. $7\overline{)28}$

9. $8\overline{)48}$ 10. $3\overline{)9}$ 11. $4\overline{)32}$ 12. $2\overline{)2}$

13. $6\overline{)36}$ 14. $9\overline{)63}$ 15. $3\overline{)24}$ 16. $6\overline{)30}$

17. $7\overline{)7}$ 18. $5\overline{)40}$ 19. $4\overline{)8}$ 20. $1\overline{)6}$

21. $8\overline{)56}$ 22. $6\overline{)12}$ 23. $8\overline{)40}$ 24. $5\overline{)15}$

25. $9\overline{)9}$ 26. $4\overline{)20}$ 27. $7\overline{)0}$ 28. $9\overline{)36}$

29. $8\overline{)16}$ 30. $5\overline{)5}$ 31. $3\overline{)18}$ 32. $1\overline{)8}$

33. $9\overline{)45}$ 34. $8\overline{)64}$ 35. $5\overline{)0}$ 36. $4\overline{)4}$

37. $8\overline{)32}$ 38. $5\overline{)35}$ 39. $7\overline{)21}$ 40. $5\overline{)25}$

41. $9\overline{)0}$ 42. $6\overline{)6}$ 43. $4\overline{)16}$ 44. $7\overline{)63}$

45. $9\overline{)54}$ 46. $7\overline{)42}$ 47. $8\overline{)72}$ 48. $4\overline{)24}$

49. $6\overline{)48}$ 50. $2\overline{)4}$ 51. $5\overline{)20}$ 52. $3\overline{)0}$

53. $7\overline{)35}$ 54. $3\overline{)3}$ 55. $4\overline{)36}$ 56. $2\overline{)18}$

57. $5\overline{)45}$ 58. $9\overline{)27}$ 59. $1\overline{)4}$ 60. $4\overline{)28}$

61. $2\overline{)14}$ 62. $8\overline{)8}$ 63. $7\overline{)49}$ 64. $6\overline{)54}$

65. $6\overline{)42}$ 66. $9\overline{)72}$ 67. $5\overline{)30}$ 68. $2\overline{)10}$

(10) Write standard numerals.

1. Eight hundred ten　　　**2.** Six hundred eighty

3. Seven hundred one　　　**4.** Five hundred nine

5. One hundred forty-six　　**6.** Two hundred thirty

Write two expanded numerals for each.

7. 848　　　**8.** 907　　　**9.** 562　　　**10.** 830

11. 715　　**12.** 346　　**13.** 189　　**14.** 234

(12) Write standard numerals.

1. Six thousand, four hundred seventy-five

2. Six thousand, seventy

3. Nine thousand, eight hundred four

4. Five thousand, three

5. Seven thousand, six hundred ninety

Write two expanded numerals for each.

6. 6,489　　**7.** 2,748　　**8.** 9,999　　**9.** 8,065

10. 5,321　　**11.** 7,952　　**12.** 2,603　　**13.** 4,315

(14) What is the value of each underlined digit?

1. 48,397　　　　**2.** 63,481　　　　**3.** 51,238

4. 70,359　　　　**5.** 35,472　　　　**6.** 483,276

7. 324,387　　　**8.** 926,047　　　**9.** 521,879

(16) What is the value of each underlined digit?

1. 4,805,706   **2.** 9,543,124

3. 5,287,312   **4.** 846,297,395

5. 96,274,165   **6.** 935,205,847

7. 43,293,871   **8.** 157,483,291

(18) Compare. Use =, >, or <.

1. 93 ⊜ 87   **2.** 58 ⊜ 54

3. 639 ⊜ 693   **4.** 725 ⊜ 527

5. 514 ⊜ 518   **6.** 847 ⊜ 873

7. 8,241 ⊜ 8,412   **8.** 9,278 ⊜ 9,287

9. 6,345 ⊜ 7,124   **10.** 7,341 ⊜ 7,348

(27) True or false?

1. $9 + 8 = 17$ **2.** $3 + 8 = 14$ **3.** $9 + 4 = 8 + 7$

4. $15 - 8 = 9$ **5.** $12 = 7 + 5$ **6.** $3 + 7 = 7 + 4$

7. $8 = 16 - 9$ **8.** $15 = 8 + 6$ **9.** $5 + 9 = 7 + 7$

(28) Make true sentences. Use whole numbers.

1. $\square + 7 = 15$ **2.** $7 + \square = 14$ **3.** $8 - 3 = \square$

4. $\square = 9 + 6$ **5.** $15 - 9 = \square$ **6.** $9 + 3 = \square + 7$

7. $16 - \square = 9$ **8.** $\square = 3 + 8$ **9.** $6 + 9 = 8 + \square$

358

(48) Add.

1. 49
   + 6

2. 85
   + 7

3. 19
   + 8

4. 14
   + 7

5. 25
   + 7

6. 65
   + 4

7. 19
   + 9

8. 28
   + 7

9. 36
   + 6

10. 45
    + 7

11. 54
    + 8

12. 63
    + 9

(50) Add.

1. 9
   4
   3
   +7

2. 6
   9
   8
   +5

3. 4
   7
   9
   +5

4. 3
   5
   6
   +2

5. 5
   3
   7
   +6

6. 6
   7
   4
   +3

7. 3
   9
   6
   +4

8. 5
   9
   1
   +5

9. 4
   4
   9
   +6

10. 9
    6
    1
    +4

(56) Add.

1. 54
   + 39

2. 69
   +75

3. 46
   7
   +95

4. 31
   3
   +49

5. 75
   68
   + 30

6. 43
   48
   +45

7. 75
   19
   +24

8. 42
   19
   + 8

9. 37
   29
   73
   +88

10. 52
    63
    41
    +79

11. 81
    97
    38
    + 38

12. 64
    83
    46
    +56

(58) Add.

1.	329 + 436	**2.**	847 + 125	**3.**	438 + 232	**4.**	726 + 138
5.	191 + 191	**6.**	243 + 271	**7.**	451 + 273	**8.**	193 + 284
9.	986 + 479	**10.**	385 + 385	**11.**	692 + 498	**12.**	376 + 285
13.	593 876 + 477	**14.**	699 397 + 793	**15.**	487 395 482 + 749	**16.**	999 888 76 + 6

(60) Add.

1.	7,497 + 3,864	**2.**	4,872 + 9,874	**3.**	2,486 + 1,983	**4.**	4,833 + 6,148
5.	44,987 + 39,486	**6.**	74,784 + 96,877	**7.**	9,877 9,877 + 425	**8.**	43 328 + 4,123
9.	3,498 9,843 + 785	**10.**	9,999 9,999 + 9,999	**11.**	4,876 3,943 + 748	**12.**	19,876 498 + 789

(66) Add.

1.	$1.76 + 2.79	**2.**	$4.98 + .74	**3.**	$.05 + .05	**4.**	$.04 + .01
5.	$.98 .76 + .49	**6.**	$ 4.97 3.85 + 87.46	**7.**	$14.97 26.49 + 3.78	**8.**	$ 4.78 32.76 + 74.95

(68) Round to the nearest ten.

1. 68   **2.** 55   **3.** 63   **4.** 46

(70) Round to the nearest hundred.

1. 468   **2.** 734   **3.** 795   **4.** 650

Round to the nearest thousand.

5. 7,164   **6.** 6,489   **7.** 8,841   **8.** 7,500

Round to the nearest dollar.

9. $7.89   **10.** $2.63   **11.** $9.49   **12.** $4.50

(72) Estimate each sum.

1.	48	**2.**	74	**3.**	378	**4.**	$1.98
	+ 34		+78		+799		+ 3.05

5.	39	**6.**	724	**7.**	$6.98	**8.**	276
	41		326		.78		395
	+ 62		+ 924		+ 3.48		+ 450

(84) Subtract.

1.	75	**2.**	63	**3.**	42	**4.**	55
	− 8		− 9		− 8		− 7

5.	63	**6.**	21	**7.**	40	**8.**	36
	− 5		− 6		− 3		− 7

9.	97	**10.**	36	**11.**	45	**12.**	41
	−28		− 19		−27		−29

13.	391	**14.**	476	**15.**	273	**16.**	826
	− 265		− 158		− 164		−508

(86) Subtract.

1. 648 −257	**2.** 737 −373	**3.** 942 −681	**4.** 374 −293
5. 4,815 −3,904	**6.** 4,399 −2,784	**7.** 6,844 −2,910	**8.** 9,186 −4,721

(88) Subtract.

1. 984 −387	**2.** 286 −199	**3.** 875 −398	**4.** 486 −297
5. 746 −498	**6.** 782 −658	**7.** 475 −386	**8.** 841 −742
9. 4,982 −2,983	**10.** 6,843 −3,995	**11.** 6,782 −5,649	**12.** 8,244 −7,656
13. 9,884 −4,988	**14.** 3,486 − 799	**15.** 4,783 −3,948	**16.** 7,832 −4,944
17. 19,344 − 6,788	**18.** 75,678 −38,569	**19.** 79,888 −69,999	

(92) Subtract.

1. 800 −251	**2.** 700 −653	**3.** 505 −186	**4.** 807 −398
5. 4,000 −3,486	**6.** 7,000 −3,944	**7.** 8,006 −5,988	**8.** 7,007 −5,848
9. 20,307 −14,299	**10.** 35,000 −26,341	**11.** 20,600 − 4,963	

(97) Subtract.

1. $ .39
 − .18

2. $4.98
 −2.87

3. $3.64
 −1.58

4. $9.62
 −8.76

5. $12.97
 − 8.48

6. $18.42
 −16.97

7. $20.00
 −15.85

8. $49.76
 −38.29

9. $9.08
 −6.49

10. $8.72
 − .98

11. $4.86
 −1.97

12. $93.27
 −79.38

(100) Estimate the differences.

1. 82
 −49

2. 79
 −25

3. 293
 −127

4. 855
 −332

5. $7.25
 −2.98

6. $6.87
 −4.93

7. 3,294
 −1,983

8. 7,543
 −2,149

(158) Multiply.

1. 8 × 10

2. 10 × 9

3. 14 × 10

4. 4 × 100

5. 100 × 8

6. 19 × 100

7. 5 × 1,000

8. 1,000 × 8

9. 23 × 1,000

(162) Multiply.

1. 5 × 70

2. 90 × 8

3. 80 × 7

4. 300 × 9

5. 6 × 700

6. 9 × 600

7. 900 × 4

8. 7 × 600

9. 500 × 4

10. 5,000 × 9

11. 8 × 6,000

12. 4,000 × 7

(164) Multiply.

1. 20×20 **2.** 20×30 **3.** 30×40

4. 70×60 **5.** 90×70 **6.** 500×90

7. 900×90 **8.** 80×500 **9.** 700×30

(168) Multiply.

1. 21	**2.** 72	**3.** 41	**4.** 84
$\times 4$	$\times 3$	$\times 9$	$\times 2$

5. 121	**6.** 212	**7.** 423	**8.** 711
$\times 3$	$\times 4$	$\times 3$	$\times 7$

(172) Multiply.

1. 62	**2.** 94	**3.** 27	**4.** 49
$\times 7$	$\times 3$	$\times 6$	$\times 5$

5. 78	**6.** 49	**7.** 65	**8.** 72
$\times 4$	$\times 3$	$\times 4$	$\times 5$

9. 83	**10.** 95	**11.** 75	**12.** 63
$\times 8$	$\times 9$	$\times 8$	$\times 7$

(174) Multiply.

1. 115	**2.** 414	**3.** 827	**4.** 407
$\times 2$	$\times 7$	$\times 3$	$\times 9$

5. 116	**6.** 748	**7.** 309	**8.** 616
$\times 3$	$\times 2$	$\times 4$	$\times 4$

9. 3,416	**10.** 5,823	**11.** 5,219	**12.** 9,282
$\times 4$	$\times 3$	$\times 4$	$\times 3$

(176) Multiply.

1. 487 × 6	**2.** 795 × 5	**3.** 489 × 7	**4.** 642 × 4
5. 788 × 8	**6.** 497 × 9	**7.** 375 × 3	**8.** 436 × 3
9. 999 × 2	**10.** 999 × 9	**11.** 875 × 8	**12.** 487 × 7
13. 1,234 × 5	**14.** 6,985 × 4	**15.** 3,987 × 5	**16.** 4,286 × 3
17. 7,248 × 6	**18.** 9,287 × 2	**19.** 7,948 × 7	**20.** 8,765 × 8
21. 3,275 × 9	**22.** 4,873 × 9	**23.** 8,834 × 2	**24.** 9,999 × 9
25. $ .39 × 6	**26.** $ .48 × 8	**27.** $1.76 × 3	**28.** $9.42 × 5
29. $8.75 × 9	**30.** $12.46 × 5	**31.** $19.47 × 2	**32.** $49.86 × 2

(180) Estimate the products.

1. 63 × 9	**2.** 24 × 7	**3.** 85 × 6	**4.** 91 × 5
5. 79 × 4	**6.** 57 × 3	**7.** 247 × 2	**8.** 389 × 7
9. 654 × 5	**10.** 929 × 8	**11.** 832 × 6	**12.** 764 × 9

(182) Multiply.

1.	35 × 20	**2.**	76 × 30	**3.**	84 × 90	**4.**	48 × 40
5.	75 × 80	**6.**	63 × 70	**7.**	349 × 50	**8.**	883 × 40
9.	583 × 70	**10.**	747 × 80	**11.**	964 × 50	**12.**	438 × 60

(183) Multiply.

1.	54 × 36	**2.**	97 × 25	**3.**	48 × 39	**4.**	75 × 43
5.	86 × 58	**6.**	49 × 63	**7.**	75 × 84	**8.**	87 × 92
9.	86 × 77	**10.**	48 × 23	**11.**	97 × 58	**12.**	65 × 65
13.	$.49 × 56	**14.**	$.37 × 98	**15.**	$.85 × 63	**16.**	$.94 × 75

(185) Multiply.

1.	324 × 92	**2.**	583 × 47	**3.**	297 × 56	**4.**	763 × 81
5.	864 × 63	**6.**	758 × 49	**7.**	935 × 77	**8.**	354 × 98
9.	$2.49 × 51	**10.**	$5.98 × 76	**11.**	$9.75 × 59	**12.**	$7.63 × 94

(190) Divide.

1. 8)560　**2.** 7)490　**3.** 5)150　**4.** 6)420

5. 9)360　**6.** 3)150　**7.** 4)1,600　**8.** 7)3,500

9. 6)3,600　**10.** 8)6,400　**11.** 5)3,500　**12.** 9)5,400

(198) Divide.

1. 3)123　**2.** 2)68　**3.** 3)69　**4.** 2)124

5. 5)255　**6.** 7)217　**7.** 4)92　**8.** 6)324

9. 7)322　**10.** 9)306　**11.** 6)264　**12.** 7)231

13. 8)432　**14.** 6)384　**15.** 7)539　**16.** 4)312

(200) Divide.

1. 3)789　**2.** 4)968　**3.** 2)568　**4.** 6)3,186

5. 9)6,579　**6.** 6)2,796　**7.** 8)2,560　**8.** 6)2,250

9. 3)552　**10.** 2)750　**11.** 4)1,764　**12.** 5)2,405

13. 7)4,312　**14.** 8)3,048　**15.** 4)2,576　**16.** 9)6,426

(204) Divide.

1. 7)23　**2.** 8)68　**3.** 6)41　**4.** 4)30

5. 3)278　**6.** 4)250　**7.** 6)365　**8.** 7)500

9. 2)161　**10.** 3)497　**11.** 8)1,780　**12.** 9)5,000

13. 6)4,329　**14.** 9)7,148　**15.** 4)1,253　**16.** 7)4,386

(206) Divide.

1. $30\overline{)94}$ **2.** $50\overline{)183}$ **3.** $50\overline{)450}$ **4.** $60\overline{)371}$

5. $80\overline{)493}$ **6.** $30\overline{)270}$ **7.** $70\overline{)490}$ **8.** $90\overline{)571}$

9. $20\overline{)620}$ **10.** $80\overline{)984}$ **11.** $30\overline{)620}$ **12.** $70\overline{)5,000}$

13. $70\overline{)2,364}$ **14.** $50\overline{)4,837}$ **15.** $30\overline{)1,964}$

(214) Find the average.

1. 6, 12 **2.** 7, 15, 5

3. 6, 8, 10, 12 **4.** 12, 12, 12

5. 60, 80, 40 **6.** 30, 50, 80, 40

7. 23, 45, 86, 90 **8.** 4, 9, 6, 5

(216) Divide.

1. $5\overline{)\$.95}$ **2.** $8\overline{)\$.72}$ **3.** $4\overline{)\$.72}$ **4.** $3\overline{)\$.93}$

5. $6\overline{)\$1.92}$ **6.** $9\overline{)\$5.67}$ **7.** $8\overline{)\$4.56}$ **8.** $7\overline{)\$2.31}$

9. $4\overline{)\$3.56}$ **10.** $5\overline{)\$3.45}$ **11.** $3\overline{)\$1.86}$ **12.** $8\overline{)\$5.92}$

(225) Complete.

1. $\frac{1}{4}$ of 8 = **2.** $\frac{1}{5}$ of 20 =

3. $\frac{1}{2}$ of 36 = **4.** $\frac{1}{3}$ of 18 =

5. $\frac{1}{6}$ of 36 = **6.** $\frac{1}{8}$ of 40 =

7. $\frac{1}{7}$ of 56 = **8.** $\frac{1}{9}$ of 63 =

368

(234) Compare. Use >, <, or =.

1. $\frac{3}{5} \equiv 1$

2. $1 \equiv \frac{2}{5}$

3. $1 \equiv \frac{7}{5}$

4. $\frac{5}{5} \equiv 1$

5. $\frac{7}{8} \equiv 1$

6. $\frac{5}{2} \equiv 1$

7. $\frac{9}{9} \equiv 1$

8. $1 \equiv \frac{3}{4}$

9. $1 \equiv \frac{7}{6}$

(248) Add.

1. $\begin{array}{r} \frac{1}{8} \\ +\frac{2}{8} \\ \hline \end{array}$

2. $\begin{array}{r} \frac{1}{4} \\ +\frac{2}{4} \\ \hline \end{array}$

3. $\begin{array}{r} \frac{3}{9} \\ +\frac{4}{9} \\ \hline \end{array}$

4. $\begin{array}{r} \frac{6}{8} \\ +\frac{1}{8} \\ \hline \end{array}$

5. $\begin{array}{r} \frac{5}{10} \\ +\frac{2}{10} \\ \hline \end{array}$

6. $\begin{array}{r} \frac{4}{7} \\ +\frac{2}{7} \\ \hline \end{array}$

7. $\begin{array}{r} \frac{1}{6} \\ +\frac{4}{6} \\ \hline \end{array}$

8. $\begin{array}{r} \frac{1}{3} \\ +\frac{1}{3} \\ \hline \end{array}$

(250) Subtract.

1. $\begin{array}{r} \frac{7}{8} \\ -\frac{1}{8} \\ \hline \end{array}$

2. $\begin{array}{r} \frac{3}{4} \\ -\frac{1}{4} \\ \hline \end{array}$

3. $\begin{array}{r} \frac{5}{10} \\ -\frac{3}{10} \\ \hline \end{array}$

4. $\begin{array}{r} \frac{11}{12} \\ -\frac{9}{12} \\ \hline \end{array}$

5. $\begin{array}{r} \frac{4}{6} \\ -\frac{1}{6} \\ \hline \end{array}$

6. $\begin{array}{r} \frac{13}{7} \\ -\frac{8}{7} \\ \hline \end{array}$

7. $\begin{array}{r} \frac{5}{6} \\ -\frac{1}{6} \\ \hline \end{array}$

8. $\begin{array}{r} \frac{5}{5} \\ -\frac{3}{5} \\ \hline \end{array}$

(254) Compare. Use > or <.

1. $\frac{2}{3} \equiv \frac{3}{4}$

2. $\frac{5}{8} \equiv \frac{3}{4}$

3. $\frac{7}{10} \equiv \frac{1}{2}$

4. $\frac{3}{12} \equiv \frac{1}{6}$

5. $\frac{4}{5} \equiv \frac{1}{2}$

6. $\frac{5}{6} \equiv \frac{2}{3}$

7. $\frac{3}{4} \equiv \frac{5}{6}$

8. $\frac{1}{2} \equiv \frac{7}{10}$

9. $\frac{4}{9} \equiv \frac{1}{3}$

369

(256) Add.

1. $\frac{1}{2}$
   $+\frac{1}{4}$

2. $\frac{1}{4}$
   $+\frac{1}{6}$

3. $\frac{2}{3}$
   $+\frac{1}{6}$

4. $\frac{1}{5}$
   $+\frac{1}{3}$

5. $\frac{2}{3}$
   $+\frac{1}{12}$

6. $\frac{2}{3}$
   $+\frac{3}{4}$

7. $\frac{1}{2}$
   $+\frac{1}{3}$

8. $\frac{3}{8}$
   $+\frac{3}{4}$

9. $\frac{2}{5}$
   $+\frac{3}{4}$

10. $\frac{1}{3}$
    $+\frac{4}{5}$

11. $\frac{2}{3}$
    $+\frac{5}{6}$

12. $\frac{3}{8}$
    $+\frac{3}{4}$

(258) Subtract.

1. $\frac{7}{10}$
   $-\frac{1}{2}$

2. $\frac{10}{12}$
   $-\frac{3}{4}$

3. $\frac{5}{6}$
   $-\frac{3}{4}$

4. $\frac{4}{5}$
   $-\frac{1}{2}$

5. $\frac{2}{3}$
   $-\frac{1}{2}$

6. $\frac{3}{4}$
   $-\frac{2}{3}$

7. $\frac{3}{4}$
   $-\frac{1}{2}$

8. $\frac{6}{9}$
   $-\frac{2}{3}$

9. $\frac{9}{10}$
   $-\frac{3}{5}$

10. $\frac{7}{8}$
    $-\frac{1}{3}$

11. $\frac{5}{9}$
    $-\frac{1}{3}$

12. $\frac{3}{5}$
    $-\frac{1}{4}$

(262) Write mixed numerals.

1. $\frac{3}{2}$

2. $\frac{4}{3}$

3. $\frac{5}{4}$

4. $\frac{6}{4}$

5. $\frac{9}{7}$

6. $\frac{9}{8}$

7. $\frac{10}{7}$

8. $\frac{9}{5}$

9. $\frac{13}{8}$

10. $\frac{11}{6}$

11. $\frac{11}{8}$

12. $\frac{15}{9}$

13. $\frac{13}{7}$

14. $\frac{8}{5}$

15. $\frac{12}{8}$

370

(264) Add. Give the sum as 1 or a mixed numeral.

1. $\frac{1}{2}$
$+\frac{1}{2}$

2. $\frac{2}{5}$
$+\frac{4}{5}$

3. $\frac{3}{8}$
$+\frac{6}{8}$

4. $\frac{4}{5}$
$+\frac{3}{5}$

5. $\frac{7}{8}$
$+\frac{3}{8}$

6. $\frac{4}{10}$
$+\frac{6}{10}$

7. $\frac{3}{4}$
$+\frac{3}{4}$

8. $\frac{9}{12}$
$+\frac{7}{12}$

9. $\frac{4}{7}$
$+\frac{3}{7}$

10. $\frac{5}{8}$
$+\frac{7}{8}$

11. $\frac{7}{9}$
$+\frac{5}{9}$

12. $\frac{5}{6}$
$+\frac{5}{6}$

13. $\frac{5}{7}$
$+\frac{5}{7}$

14. $\frac{4}{5}$
$+\frac{4}{5}$

15. $\frac{6}{8}$
$+\frac{5}{8}$

16. $\frac{8}{9}$
$+\frac{3}{9}$

(266) Add.

1. $7\frac{1}{3}$
$+2\frac{1}{3}$

2. $6\frac{4}{7}$
$+3\frac{1}{7}$

3. $9\frac{1}{5}$
$+7$

4. $9\frac{1}{5}$
$+7\frac{3}{5}$

5. $8\frac{3}{8}$
$+2\frac{4}{8}$

6. 6
$+7\frac{2}{3}$

7. $8\frac{1}{9}$
$+7\frac{3}{9}$

8. $17\frac{3}{7}$
$+24\frac{2}{7}$

(268) Subtract.

1. $9\frac{2}{3}$
$-3\frac{1}{3}$

2. $6\frac{7}{10}$
$-2\frac{5}{10}$

3. $3\frac{7}{9}$
$-2\frac{1}{9}$

4. $6\frac{7}{8}$
-4

5. $8\frac{9}{10}$
$-3\frac{9}{10}$

6. $17\frac{4}{7}$
$-8\frac{1}{7}$

7. $36\frac{1}{2}$
-19

8. $12\frac{3}{5}$
$-8\frac{1}{5}$

371

(54) Solve. If there is not enough information, write "not enough information." If there is extra information, tell what it is.

1. On Tuesday, Kikuo worked 3 hours raking leaves. On Friday he worked 2 hours. On Saturday he worked 6 hours. How many hours did he work on Friday and Saturday?

2. Mr. Nakamura paid Kikuo $1 an hour for raking leaves. He worked most of the afternoon. How much did he earn?

3. Mrs. Anderson bought a new garden hose. She gave the clerk a $20 bill. How much change did she receive?

4. There are 4 cakes for the class party. There are also 3 pies and 4 dozen cookies. How many pies and cakes in all?

5. Sara worked for 6 hours last Saturday. How much did she earn?

(75) Solve these problems.

1. Bob went to school 21 days in April and 19 days in May. How many days did he attend during these two months?

2. Janell earned $5.69 selling papers. Her brother earned $7.35. How much did they earn together?

3. Sheila and Charles were running for school president. Sheila got 1,734 votes. Charles got 1,247 votes. How many votes was this in all?

(95) Solve these problems.

1. Cesar's book holds 1,000 stamps. He has 435 stamps. How many more stamps does he need to fill the book?

2. Mrs. White Feather drove 2,462 kilometers in May. In June she drove 2,808 kilometers. How many more kilometers did she drive in June?

3. Christine read 178 pages last week. This week she read 225 pages. How many more pages did she read this week?

4. Mr. Melandez owns a gas station. In one week he sold 16,700 liters of gas. The next week he sold 17,400 liters. How many liters did he sell in all?

(100) Solve these problems.

1. A baseball glove costs $8.78 and a uniform costs $14.98. Estimate how much more the uniform costs.

2. The school bus holds 60 people. Mrs. Green's class has 28 children. Miss Katz's class has 19. Mr. Jones' class has 23. Will one bus be enough to take them all to the zoo? Estimate to find out.

3. Monday, 421 people visited the school Science Fair. Tuesday, 235 people went to the Fair. Estimate how many more went on Monday than on Tuesday.

4. George has 66¢. He spent 29¢ on a coin collecting book. About how much money does he have left?

(187) Solve these problems.

1. A bottle of root beer costs 17¢. How much does a case of 24 bottles cost?

2. Linda went bowling. Her scores were 110, 121, and 97. What was her total score for the three games?

3. Jerry walked to school 5 times a week for 39 weeks. How many times did he walk to school?

4. Mr. Ting bought a case of 50 light bulbs. He returned a dozen of them because they were broken. How many were left?

5. Mrs. Brien bought 3 bicycles for her children. She paid $69.48 for each. What was the total cost?

(202) Solve these problems.

1. Francisca bought 3 notebooks for $.59 each and a ball point pen for $1.49. How much did she spend for these items?

2. Mr. Norris brought 3 dozen apples to class. The class ate 28 of them. How many apples were left?

3. Al bought a book for $4.98 and paints for $3.95. He paid with a $10 bill. How much did he have left?

4. In a classroom, there were 6 rows with 5 children in each row. The class divided into 2 equal groups. How many children were in each group?

5. There were 573 passengers on a train going to Chicago. At a stop 146 passengers got off and 82 got on. How many are on the train now?

(209) Solve these problems.

1. Mr. Little Crow owns a flower shop. He can fit 9 plants on a shelf. He has 83 plants. About how many shelves does he need?

2. Pat has 64 meters of electric cord. She uses 3 meters to make a lamp. About how many lamps can she make with the cord?

3. Jill picked 55 baskets of apples in 6 hours. About how many did she pick in 1 hour?

4. Dan's doctor told him that his heart beats 4,320 times in one hour. About how many times does it beat in one minute?

(227) Write $+$, $-$, $\times$, or $\div$ to show which operation or operations you would use. Do not solve.

1. George baked 6 dozen cookies for the class picnic. How many cookies did he bake in all?

2. A farmer planted 250 tomato plants in 5 rows. How many plants were in each row?

3. Mack swam 3 lengths of the pool. The pool is 150 yards long. How many yards did he swim in all?

4. Tom counted 46 cars on a passing train. Carol counted 41. How many more did Tom count?

5. Jerry came home from shopping with groceries worth $5.86 and a shirt that cost $3.49. How much change did he have from a $10 bill?

375

(271) Solve these problems.

1. Sue mixed $\frac{1}{2}$ liter of orange juice with $\frac{1}{4}$ liter of grapefruit juice. How much juice did she have?

2. Nancy is $1\frac{2}{10}$ meters tall. Dora is $1\frac{6}{10}$ meters tall. How much taller is Dora?

3. Jan planted $\frac{1}{4}$ of her garden with tomatoes. She planted $\frac{1}{8}$ with peas. What part of the garden was planted with tomatoes and peas?

4. A rope was $9\frac{4}{5}$ meters long. $2\frac{1}{5}$ meters was cut off. How long was it then?

5. The gas tank in Ms. Vazquez's car holds $75\frac{1}{2}$ liters. She put $60\frac{1}{2}$ liters into the tank. How much more gasoline is needed to fill the tank?

6. Cheryl worked $5\frac{1}{4}$ hours on Monday. On Tuesday she worked $7\frac{1}{4}$ hours. How many hours did she work on both days?

7. Bob ran $\frac{3}{5}$ kilometer. Jerry ran $\frac{8}{10}$ kilometer. How much farther did Jerry run?

8. Lulu ran a kilometer in $4\frac{1}{10}$ minutes. Jane ran it in $4\frac{5}{10}$ minutes. How much longer did it take Jane?

TABLE OF MEASURES

Length

1 meter (m) = 100 centimeters (cm)
1 kilometer (km) = 1,000 meters

Liquid

1 liter (L) = 2 half liters
1 half liter = 2 quarter liters

Weight

1 kilogram (kg) = 1,000 grams (g)
1 metric ton (t) = 1,000 kilograms

Time

1 minute = 60 seconds
1 hour = 60 minutes
1 day = 24 hours
1 week = 7 days

GLOSSARY

This glossary contains an example, an illustration, or a brief description of important terms used in this book.

Addends   Numbers that are added.
   Example $5 + 6 = 11$ 5 and 6 are addends.

Angle   A figure formed by two rays with a common endpoint. This is $\angle ABC$ or $\angle B$.

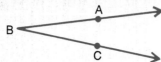

Area   The number of square units contained in a surface. The area of this figure is 10 square units.

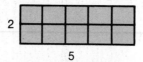

Average   A number used to represent a set of numbers. The average of 8, 4, and 3 is $\frac{8 + 4 + 3}{3}$ or 5.

Bar graph   A graph that shows information. It uses bars of different lengths.

Circle   A simple closed curve with all points the same distance from the center.

Closed curve   A curve that ends where it starts.

Common point A point where lines or line segments cross or touch each other. *P* is a common point of these two lines.

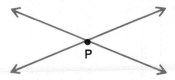

Compass A tool used to draw circles.
Cone A figure in space of this shape.

Counting numbers The numbers 1, 2, 3, and so on.
Cube A figure in space of this shape. Each of its 6 faces is a square.

Cubic measure We use cubic measure when we want to find the volume or the number of cubes that will fit inside a figure.
Cylinder A figure in space of this shape.

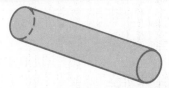

Degree The unit used when we measure temperatures with a thermometer.
Denominator The bottom number in a fraction.

Example $\frac{2}{7}$ ← denominator

Diagonal   A line segment from one corner to the opposite corner of a rectangle.

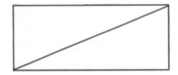

Diameter   A line segment going through the center of a
circle. It has both endpoints on the circle. $\overline{CD}$ is a
diameter.

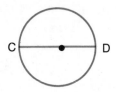

Difference   The answer in subtraction.
    Example $7 - 4 = 3$ 3 is the difference.
Digit   Any one of the ten basic numerals:
  0, 1, 2, 3, 4, 5, 6, 7, 8, 9

Equation   A number sentence with an equals sign, "=".
    Example $7 + 5 = 12$
Equivalent fractional numerals   Fractional numerals
that name the same number.
    Example $\frac{2}{3} = \frac{8}{12}$
Even number   A number that has 2 as a factor. 8 is
even because $2 \times 4 = 8$.
Expanded numeral   A name for a number that shows
the value of the digits.
    Example $398 = 300 + 90 + 8$

Factors   Numbers to be multiplied.
    Example $3 \times 4 = 12$ 3 and 4 are factors.

380

Flip　This is an example of a flip. The figure does not change size or shape.

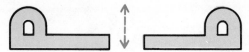

Fraction　A number named by such numerals as $\frac{2}{3}, \frac{1}{2}, \frac{5}{1}$.

Fractional numeral　Numerals such as $\frac{2}{3}, \frac{1}{2}, \frac{5}{1}$. They are names for fractions.

Function machine　A machine that follows a rule. The rule for this machine is add 3.

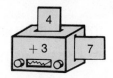

Geometry　The study of figures and shapes.

Graph　Information shown by the use of pictures, dots, or bars.

Grouping property of addition　The grouping of numbers added does not change the sum.
Example　$(2 + 5) + 3 = 2 + (5 + 3)$

Grouping property of multiplication　The grouping of numbers multiplied does not change the product.
Example　$(3 \times 2) \times 4 = 3 \times (2 \times 4)$

Inequality　A number sentence with $>$ or $<$ in it.
Examples　$8 > 5 + 2$　　$9 < 10 + 3$

Intersect　For figures to cross or touch.

Line　A straight path that goes forever in both directions. This line is called line $\overleftrightarrow{CD}$ or $\overleftrightarrow{DC}$.

Line of symmetry A line of folding so that the two halves of a figure match.

Line segment A straight path with two endpoints. This line segment is called line segment $\overline{GH}$ or $\overline{HG}$.

Mixed numeral A numeral such as $1\frac{1}{2}$, $2\frac{3}{4}$, $9\frac{4}{7}$.

Multiple The product of a number and any whole number.

Example Multiples of 3: 3, 6, 9, 12, and so on.

Multiplication-addition property A factor may be distributed over two or more addends.

Example $3 \times (2 + 4) = (3 \times 2) + (3 \times 4)$

Number line A line on which numbers are matched to points.

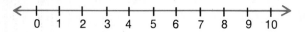

Number sentence A number sentence tells about numbers and their relations.

Examples $4 + 3 = 7$, $7 - 4 = 3$, $7 > 3$, $3 < 7$

Numeral A name for a number.

Numerator The top number in a fraction.

Example $\frac{2}{7}$ ⟵ numerator

Odd number A number that is not even. 9 is an odd number.

382

Open number sentence   A number sentence containing one or more frames. An open sentence is neither true nor false until we replace the frames.
Examples $\square + 4 = 7$ $\square + \square = 6$ $\square + \triangle = 7$

Order property of addition   The order of numbers added does not change the sum.
Example $4 + 3 = 3 + 4$

Order property of multiplication   The order of numbers multiplied does not change the product.
Example $6 \times 2 = 2 \times 6$

Ordered pair   A pair of numbers where order is important.

Parallel lines   Lines are parallel if they will never intersect.

Parentheses   These marks, ( ). The parentheses tell us to work inside them first.
Example $7 + (6 + 3) = 7 + 9$

Path   A path is a continuous set of points.

Perimeter   The distance around a geometric figure. The perimeter of this figure is $3 + 4 + 1 + 7$ or 15 units.

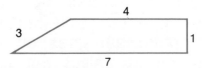

Periods in numerals   Groups of three digits in a numeral. They are separated by a comma.

Pictograph A graph that uses pictures to show information.

Point A point is a location in space. This is point *R*.

• R

Polygon A simple closed curve made of line segments.

Probability The chance of something happening. In a coin toss the chance (probability) of getting heads is one out of two.

Product The answer in multiplication.

Example 7 × 3 = 21   21 is the product.

Quotient The answer in division.

Example 21 ÷ 3 = 7   7 is the quotient.

Radius Any line segment from the center of a circle to a point on the circle $\overline{AB}$ is a radius.

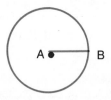

Ray A straight path that goes on forever in one direction. This ray is called ray $\overrightarrow{KL}$. It has one endpoint.

Rectangle A figure formed by four right angles. Its opposite sides are the same length.

Rectangular prism A figure in space of this shape. Each of its 6 faces is a rectangle.

Remainder In the division 14 ÷ 3, the quotient is 4 and the remainder is 2.

Right angle An angle that looks like a corner of a square.

Set Any group or collection of things.

Sides The two rays that form an angle are called sides. The lines that form a figure are its sides.

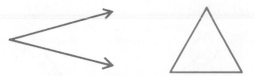

Simple closed curve A curve that begins and ends at the same point. It does not intersect itself.

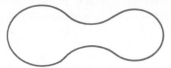

Slide   This is an example of a slide. The figure does not change size or shape.

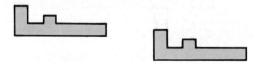

Sphere   A figure in space of this shape.

Square   A rectangle whose 4 sides have the same length.

Standard numeral   The usual or common name for a numeral. The standard numeral for fifteen is 15.

Sum   The answer in addition.

  Example $4 + 7 = 11$ 11 is the sum.

Symmetric   These figures can be folded so that one half will exactly fit on the other half. The figures are, therefore, symmetric.

Triangle   A polygon with 3 sides. This is triangle *ABC*.

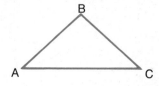

Turn This is an example of a turn. The figure does not change size or shape.

Vertex A corner point in a figure; *A, B, C,* and *D* are vertices.

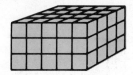

Volume The measure of the inside of a space figure. The volume of this box is 5 × 4 × 3 or 60 cubic units.

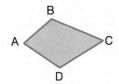

Whole numbers The numbers 0, 1, 2, 3, and so on.

SYMBOL LIST

INDEX

A

Activity, 57, 74, 94, 109, 115, 122, 134, 151, 186, 213, 282–283, 290–291, 292–293, 338–339, 342–343

Addend(s)
grouping of, 36–37, 50–51 • meaning of, 34–35 • missing, 39–40, 78 • more than two, 50–51 • order of, 36–37, 50–51

Addition
as opposite operation of subtraction, 42 • basic facts, 38 • checking, 52–53 • estimating sums in, 72–73 • expanded form in, 48–49 • mixed numerals in, 264–267 • money in, 66 • multiplication-addition property, 144, 166–167 • of fractions, different denominators, 256–257 • of fractions, same denominators, 248–249 • of hours and minutes, 310 • of hundreds, no regrouping, 52–53 • of hundreds, regrouping, 58–59 • of tens, regrouping, 48–49 • of thousands, regrouping, 60–61 • on the number line, 34–35 • properties of, 36–37 • regrouping in, 48–49, 56–57 • related to multiplication, 126–127 • short form in, 48–49 • sum in, 34–35 • with measures, 304–305, 310–311 • with more than two addends, 50–51

Addition properties, 36–37, 144, 166–167

am, 308

388

Angle(s)
comparing, 110–111 • in a triangle, 276–277 • naming, 110–111 • right, 110–111 • sides of, 110–111 • vertex of, 110–111

Area
meaning of, 322–323 • multiplying to find, 324–325 • of a rectangle, 322–323 • of a square, 322–323

Array, 126–127

Average, 214–215

B

Bar graph, 340–343

Basic facts
addition, 38 • division, 191 • multiplication, 160 • subtraction, 41

Brainteaser(s), 5, 45, 51, 62, 89, 102, 103, 107, 155, 173, 175, 218, 219, 237, 239, 263, 285, 327, 341, 347

C

Career
advertising workers, 311 • air traffic controllers, 45 • auto part sales, 113 • barbers, 133 • botanists, 351 • ceramic engineers, 281 • electricians, 90 • geologists, 217 • patternmakers, 271 • pharmacists, 187 • radio and TV announcers, 243 • school lunchroom managers, 21 • telephone workers, 75

Line segment, 106–107
Liter, 301

M

Measurement
addition and, 304–305 •
customary system, 314–319 •
metric system of, 298–307 • of
length, 298–300, 312–315 • of
liquids, 301, 316 • of temperature,
306–307, 319 • of time, 308–311
• of weight, 302–303, 317–318 •
subtraction and, 304–305
Meter, 299–300
Metric system
capacity, 301 • length, 298–300 •
temperature, 306–307 • weight,
302–303
Metric ton, 302–303
Mile, 314–315
Mini-problems, 45, 67, 90, 209, 226,
261
Missing factor, 129–130, 190
Mixed numeral(s)
addition using, 264–267 •
meaning of, 262–263 •
subtraction using, 268–269
Money
addition with, 66 • division with,
216 • estimating sums with,
72–73 • making change, 98–99 •
multiplication with, 176–178 •
notation, 64–65 • rounding with,
70–71 • subtraction with, 97–101
Multiple(s)
meaning of, 152–153 • of a
hundred, 158–159 • of ten,
158–159, 164–165, 182, 196–197,
206–208, 212 • of a thousand,
158–159
Multiplication
array in, 126–127 • as opposite
operation of division, 150 • basic
facts, 160 • by multiples of ten,
164–165, 182 • by one digit, no

regrouping, 168–169 • by
one digit, regrouping, 174–175 •
estimating products, 180–181 •
expanded form for, 168–169 •
factors in, 126–127 • money in,
176–178 • product in, 126–127 •
properties of, 144–145, 162–163,
166–167 • regrouping in,
172–173 • regrouping more than
once in, 176–177 • related to
addition, 126–127 • related to
division, 129–130 • short form
in, 168–169 • three digits by two
digits, 185–186 • two digits by
two digits, 183–184 • zero in, 135
Multiplication-addition property,
144–145, 166–167
Multiplication basic facts
one as a factor, 136–137 • two
as a factor, 138 • three as a
factor, 140 • four as a factor,
142–143 • five as a factor,
142–143 • six as a factor,
146–147 • seven as a factor,
146–147 • eight as a factor,
146–147 • nine as a factor,
148–149
Multiplication properties, 128,
136–137, 144–145, 162–163
Multiplication table, 134, 148–149

N

Number(s)
average of, 214–215 • comparing,
18–19 • counting, vi–1 • even,
139 • factors of, 152–153 •
multiples of, 152–153 • odd, 139
• order of, 2–3 • rounding, 68–71
• through 99, 7–9 • through 999,
10–11 • through 9,999, 12–13 •
through 999,999, 14–15 •
through 999,999,999, 16–17 •
used to tell "how many," 2–3 •
used to tell "which one," 2–3 •
whole, vi–1

ANSWERS

This section contains answers to developmental items only.

CHAPTER 1 • PAGE vi
    1.a. 1   **b.** 2; 7; 10; 100   **2.b.** 1
    3.a. 0   **b.** 4; 5; 0; 99   **c.** The numbers continue without end.

PAGE 2
    1.a. 3   **b.** 2   **c.** 0
    2.a. fourth or 4th   **b.** fifth or 5th
      c. first or 1st   **d.** second or 2nd
    3.a. first, second, third, . . ., fifteenth
      b. thirtieth, thirty-first, thirty-second, . . ., forty-first

PAGES 4–5
    1.a. 7   **b.** 28   **c.** 16
    2.a. 9   **b.** 90
    3.a. 39   **b.** 43   **c.** 49   **d.** 234
    4.a. LXV   **b.** XLIX   **c.** CCXXXVI   **d.** CCXLIV

PAGE 7
    1.a. 4 tens   **b.** 2 ones   **2.a.** 32   **b.** 79

PAGE 8
    1.a. standard numeral, 48   **b.** expanded numerals
    2.a. 5   **b.** 1   **c.** 3   **d.** 30
    3.a. 67   **b.** 41   **c.** 83   **d.** 17
    4.a. 8   **b.** 4

PAGE 10
    1.a. 2; 3; 4   **b.** 2 bags of 100, 3 bags of 10, 4 ones
    2.a. 4 hundreds + 5 tens + 8; 400 + 50 + 8
      b. 6 hundreds + 9 tens + 3; 600 + 90 + 3
      c. 7 hundreds + 0 tens + 1; 700 + 0 + 1   **3.a.** 3; 2; 4   **b.** 30

PAGE 12
    1. 5; 4; 3; 2   **2.a.** 5; 3   **b.** 400; 50   **3.** 400; 50
    4.a. 3 thousands + 4 hundreds + 9 tens + 6;
        3,000 + 400 + 90 + 6
      b. 2 thousands + 4 hundreds + 3 tens + 8;
        2,000 + 400 + 30 + 8
      c. 5 thousands + 3 hundreds + 7 tens + 0;
        5,000 + 300 + 70 + 0
    5.a. 3,000   **b.** 30   **c.** 300

PAGES 14–15
    1. ten thousands; hundred thousands
    2.a. 4,000   **b.** 800,000   **c.** 600   **d.** 30   **e.** 2

PAGES 14–15 (continued)
  3.a. 700,000 + 30,000 + 8,000 + 200 + 60 + 1
    b. 400,000 + 90,000 + 6,000 + 200 + 80 + 5
  4. 3; ones; tens; hundreds   **5.** a comma
  6.a. thirty-four thousand, eight hundred ninety-four
    b. forty thousand, seven hundred sixty-five
    c. fifty-six thousand, one hundred thirty-nine
    d. two hundred sixty-three thousand, one hundred forty-seven
    e. five hundred eight thousand, six hundred four
    f. eight hundred forty thousand, three

PAGE 16
  1.a. one millions; 4   **b.** 0; 7   **c.** 291; 853; 704
  2.a. two million, three hundred eighty-nine thousand, two hundred eighty-six
    b. four million, two hundred thousand, three hundred ninety-one
    c. thirteen million, four hundred eighty-six thousand, two hundred ninety-one
    d. sixty-eight million, two hundred ninety-seven thousand, four hundred one
    e. three hundred million, three hundred thousand, three hundred
    f. seven hundred fourteen million, six hundred three
  3. 300,000,000; 60,000,000; 2,000

PAGE 18
  1.a. <   **b.** >   **c.** =   **d.** <   **e.** >   **f.** <
  2.a. 7 hundreds > 4 hundreds
    b. 6 thousands < 7 thousands
  3.a. <   **b.** <   **c.** >   **d.** <   **e.** =   **f.** >

PAGE 20
  1. 9, 2, 5, 3, 0   **2.** 13, 16, 19, 22

CHAPTER 2 • **PAGES 24–25**
  1.a. subtract 2; add 4; subtract 3   **b.** 6; 5; 9
  2. Inputs: 0, 3; Outputs: 9, 14, 5
  3. Inputs: 5; Outputs: 5, 7

PAGE 26
  1.a. Three plus six is equal to nine.
    b. Nine is greater than seven.
    c. Seven is less than eight.
  2.a. inequality   **b.** equation   **c.** inequality

PAGE 27

1.a. true **b.** false **c.** true

2.a. 2 **b.** 3 **c.** 1

PAGES 28–29

1.a. Christopher Columbus **b.** Answers may vary. Ex: George Washington

2.a. 12 **b.** Answers may vary. Ex: 20

3.a. 13 **b.** 6 **c.** 4 **d.** 7 **e.** 14 **f.** 4 **4.a.** F **b.** O **c.** T

PAGE 30

1.a. Answers may vary. Ex: $4 + 2 = 6$

b. Answers may vary. Ex: $3 - 1 = 2$

2.a. $3 + 3 = 6$ **b.** Answers may vary. Ex: $5 + 0 = 5$

PAGES 34–35

1.b. 13 **c.** 7, 6; 13

2.b. 12 **c.** 8, 4; 12

3.a. 7 **b.** 8 **c.** 7 **d.** 15 **e.** 5 **f.** 10 **g.** 13 **h.** 12

4.a. $=$ **b.** $=$ **c.** $<$ **d.** $>$

PAGES 36–37

1.a. $10 + 4$; 14; $7 + 7$; 14 **b.** yes

2.a. 7 **b.** 12

3.a. 8 **b.** 8 **c.** 9

4.a. property of zero **b.** order property **c.** grouping property

5.a. 34 **b.** 12

PAGES 39–40

1.b. 7 **2.b.** 5

3.a. 7; 7 **b.** 6; 6

4.a. 8 **b.** 8 **c.** 9 **d.** 1 **e.** 4 **f.** 5 **g.** 0 **h.** 4

PAGE 42

1.a. 4 **b.** 7 **2.** 8

CHAPTER 3 • PAGES 48–49

1. 1 ten $+$ 7; 17 **2.a.** 1; 3; 34

b. 14; 1; 4; small 1 in the tens place, 4 in the ones place

3.a. 28 **b.** 49 **c.** 31 **d.** 55

PAGE 50

1.a. 19 **b.** 21 **2.a.** 20 **b.** Sharon added from bottom to top; 20

c. 20 **3.a.** 18 **b.** 11 **c.** 20 **d.** 22 **e.** 20

PAGE 52

1.a. 2 hundreds $+$ 3 tens $+$ 7 **b.** 237

$+$ 4 hundreds $+$ 2 tens $+$ 1 $+$ 421

6 hundreds $+$ 5 tens $+$ 8 $= 658$ 658

2.a. 59 **b.** 688 **c.** 8,787 **d.** 989

PAGE 54

1. cost of kite   **2.** $50 + 14 = 64$ cents   **3.** no

4. number of blue marbles

5. Answers may vary. Ex: 9 blue marbles; $8 + 9 = 17$ marbles

PAGE 56

1.a. 14 **b.** small 1 over the tens place, 4 in the ones place   **c.** 9

2.a. 75   **b.** 133   **c.** 110   **d.** 77

3.a. 23 **b.** 2; 3 **c.** small 2 over the tens place, 3 in the ones place

   d. 9   **4.a.** 79   **b.** 106   **c.** 110   **d.** 84

PAGE 58

1.a. 17   **b.** small 1 over tens place, 7 in ones place   **c.** 694

2.a. 12 **b.** small 1 over hundreds place, 2 in tens place   **c.** 819

3.a. 1,022   **b.** 860   **c.** 1,863   **d.** 1,123

PAGE 60

1.a. 10; small 1 over thousands place, 0 in hundreds place   **b.** 12

   c. 12,051

2.a. 14,180   **b.** 41,071   **c.** 47,861

PAGES 64–65

1.a. eighty-four cents   **b.** eighty-four cents

   c. ninety-eight cents   **d.** ninety-eight cents

   e. six cents   **f.** six cents   **g.** one cent   **h.** one cent

2.a. 47¢; $.47   **b.** 11¢; $.11   **c.** 8¢; $.08   **d.** 2¢; $.02

3.a. nine dollars and eighty-six cents

   b. seven dollars and four cents

   c. nineteen dollars and eighty-seven cents

   d. twenty-nine dollars and eight cents

   e. one hundred thirty-four dollars and seventy-two cents

   f. two thousand, one hundred thirty-three dollars and five cents

4. a point

5.a. $7.31; 731¢   **b.** $6.04; 604¢   **c.** $3.45; 345¢

6.a. 5   **b.** 6   **c.** 0   **d.** 2   **e.** 3   **f.** 1

PAGE 66

1.a. 22; 2 in the tens of cents place, 2 in the ones of cents place

   b. 27; 2 in the ones of dollars place, 7 in the tens of cents place

   c. 16   **2.** $9.47

PAGES 68–69

1.a. exact   **b.** about 50

2.a. yes   **b.** yes   **c.** 55   **d.** 50

3.a. 20   **b.** 30   **c.** 30   **d.** 90

4. Neither; it is halfway.

5.a. 30   **b.** 20   **c.** 90   **d.** 80   **e.** 50

PAGES 70–71

1.a. 300   **b.** 900   **2.** Neither; it is halfway.

3.a. 2,000   **b.** 6,000   **c.** 4,000   **d.** 5,000
4.a. 50   **b.** more
5.a. $4.00   **b.** $6.00   **c.** $8.00   **d.** $2.00

PAGE 72
1.a. nearest hundred: 435 to 400, 541 to 500,
    394 to 400, 550 to 600   **b.** 20
2.a. $400 + 800 = 1,200$
   b. $300 + 300 + 700 + 200 = 1,500$
3.a. $40 + 80 = 120$ **b.** $80 + 40 + 80 = 200$
4.a. $5.00 + $4.00 + $5.00 = $14.00   **b.** $13.91

CHAPTER 4 • **PAGE 78**
1. 6; 6   **2.** no   **3.** c, e
PAGE 79
1.a. 9 tens; 90   **b.** 4 thousands; 4,000
2.a. 80   **b.** 800   **c.** 8,000   **d.** 7,000
PAGE 80
1.a.

$$\begin{array}{r} 7 \text{ tens} + 5 \\ - 2 \text{ tens} + 1 \\ \hline 5 \text{ tens} + 4 \end{array}$$

b.

$$\begin{array}{r} 75 \\ - 21 \\ \hline 54 \end{array}$$

2.a. 62   **b.** 422   **c.** 401   **d.** 40
PAGE 81
1. Go back and subtract again.   **2.** 223
PAGE 82
1.a. 9; 9; 19   **b.** 8; 8; 18   **c.** 4; 1; 12
2.a. 7; 17   **b.** 3; 13   **c.** 4; 18
PAGES 84–85
1.a. can't subtract ones.   **b.** 6 tens + 14   **c.** 3 tens + 6; 36
2.a. can't subtract ones.   **b.** 4 hundreds + 2 tens + 18
   c. 2 hundreds + 1 ten + 9; 219

3.a.

$$\begin{array}{r} \overset{5}{\cancel{6}} \text{ tens} + \overset{14}{\cancel{4}} \\ - 2 \text{ tens} + 8 \\ \hline 3 \text{ tens} + 6 = 36 \end{array}$$

b.

$$\begin{array}{r} 5 \text{ hundreds} + \overset{3}{\cancel{4}} \text{ tens} + \overset{13}{\cancel{3}} \\ - 2 \text{ hundreds} + 1 \text{ ten } + 8 \\ \hline 3 \text{ hundreds} + 2 \text{ tens} + 5 = 325 \end{array}$$

4.a. 25   **b.** 23   **c.** 317   **d.** 36
PAGES 86–87
1.a. can't subtract tens.   **b.** 5 hundreds + 13 tens + 8
   c. 1 hundred + 8 tens + 5; 185
2.a. can't subtract hundreds
   b. 3 thousands + 16 hundreds + 3 tens + 8   **c.** 2,711

    3.a. 454   **b.** 75   **c.** 2,332   **d.** 191

PAGE 88
    1.a. 229   **b.** 482   **c.** 89
    2.a. 2,858   **b.** 13,215   **c.** 54,779

PAGE 91
    1.a. 10   **b.** 699   **2.a.** 69   **b.** 399

PAGES 92–93
    1.a. 6 cannot be subtracted from 5, and 2 cannot be subtracted from 0.
    b. 29 tens + 15   **c.** 179   **2.a.** 599 tens + 13   **b.** 3,214
    3.a. 153 **b.** 2,519 **c.** 806 **4.a.** 1,885 **b.** 4,584 **c.** 5,176
    d. 5,552

PAGES 98–99
    1. 3 quarters: $2.50, $2.75, $3.00   **2.** 1 penny: $3.50
        2 dollars: $4.00, $5.00   2 quarters: $3.75, $4.00
                                      1 dollar: $5.00
                                      1 $5-bill: $10.00

    3.a. 3 dollars: $1.00, $2.00, $3.00
           3 quarters: $3.25, $3.50, $3.75
           1 nickel: $3.80
           1 penny: $3.81
    3.b. 1 $10-bill: $10.00
           2 dollars: $11.00, $12.00
           3 quarters: $12.25, $12.50, $12.75
           4 pennies: $12.76, $12.77, $12.78, $12.97

PAGE 100
    1.a. nearest hundred **b.** yes; she has about 300 kilometers to go.
    2.a. no   **b.** 2,040

CHAPTER 5 • **PAGES 104–105**
    1. waterhole, old tree, tree stump   **2.** point W; point Y
    4.a. point P **b.** red

PAGE 106
    1.d. one   **e.** an unending number   **2.** $\overleftrightarrow{XY}$; $\overleftrightarrow{YX}$
    3.a. line segment MN **b.** line segment NM
      c. line segment AB **4.a.** 3   **b.** 6   **c.** 0   **5.** $\overline{AB}$, $\overline{BC}$, $\overline{AC}$

PAGE 108
    1.b. forever   **c.** It goes on forever.
    2.a. $\overrightarrow{XY}$ **b.** $\overrightarrow{LM}$ **c.** $\overrightarrow{CD}$ **3.c.** $\overrightarrow{XC}$, $\overrightarrow{XB}$

PAGE 110
    2.a. $\overrightarrow{ML}$, $\overrightarrow{MN}$ **b.** M **c.** in the middle; in the middle

3.a. no   **b.** yes   **c.** yes
4.a. ∠XYZ, ∠ZYX   **b.** ∠HIJ, ∠JIH   **c.** ∠DEF, ∠FED
PAGE 114
  1.c. a line
  2.a. no   **b.** no   **c.** yes   **d.** no   **e.** yes   **f.** yes
  3.a. $\overleftrightarrow{DE}$, $\overleftrightarrow{ED}$ **b.** $\overleftrightarrow{XY}$, $\overleftrightarrow{YX}$ **c.** $\overleftrightarrow{MN}$, $\overleftrightarrow{NM}$
PAGES 116–117
  2.b. no   **c.** no   **3.a.** no   **b.** yes   **5.** a; c
PAGES 118–119
  1.a. no   **b.** no   **2.a.** yes   **b.** yes
  3.a. yes **b.** no **4.a.** closed **b.** curve **c.** simple closed
  d. closed
PAGE 120
  1.c. yes   **2.a.** $\overline{LN}$, $\overline{LO}$ **b.** same   **3.a.** $\overline{CD}$ **b.** same

CHAPTER 6 • **PAGES 126–127**
  1.a. $2 \times 8 = 16$ **b.** $4 \times 5 = 20$
  2.a. 4, 9; 36   **b.** 7, 7; 49
  3.a. $6 + 6 = 12$; 12   **b.** $3 + 3 + 3 = 9$; 9   **c.** $5 + 5 + 5 + 5 = 20$; 20
  4.a. 18   **b.** 28   **c.** 6
PAGE 128
  1.a. 36   **b.** 42   **2.** 2
PAGE 129
  1.a. 8; 8   **b.** 4; 4   **c.** 5; 5
  2.a. 5; 4   **b.** 3   **3.a.** 4   **b.** 4   **4.b.** 2
PAGE 131
  1.a. 4   **b.** 4
  2.a.

$$\begin{array}{r} 8 \\ -4 \\ \hline 4 \\ -4 \\ \hline 0 \end{array} \quad 8 \div 4 = 2$$

  b.

$$\begin{array}{r} 15 \\ -5 \\ \hline 10 \\ -5 \\ \hline 5 \\ -5 \\ \hline 0 \end{array} \quad 15 \div 5 = 3$$

PAGE 135
  1.a. yes   **b.** 0; 0   **2.** order property
  3.a. 0; 0   **b.** 0; 0   **c.** 0; 0
PAGES 136–137
  1.a. yes   **b.** the other factor   **2.a.** 8   **b.** 8
  3.a. 7   **b.** 6   **c.** 1
  4.a. 1   **b.** 1   **5.a.** 1   **b.** 1   **c.** 1

PAGE 138

1.a. $3 + 3 = 6$ **b.** $4 + 4 = 8$ **c.** $6 + 6 = 12$
  d. $7 + 7 = 14$ **e.** $8 + 8 = 16$ **f.** $9 + 9 = 18$

2.a. $6 \div 2 = 3, 6 \div 3 = 2, 3 \times 2 = 6$
  b. $8 \div 2 = 4, 8 \div 4 = 2, 4 \times 2 = 8$
  c. $12 \div 2 = 6, 12 \div 6 = 2, 6 \times 2 = 12$
  d. $14 \div 2 = 7, 14 \div 7 = 2, 7 \times 2 = 14$
  e. $16 \div 2 = 8, 16 \div 8 = 2, 8 \times 2 = 16$
  f. $18 \div 2 = 9, 18 \div 9 = 2, 9 \times 2 = 18$

PAGE 139

1.a. 4, 6, 8, 0, 2, 4; even   **b.** 30, 32, 34, 36, 38, 40
2.a. 5, 7, 9, 1, 3, 5; odd   **b.** 31, 33, 35, 37, 39, 41

PAGE 140

1.a. $5 + 5 + 5 = 15$ **b.** $6 + 6 + 6 = 18$
  c. $7 + 7 + 7 = 21$ **d.** $9 + 9 + 9 = 27$
2.a. $3 \times 5 = 15$ **b.** $3 \times 6 = 18$ **c.** $3 \times 7 = 21$ **d.** $3 \times 9 = 27$
3.a. $18 \div 6 = 3, 18 \div 3 = 6$ **b.** $24 \div 3 = 8,$
    $24 \div 8 = 3$ **c.** $27 \div 9 = 3, 27 \div 3 = 9$
4.a. 3   **b.** 3   **c.** 3   **d.** 4

PAGES 142–143

1.a. 4; 20   **b.** 4; 24   **2.a.** 28   **b.** 32   **c.** 36   **3.** 24; 24
4.a. 5; 40   **b.** 5; 45   **5.** 30; 30
6.a. $28 \div 7 = 4, 28 \div 4 = 7$ **b.** $40 \div 5 = 8, 40 \div 8 = 5$
  c. $36 \div 9 = 4, 36 \div 4 = 9$ **d.** $20 \div 4 = 5, 20 \div 5 = 4$
  e. $35 \div 7 = 5, 35 \div 5 = 7$ **f.** $45 \div 5 = 9, 45 \div 9 = 5$

PAGE 144

1. 2   **2.a.** 1   **b.** 2; 4
3.a. Paula: $5 + 1$; José: $3 + 3$
  b. multiplication-addition property   **c.** yes
  d.

4×9	4×9
$4 \times (6 + 3)$	$4 \times (4 + 5)$
$(4 \times 6) + (4 \times 3)$	$(4 \times 4) + (4 \times 5)$
$24 + 12$	$16 + 20$
36	36

There are still more ways to find the answer.

PAGES 146–147

1.a. 1, 1, 36, 6, 42   **b.** 1, 7, 1, 42, 6, 48
2. Answers may vary. Ex:

$$6 \times 9$$
$$6 \times (6 + 3)$$
$$(6 \times 6) + (6 \times 3)$$
$$36 + 18$$
$$54$$

PAGES 146–147 (continued)

3.a. $42 \div 6 = 7$; $42 \div 7 = 6$ **b.** $48 \div 8 = 6$; $48 \div 6 = 8$
   c. $54 \div 6 = 9$; $54 \div 9 = 6$

4.a. 1, 1, 42, 7, 49   **b.** 1, 7, 1, 49, 7, 56, 56

5. Answers may vary. Ex:
$$7 \times 9$$
$$7 \times (6 + 3)$$
$$(7 \times 6) + (7 \times 3)$$
$$42 + 21$$
$$63$$

6. $56 \div 7 = 8$, $56 \div 8 = 7$; $63 \div 9 = 7$, $63 \div 7 = 9$

7. Answers may vary.

   a. Ex:
$$8 \times 8$$
$$8 \times (5 + 3)$$
$$(8 \times 5) + (8 \times 3)$$
$$40 + 24$$
$$64$$

   b. Ex:
$$8 \times 9$$
$$8 \times (6 + 3)$$
$$(8 \times 6) + (8 \times 3)$$
$$48 + 24$$
$$72$$

8.a. 8   **b.** 9   **c.** 8

PAGES 148–149

2. 9   **3.a.** The tens digit is always one less.   **b.** Always add to 9.
4. 5; 4; 54   **5.a.** 72   **b.** 27   **c.** 45   **6.a.** 7   **b.** 9   **c.** 9

PAGE 150

1.a. 16   **b.** 8   **2.** 15

PAGES 152–153

1.a. 20, 10, 4   **b.** 4, 5, 10, 20
2.a. 1, 3, 5, 15   **b.** 1, 3, 9
   c. 1, 2, 3, 4, 6, 8, 12, 24   **d.** 1, 7
3.a. yes, $3 \times 5 = 15$ **b.** yes, $3 \times 9 = 27$ **c.** no
4.a. yes   **b.** yes   **c.** no
5.a. 6, 12, 18, 24, 30, 36, 42, 48   **b.** 9, 18, 27, 36, 45, 54, 63, 72
   c. 8, 16, 24, 32, 40, 48, 56, 64

PAGE 155 (Answers may vary.)

1. Ex. 7 children.
   4 cookies each.
   How many cookies
   in all? 28

2.a. Ex. 7 red candles.
   8 blue candles.
   How many candles
   in all? 15

b. Ex. 12 apples.
   9 are eaten.
   How many apples
   are left? 3

c. Ex. 12 crayons.
   3 children.
   How many crayons
   for each child? 4

CHAPTER 7 • PAGES 158–159

1.a. 70   **b.** 180   **c.** 32,400   **2.a.** 2,000   **b.** 52,000   **c.** 483,000

402

    3.a. 130   **b.** 300   **c.** 265,000   **4.a.** 10   **b.** 6   **c.** 10
    5.a. 2   **b.** 100   **6.a.** 1,000   **b.** 1,000

PAGES 162–163
    1.a. 8, 40; 10, 40   **b.** 5
    2.a. 100; 100; 32; 100; 3,200
    b. 1,000; 1,000; 32; 1,000; 32,000
    3.a. 420   **b.** 100; 5,600   **c.** 1,000; 24,000
    4.a. 560   **b.** 54,000
    5.a. 240   **b.** 2,800   **c.** 40,000   **d.** 4,900   **e.** 48,000   **f.** 90

PAGES 164–165
    1.a. 10; 10; 10; 10; 100; 600
    b. 10; 10; 36; 1,000; 36,000
    c. 100; 10; 100; 18; 1,000; 18,000
    2.a. 1,200   **b.** 5,600   **c.** 32,000   **d.** 18,000

PAGES 166–167
    1.a. 8; 10; 8; 40; 32; 72
    b. 2; 10; 2; 300; 60; 360
    2.a. 5; 120; 15; 1,035
    b. 10; 4; 4,000; 200; 80; 4,280
    3.a. 93   **b.** 2,048   **c.** 4,260   **d.** 10,560

PAGES 168–169
    1.a. 1; 30   **b.** 3; 2; 3; 60   **2.a.** 6   **b.** 18
    3.a. 48   **b.** 568   **c.** 270   **d.** 108
    4.a. 1,566   **b.** 1,828   **c.** 1,284

PAGES 172–173
    1.a. 3; 5; 70   **b.** 4; 8; 4; 60   **2.a.** 15   **b.** 1; 5
    c. 1 in the tens place, 5 in the ones place   **d.** 35   **e.** 36
    3.a. 81   **b.** 136   **c.** 235   **d.** 702

PAGES 174–175
    1.a. 28; small 2 above the tens place, 8 in the ones place
    b. 7; 9   **c.** 5,698
    2.a. 8 **b.** 20; small 2 above the hundreds place, 0 in the tens place
    c. 4; 6 **d.** 12,608 **3.a.** 868 **b.** 1,848 **c.** 7,917 **d.** 14,469

PAGES 176–177
    1.a. 2,436   **b.** 6,384   **c.** 3,555
    2.a. 19,488   **b.** 71,532   **c.** 17,175   **d.** 31,388
    3. Dollar sign and decimal point were put in product.
    4.a. $4.58   **b.** $6.24   **c.** $.63   **d.** $101.96

PAGE 180
    1.a. 630   **b.** $3.20   **2.a.** $70 \times 6 = 420$
    b. $\$.40 \times 9 = \$3.60$ **c.** $\$.80 \times 4 = \$3.20$ **d.** $40 \times 6 = 240$
    3.a. 1,500   **b.** 500; 3,500   **c.** $8; $48

PAGE 180 (continued)
    4.a. $500 \times 5 = 2,500$ **b.** $\$7 \times 4 = \$28$
      c. $700 \times 6 = 4,200$ **d.** $\$7 \times 7 = \$49$
PAGE 182
    1. 10; 10; 10; 720
    2.a. 78; 780   **b.** 343; 3,430   **c.** 5,712; 57,120
PAGE 183
    1.a. 76   **b.** 1,520   **c.** 1,596
    2.a. 1,248   **b.** 5,922   **c.** 4,250; 4,845   **d.** 1,710; 2,166
    3.a. 1,617   **b.** 1,702   **c.** 6,630   **d.** $74.26
PAGE 185
    1. 44,496
    2.a. 10,406   **b.** 85,848   **c.** 19,740   **d.** $643.80

CHAPTER 8 • PAGE 190
    1.a. 3, 3, 3, 30, 30, 30, 300, 300, 300
      b. 4, 4, 4, 40, 40, 40, 400, 400, 400
    2.a. 50   **b.** 400   **c.** 700
PAGES 192–193
    1.a. 5; 5; 2   **b.** 12   **2.** 10; 2; 12   **3.a.** 13   **b.** 23
    4.a. 1   **b.** 2   **c.** 3   **5.a.** 2   **b.** 4
PAGES 194–195
    1.a. 20, 120, 18   **b.** 3, 18, 0, 23   **c.** 138
    2.a. 4, 5, 4, 13   **b.** 10, 3, 13   **3.a.** 12   **b.** 18   **c.** 27   **d.** 36
PAGES 196–197
    1.a. 50; 10   **b.** 60
    2.a. 6 can go in 10 more times.
      b. can't subtract 300 from 252   **c.** 40
    3.a. yes   **b.** no   **c.** 60
    4.a. 80   **b.** 20   **c.** 30   **d.** 80
PAGES 198–199
    1.a. yes; yes; no   **b.** 60   **c.** 65
    2.a. 44   **b.** 33   **c.** 22   **d.** 66
PAGE 200–201
    1.a. yes; yes; no   **b.** 700   **c.** 20   **d.** 729
    2.a. 200   **b.** 400   **c.** 700
    3.a. 284   **b.** 639   **c.** 406
PAGE 202
    1.a. 15 people   **b.** 13 people
    2.a. $11.46   **b.** $8.54   **3.a.** 36 apples   **b.** $2.52

    1.a. 5   **b.** 6   **c.** $5 \times 7 = 35, 35 + 6 = 41$

    2. 0   **3.a.** 0, 1, 2   **b.** yes

    4.a. 0, 1, 2, 3,   **b.** yes

    5.a. 8 r 2   **b.** OK   **c.** 8 r 3

    6.a. 6 r 3   **b.** 41 r 1   **c.** 714 r 2

    1.a. yes   **b.** 6; 6 r 26

    2.a. 9 r 6   **b.** 9 r 24   **c.** 7 r 53

    3.a. yes; no   **b.** 20   **c.** 8   **d.** 28 r 4

    4.a. 60   **b.** 30   **c.** 20   **5.a.** 27 r 6   **b.** 32 r 27   **c.** 96 r 34

    1.a. 40; 4 in tens place   **c.** 49

    b. 9; in the ones place

$$\times 7$$

$$343 + 5 = 348$$

    2. Estimate 400. Write 4 in hundreds place.

        Estimate 90. Write 9 in tens place.   497

        Estimate 7. Write 7 in ones place. Check the division. $\times 3$

                                                 1491

                                                 $+ 1$

                                                 1492

    3.a. 97   **b.** 64   **c.** 480 r 1   **d.** 982

    1.a. 20; 2 in tens place   **b.** 3; in the ones place

    2.a. 19 r 37   **b.** 62 r 20   **c.** 55 r 50

    1.a. 95; 75   **b.** 255   **c.** 3   **d.** 85   **2.** 18 pts

    3.a. 4   **b.** 7   **c.** 75

    1.a. 57   **b.** $.57 or 57¢

    2.a. $.25 or 25¢   **b.** $.75 or 75¢   **c.** $.09 or 9¢

    1.a. 2; 3   **b.** $\frac{2}{3}$ **c.** two thirds

    2.a. 5 out of 6   **b.** $\frac{5}{6}$ **c.** five sixths

    3.a. zero halves, one half, two halves, three halves, four halves,
        five halves   **b.** zero thirds, one third, two thirds, . . . ,
        five thirds   **c.** zero fourths, one fourth, two fourths, . . . ,
        five fourths   **d.** zero tenths, one tenth, two tenths, . . . ,
        five tenths

    4.a. 1; 8   **b.** 2; 7   **c.** 5; 6   **d.** 7; 2   **e.** 0; 3

PAGE 222

    1.a. no   **b.** no   **c.** yes

    2.a. 3 parts shaded out of 10   **b.** 1 part shaded out of 6

    c. 3 parts shaded out of 8   **d.** 7 parts shaded out of 7

PAGE 223

    1.a. yes   **b.** no   **c.** yes   **2.a.** $\frac{0}{8}$ **b.** $\frac{5}{5}$

    3.a. 7   **b.** $\frac{2}{7}$ **c.** $\frac{1}{7}$ **d.** $\frac{4}{7}$

PAGE 225

    1.a. 4; 4   **b.** 3; 3   **2.a.** 4   **b.** 5

PAGE 228

    1.a. $\frac{1}{3}$ **b.** $\frac{2}{6}$ **c.** yes   **d.** 2

    2.a. $\frac{3}{6}, \frac{1}{2}$ **b.** $\frac{3}{6} = \frac{1}{2}$ **3.** $\frac{1}{4}; \frac{2}{8}$

PAGE 230

    1.a. 10; 5   **b.** 2; 1   **c.** 1

    2.a. $\frac{1}{3}, \frac{2}{6}$ **b.** $\frac{1}{3} = \frac{2}{6}$ **3.** $\frac{1}{2}, \frac{4}{8}$

PAGES 232–233

    1.a. fourths **b.** zero fourths, one fourth, two fourths, . . . ,
    twelve fourths

    2.a. right; >   **b.** left; <

    3.a. <   **b.** >   **c.** >   **d.** <   **e.** =   **f.** <

PAGES 234–235

    1.a. $\frac{0}{2}, \frac{0}{3}, \frac{0}{4}, \frac{0}{5}$ **b.** 0   **c.** $\frac{2}{2}, \frac{3}{3}, \frac{4}{4}, \frac{5}{5}$ **d.** They are the same.

    2.a. $\frac{6}{6}$ **b.** $\frac{0}{6}, \frac{1}{6}, \frac{2}{6}, \frac{3}{6}, \frac{4}{6}, \frac{5}{6}, \frac{6}{6}$ **c.** Denominators are greater.

    d. $\frac{7}{6}, \frac{8}{6}, \frac{9}{6}, \frac{10}{6}, \frac{11}{6}, \frac{12}{6}$ **e.** Numerators are greater.

    3.a. <   **b.** >   **c.** =

PAGE 236

    1.a. $\frac{2}{8}$ **b.** $\frac{3}{4}$ **2.a.** 1 **b.** 0 **c.** 2 **d.** 0 **e.** 2 **f.** 4

    3.a. T   **b.** F   **c.** T

PAGES 238–239

    1.a. Increase by one; increase by two.

    b. $\frac{5}{10}$ **c.** $\frac{6}{12}, \frac{7}{14}, \frac{8}{16}, \frac{9}{18}, \frac{10}{20}$

    2.a. keeps going   **b.** an unending number

    3.a. Numerators add 2; denominators add 3.

    b. $\frac{12}{18}, \frac{14}{21}, \frac{16}{24}$ **c.** $\frac{4}{6}, \frac{6}{9}, \frac{8}{12}, \frac{10}{15}, \frac{12}{18}, \ldots$

    4.a. $\frac{4}{16}, \frac{5}{20}, \frac{6}{24}, \frac{7}{28}$ **b.** $\frac{8}{20}, \frac{10}{25}, \frac{12}{30}, \frac{14}{35}$

1.a. $\frac{1 \times 5}{4 \times 5}$ **b.** $\frac{1 \times 6}{4 \times 6}$ **2.a.** $\frac{7}{28}$ **b.** $\frac{7}{28}$

3.a. 3; 6; 12; 16; $\frac{15}{20}$; $\frac{18}{24}$ **b.** $\frac{3}{4}, \frac{6}{8}, \frac{9}{12}, \frac{12}{16}, \frac{15}{20}, \frac{18}{24}$

4.a. $\frac{2}{10}, \frac{3}{15}, \frac{4}{20}, \frac{5}{25}$ **b.** $\frac{4}{6}, \frac{6}{9}, \frac{8}{12}, \frac{10}{15}$ **c.** $\frac{2}{24}, \frac{3}{36}, \frac{4}{48}, \frac{5}{60}$

PAGE 242

1.a. 24, 24   **b.** yes   **c.** yes   **2.a.** yes   **b.** no   **c.** no

CHAPTER 10 • **PAGES 248–249**

1.a. $\frac{2}{8}, \frac{1}{8}$ **b.** 3

2.a. $\frac{1}{5}$ and $\frac{2}{5}$ **b.** 3

3. Add the numerators; keep same denominators.

4.a. 2   **b.** 2; 6

5.a. $\frac{3}{4}$ **b.** $\frac{4}{5}$ **c.** $\frac{4}{6}$

PAGES 250–251

1. 1   **2.** 4

3. Subtract numerators; keep same denominators.

4.a. 9, 5   **b.** 11, $\frac{6}{11}$

5.a. $\frac{5}{8}$ **b.** $\frac{7}{12}$ **c.** $\frac{0}{5}$

PAGE 253

1.a. yes   **b.** $<$ **c.** $<$

2.a. $<$ **b.** $>$ **c.** $<$

PAGES 254–255

1. $<$ **2.a.** 2, 3, 4   **b.** $\frac{2}{3}, \frac{4}{6}, \frac{6}{9}, \frac{8}{12}$ **c.** $\frac{3}{6}, \frac{4}{6}$ **d.** 3, 4   **e.** $<, <$

3.a. $\frac{1}{3}, \frac{2}{6}, \frac{3}{9}, \frac{4}{12}; \frac{1}{4}, \frac{2}{8}, \frac{3}{12}, \frac{4}{16}$ **b.** $\frac{4}{12}; \frac{3}{12}$ **c.** $>$ **4.** $>$

PAGES 256–257

1.a. $\frac{1}{3}, \frac{2}{6}, \frac{3}{9}; \frac{1}{6}, \frac{2}{12}, \frac{3}{18}$ **b.** $\frac{2}{6}, \frac{1}{6}$ **c.** 2; 1; 2; 1; 3

2.a. 4; 3; 7   **b.** 5; 4; 9

3.a. $\frac{5}{8}$ **b.** $\frac{5}{6}$ **c.** $\frac{11}{12}$

PAGES 258–259

1.a. $\frac{1}{3}, \frac{2}{6}, \frac{3}{9}, \frac{1}{6}, \frac{2}{12}$ **b.** $\frac{2}{6}, \frac{1}{6}$ **c.** 2, 1, 2, 1, 1

2.a. 8, 3, 5   **b.** 8, 5, 3

3.a. $\frac{2}{6}$ **b.** $\frac{1}{6}$ **c.** $\frac{7}{15}$

1.a. 3   **b.** $\frac{3}{2}$ **c.** 1   **d.** $\frac{1}{2}$ **e.** $1\frac{1}{2}$

2.a. $\frac{5}{3}, 1\frac{2}{3}$ **b.** $\frac{5}{4}, 1\frac{1}{4}$

3.a. $\frac{1}{5}; 1\frac{1}{5}$ **b.** $\frac{3}{6}; 1; \frac{3}{6}; 1\frac{3}{6}$

4.a. $1\frac{2}{5}$ **b.** $1\frac{3}{8}$ **c.** $1\frac{2}{7}$

1.a. 8   **b.** 1   **c.** yes

2.a. 1   **b.** $\frac{2}{5}, 1\frac{2}{5}$

3.a. 1   **b.** $1\frac{3}{10}$ **c.** $1\frac{2}{6}$

1.a. $\frac{4}{6}$ **b.** 5   **c.** five and four sixths

2.a. $7\frac{2}{3}$ **b.** $16\frac{3}{5}$ **c.** $146\frac{4}{7}$ **d.** $51\frac{1}{8}$

1.a. $\frac{3}{6}$ **b.** 4   **c.** four and three sixths

2.a. $2\frac{1}{3}$ **b.** $2\frac{2}{4}$ **c.** 18 or $18\frac{0}{8}$ **d.** $38\frac{3}{5}$

CHAPTER 11 • **PAGE 274**

1.c. yes

1.a. 3   **b.** $\overline{AB}, \overline{BC}$ **2.a.** 2   **b.** $\angle MLN, \angle LNM$

3.a. 2   **b.** B, C **4.** $\triangle RST$

1.a. 4   **b.** $\overline{AB}, \overline{BC}, \overline{CD}, \overline{DA}$ **c.** 4; 4; 4

2.a. $\overline{AB}$ and $\overline{DC}$ **b.** same   **c.** same

3.a. yes; its two pairs of parallel lines form right angles.   **b.** same

4.a. rectangle   **b.** neither   **c.** square and rectangle   **d.** rectangle

1.a. $\triangle ACD, \triangle ABC$ **b.** $\overline{BD}$

2.a.–c. They are the same length.

1.d. no   **2.d.** no

3.a. slide   **b.** neither   **c.** slide   **d.** turn   **e.** neither   **f.** neither

2.d. no   **e.** no   **f.** yes

3.a. yes   **b.** no   **c.** yes

1.a. yes   **b.** no   **c.** no   **d.** yes

3.a. 2   **b.** an unending number
5. Answers may vary. Ex: door, window, desk, chalkboard, etc.
PAGES 290–291
5.a. 6   **b.** square   **c.** 12; 8   **6.a.** no   **b.** 6; 12; 8
PAGES 292–293
1.a. circle   **b.** circle   **c.** rectangle
2.a. yes   **b.** no   **c.** yes   **3.d.** circle
PAGE 294
1. yes   **2.** circle   **3.** circle

CHAPTER 12 • PAGE 298
1.a. 2 cm   **b.** 2 cm
PAGES 299–300
1.a. 300 **b.** 100; 600 **2.a.** 4 **b.** 2; 2 **3.a.** 800 **b.** 500 **c.** 7 **d.** 9
4.a. 8; 25   **b.** 5; 5   **c.** 642   **d.** 309   **5.** 4 km
6.a. 2,000 **b.** 5 **c.** 793 **d.** 9,500 **7.a.** cm **b.** km **c.** m or cm
PAGE 301
1. 2   **2.a.** 4   **b.** 4   **c.** 1   **d.** 2
PAGES 302–303
1.a. 2 **b.** 1; 500   **c.** 3; 325   **2.a.** 3,000   **b.** 9,000   **c.** 5,625
3.a. 5,000   **b.** 9,986   **c.** 3; 486
4.a. g   **b.** kg   **c.** t   **d.** g   **e.** t   **f.** kg
PAGES 304–305
1.a. 732 m   **b.** 10 km   **c.** 10 km 732 m
2.a. 135 m 67 cm   **b.** 127 km 829 m
3.a. 1,059 kg 519 g   **b.** 145 t 983 kg
4.a. 13 m 51 cm   **b.** 678 kg 266 g
PAGES 306–307
1.a. 0°C **b.** 100° **2.a.** 28°C **b.** 15°C **c.** A **3.a.** 15° **b.** −5°C
PAGES 308–309
1.a. 1:08; 8; 1   **b.** 12:55; 5; 1   **2.a.** am   **b.** pm
3. 180 min; 480 min   **4.** 120 sec; 600 sec
PAGE 310
1.a. 7:00 pm   **b.** 10:21 am   **c.** 1:00 am
2.a. 7:15 am   **b.** 11:00 pm   **c.** 8:25 pm   **3.** 9:54   **4.** 4:15
PAGES 312–313
1.a. $2\frac{1}{4}$ in.   **b.** $1\frac{1}{2}$ in.   **3.a.** 8   **b.** $1\frac{3}{8}$ inches
4.a. $1\frac{1}{8}$ in.   **b.** $\frac{5}{8}$ in.
6. $1\frac{5}{8}$ in.   **7.a.** $\frac{7}{8}$ in.   **b.** $\frac{7}{8}$ in.   **c.** $1\frac{1}{8}$ in.

1.a. 24 **b.** 12; 60 **c.** 36 **d.** 108 **2.a.** 12 **b.** 216 **3.a.** 4 **b.** 7
4.a. 10,560 **b.** 47,520 **5.a.** in. **b.** mi

PAGE 316

1.a. 4 **b.** 16 **2.a.** 7 pt **b.** 9 qt

PAGE 317

1.a. 32 **b.** 160 **2.** 4 oz **3.a.** 6 **b.** 1 **c.** 1, 9 **d.** 1, 3
4.a. 4,000 **b.** 10,000 **5.a.** oz **b.** lb **c.** ton

PAGE 319

1. 32°F **2.** 66°F **3.** 48°F

PAGE 320

1.a. 2 cm; 3 cm; 4 cm **b.** 9 cm
2.a. 21 cm **b.** 26 m **c.** 24 m **d.** 28 cm
3.a. 28 cm **b.** 12 m **4.** 422 m

PAGES 322–323

1. 8 **2.a.** 3 **b.** 3 in.²
3.a. 12 in.² **b.** 10 in.² **c.** 18 cm² **d.** 9 cm²

PAGE 324

1.a. 20 **b.** 20 cm² **2.** yes
3.a. 28 m² **b.** 28 m² **4.a.** 10 m² **b.** 21 yd²

PAGE 326

1. 24 **2.a.** 16 cubic units **b.** 27 cubic units

CHAPTER 13 • PAGES 334–335

1.a. 1; 1 **b.** 1; 2 **c.** 2; 2; (2, 2)
2.a. (3, 1) **b.** (4, 2) **c.** (1, 3) **d.** (2, 5)
3.a. Miguel **b.** Julie **c.** Kayleen **d.** Laura
4. first number: Paul, Irene, Soichi, Laura, Richard, Ray;
second number: Vic, Kathy, Soichi, Kayleen, Jack
5. George, Kali, Laura, Kayleen, Camila

PAGE 336

1.a. 4 **b.** Alice; 7 **2.a.** Robert: 8, John: 5, Alice: 7, Betty: 3

PAGES 338–339

1.c. 1 symbol for 5 members; 5 is the largest number to divide
evenly into each number of members. **d.** yes

PAGE 346

1. heads, tails **2.b.** yes **c.** 1 out of 2 **d.** yes
3.a. 3 **b.** 1 **c.** 1 out of 3; 1 out of 3

PAGE 348

1.a. 4 **b.** 3 **2.a.** 8 **b.** 3 **c.** 3 out of 8
d. 2 out of 8; 2 out of 8; 1 out of 8 **3.a.** 6; 6 **b.** 2; 4 **c.** B